John Lipski

Afro-Bolivian Spanish

Lengua y Sociedad en el Mundo Hispánico
Language and Society in the Hispanic World

Editado por / *Edited by*
Julio Calvo Pérez (Universitat de València)
Luis Fernando Lara (El Colegio de México)
Matthias Perl (Universität Mainz)
Armin Schwegler (University of California, Irvine)
Klaus Zimmermann (Universität Brement)

Vol. 20

John Lipski

Afro-Bolivian Spanish

Iberoamericana · Vervuert · 2008

Bibliographic information published by Die Deutsche Nationalbibliothek.
Die Deutsche Nationalbibliothek lists this publication in the Deutsche Nationalbibliografie;
detailed bibliographic data are available on the Internet at http://dnb.ddb.de

© Iberoamericana, 2008
Amor de Dios, 1 – E-28014 Madrid
Tel.: +34 91 429 35 22
Fax: +34 91 429 53 97
info@iberoamericanalibros.com
www.ibero-americana.net

© Vervuert, 2008
Elisabethenstr. 3-9 – D-60594 Frankfurt am Main
Tel.: +49 69 597 46 17
Fax: 49 69 597 87 43
info@iberoamericanalibros.com
www.ibero-americana.net

ISBN 978-84-8489-367-7 (Iberoamericana)
ISBN 978-3-86527-389-5 (Vervuert)

Depósito Legal: B-49.067-2008

Fotografía de la cubierta: Angélica Pinedo, Tocaña. © John Lipski
Cubierta: Michael Ackermann
Impreso en España por
The paper on which this book is printed meets the requirements of ISO 9706

TABLE OF CONTENTS

LIST OF PHOTOS, FIGURES, AND MAPS

LIST OF TABLES AND CHARTS

DEDICATION

This book is dedicated to the long-suffering Afro-Bolivian community, deserving of so much more than they have ever received.

ACKNOWLEDGMENTS

This study did not develop in a vacuum, and I owe many debts of gratitude to numerous individuals and organizations. First and foremost, I express my deep thanks to Juan Angola Maconde, my tireless guide, travel companion, and friend since the inception of my research in Bolivia. Juan and I share the same name-sake (*somos tocayos*) and year of birth, and we have also shared many adventures in the search for the elusive vestiges of traditional Afro-Bolivian Spanish. A devoted activist in the cause of Bolivia's *afrodescendientes,* Juan proudly embodies the tremendous intellectual energy and creativity of Afro-Bolivians.

In Mururata, my second home in Bolivia, Antonia Pinedo is at once expert guide, insightful linguistic consultant, community activist, volunteer literacy teacher, and gracious hostess. Her husband, Ramón Barra, has shared his language, his life history, and his home with us on several occasions, and also forms part of the inner circle that circumscribes this research effort. In Coroico, Carlos Pinedo and Juana Salles, both originally from Chijchipa, also provided valuable data. Dozens of other Afro-Bolivians contributed interviews, stories, and good cheer during the course of my research. Guarantees of confidentiality preclude mentioning them all by name, but each and every one holds a permanent place in my thoughts.

In La Paz, Dr. José Mendoza of the Universidad Mayor de San Andrés facilitated my initial explorations, and invited me to teach at his university. My students at the Universidad Mayor de San Andrés and the Universidad Pública y Autónoma de El Alto sharpened my knowledge of Bolivian language and culture, and overwhelmed me with boundless Bolivian hospitality.

Funding for field research in Bolivia came from Penn State's *Africana Research Center*, the *Institute for the Arts and Humanities*, and the *College of the Liberal Arts*; I am especially grateful to Dean Susan Welch for her generous support of my research, including a sabbatical leave that enabled me to finish this project expeditiously. External funding was provided by a fellowship from the John Simon Guggenheim Memorial Foundation.

Many anonymous readers have reviewed and commented on various portions of this research. While I happily acknowledge their contributions and attribute to them any possible felicities in the manuscript, I retain sole responsibility for all shortcomings. Deserving of very special mention is my friend and favorite intellectual sparring partner, Armin Schwegler, who provided superb editorial guidance, thoughtful criticism, and suggestions that go far beyond the usual professional expectations.

As always, my research would not be possible without the loving support of my family. My wife, Beverly, has patiently tolerated my seemingly endless meanderings, and has always welcomed me back home even when I returned with so many insect bites (having run out of repellent at an unfortunate moment) that I should have been placed in quarantine instead. My children, Ursula and Michael, surely do not fathom why I am not like other dads, but suffer my idiosyncrasies without reproach.

To all, my humblest thanks.

CHAPTER 1

INTRODUCTION: AFRO-BOLIVIANS AND THEIR LANGUAGE

1.1. Introduction

The African diaspora in Spanish America involved at least eight million individuals (Andrews 2004; Eltis et al. 1999; Rout 1976), and spanned more than four centuries. Despite the magnitude of these figures, the study of the linguistic contributions of Africans and Afro-Americans to Latin American Spanish has lagged behind the legacy of Spaniards and Native Americans (Lipski 2005). In contemporary Latin America, notwithstanding racial stereotypes in literature and popular culture, there is in general no ethnically unique "Black Spanish", comparable to vernacular African-American English in the United States (Lipski 1985b, 1999d). In more recent times, the linguistic characteristics attributed to black Spanish speakers have been simply those of the lower socioeconomic classes, irrespective of race. However, in the past, the situation *was* different, as there exists ample evidence that distinctly Afro-Hispanic speech forms did exist.

The greatest obstacle in the assessment of earlier Afro-Hispanic language is the high level of prejudice, exaggeration, and stereotyping that has always surrounded the description of non-white speakers of Spanish, and which attributes to all of them a wide range of defects and distortions that frequently are no more than an unrealistic repudiation of this group. One group that did use a "special" language were the *bozales* (slaves born in Africa), who spoke European languages only with difficulty.

Literary imitations of *bozal* language began in 15th-century Portugal and early 16th-century Spain, and subsequently arose in Spanish America. Extant *bozal* imitations from Spanish America fall largely into two groups (Lipski 2005). The first consists of early colonial texts from highland mining regions (Bolivia, Peru, central Colombia, highland Mexico), whose language coincides exactly with 16th–17th-century texts from Spain, and which were probably not accurate renditions of Africans' approximations to popular Spanish but rather crude literary parodies. The second group spans the 19th century –and sometimes the first decades of the 20th– and comes from the regions where the African *bozal* presence represented the latest dates of importation: Cuba (and a few from Puerto Rico), Buenos Aires and Montevideo, and coastal Peru.

While many of these texts are also obvious parodies devoid of linguistic legit-
imacy, others are based on personal observation, and provide some insight into
the expansion of a rough Afro-Hispanic pidgin into vehicle for daily communication among Africans sharing no native language, and between Africans and
white colonials. To date, there are almost no documents from the intermediate
period, i.e., the 18th century, during which Africans in many highland regions
(Colombia, Peru, Bolivia, Mexico) often outnumbered Europeans. A possible
third source of corroborative data is the use of fragments of *bozal* language in
Afro-Cuban *Palo Monte* ceremonies (Fuentes Guerra and Schwegler 2005;
Schwegler 2006). Some *santería* practitioners when in a trance speak in what
they claim to be the language of their *bozal* ancestors (Castellanos 1990),
although such assertions cannot be independently verified.

Although most *bozal* Spanish specimens reflect only non-native usage by
speakers of African languages, data from some texts –all from the Caribbean
region– have given rise to two controversial proposals, which are of great importance to general Spanish dialectology. The first is that Afro-Hispanic language in
the Caribbean and possibly elsewhere coalesced into a stable creole (i.e., one
that had consistent structural characteristics, and eventually developed into a
native language).[1] The second proposal is that this earlier Afro-Hispanic pidgin
or perhaps creole extended beyond the pale of slave barracks and plantations,
and permanently affected the evolution of a broader spectrum of Spanish
dialects, particularly in the Caribbean. The parameters and participants in this
ongoing debate are well represented in extant bibliography and will not be enu-
merated here.[2] A related possibility –one that has not been sufficiently explored
in the realm of Afro-Hispanic language contacts– is the formation of a *semicreole*, i.e., a partially restructured version of the input (lexifier) language, in this
case Spanish, but without the radical break in trans-generational transmission
that characterizes creolization. Holm applies this slippery term to describe situations where "people with different first languages shift to a typologically distinct

[1]   A corollary is the claim that this creole had its origins in an even earlier Afro-Portuguese
      pidgin or creole, formed in West Africa and surviving in the contemporary creoles of Cape
      Verde, São Tomé and Annobón, and in Latin America in Papiamentu (spoken in the
      Netherlands Antilles) and Palenquero (spoken in the Afro-Colombian village of El
      Palenque de San Basilio).
[2]   The debate and its protagonists are summarized in Lipski (1998b, 2005). In the Caribbean,
      matters are complicated by the introduction, in the 19th century, of other Afro-European
      creole languages when contract laborers arrived from other Caribbean islands; some of
      these creoles (e.g., Papiamentu) were similar enough to *bozal* approximations to Spanish
      to probably have influenced *bozales'* acquisition of Spanish, and to cause white observers
      to confuse the "broken Spanish" of African-born blacks with stable Afro-Atlantic creoles.

target language (itself an amalgam of dialects in contact, including fully restructured varieties) under social conditions that partially restrict their access to the target language as normally used among native speakers" (2000: 10). Vernacular Brazilian Portuguese and vernacular African-American English have been characterized as having semicreole status.

The debates over the nature of earlier Afro-Hispanic *bozal* and post-*bozal* language are partially frustrated by the scarcity of verifiable data in surviving Afro-Hispanic linguistic enclaves. In most of Latin America, "black" Spanish is confined to songs and religious rituals, often sung in remnants of remembered or memorized African languages, embellished with onomatopoeic elements felt to be "African".[3] Thus for example the *negros congos* of Panama's Caribbean coast, clustered around the former colonial slaving ports of Portobelo and Nombre de Dios, employ a special language –now becoming increasingly deformed by deliberate distortion– during Carnival season and occasionally at other times. They affirm that it embodies the collective memory of *bozal* speech from previous centuries, but in reality is little more than a dimly remembered parody of "broken" Spanish, together with a handful of words that can be correlated with *bozal* Spanish from other times and places.[4] Some Afro-Cuban ritual songs from the *Palo Monte* tradition (Fuentes Guerra and Schwegler 2005; Schwegler 2006) contain invariant verb forms, derived from the third person singular, as well as the invariant copula *son*, independently attested in Afro-Cuban Spanish (Lipski 1999c, 2002c).

In addition to ritualized speech, a few Afro-Hispanic enclaves remain isolated from the remaining Spanish-speaking population. As such, they offer a glimpse into the final stages of *bozal* speech, and the possible retention of post-*bozal* elements in natively spoken Spanish as used by descendents of Africans. Highland Ecuador's Chota Valley provides one case: surrounded by indigenous communities for whom Spanish continues to be a second language and where a local micro-dialect of Spanish has evolved that differs in subtle ways from neighboring highland varieties. A few of the oldest residents exhibit occasional traces of what might be *bozal* remnants (lapses of agreement, invariant plurals, loss of prepositions and articles), but no one speaks this way consistently, and no one in the community is capable of deliberately switching dialects. Community mem-

---

[3]   Schwegler (1996a) provides a compelling example, in his analysis of the *lumbalú* funeral chants in the Palenque de San Basilio, which contains words felt to be "African" by community members, when in reality these are, at times, highly distorted Spanish or Portuguese elements.

[4]   De la Rosa Sánchez (1988), Drolet (1980a, 1980b), Joly (1981, 1984), Laribe (1968, 1969), Lipski (1986h, 1986i, 1989a, 1997), Smith (1975), Tejeira Jaén (1974).

bers feel that they speak a "different" dialect from the remainder of the Ecuadoran highlands, but do not always correctly identify those features that separate their speech from that of neighboring areas. Opinions by Ecuadorans from outside the community are routinely erroneous, confusing the essentially Andean Chota dialect with the consonant-weak coastal dialect of Esmeraldas, Ecuador's acknowledged "black" province, under the assumption that all black Ecuadorans must speak alike.[5] Finally, some of the more isolated villages in the Colombian Chocó, nearly all of whose residents are black, exhibit subtle linguistic traits reminiscent of earlier *bozal* language, but despite rumors of "special" Afro-Colombian cryptolects still in existence, no significant departures from regional vernacular Spanish have been discovered (see M. Ruiz García 2000 and Schwegler 1991a for a confirmation that no cryptolects survive in the Chocó today). Table 1.1 illustrates the principal post-*bozal* communities investigated to date (corresponding references are in the bibliography). The same table offers a list of the principal traits that characterize these speech communities.

In view of the sparse data available to date on the survival of possibly post-*bozal* continuities in Afro-Hispanic speech communities, the search for additional specimens remains a high research priority. The present monograph describes a speech community of Highland Bolivia whose characteristics were until very recently unknown outside the remote area where its language is spoken.

1.2. Bolivia's *afrodescendientes* and their environment

The present study describes a unique Afro-Hispanic speech community, subject to linguistic analysis for the first time, and arguably representing the oldest surviving Afro-American variety of any language. It is found in the Yungas, tropical valleys surrounded by the Bolivian highlands to the northeast of the capital La Paz. The Afro-Yungas dialect differs systematically and significantly from any other variety of Bolivian Spanish, and from any natively spoken Spanish dialect elsewhere in the world. Data from the Afro-Yungueño dialect provide a window into early colonial Afro-Hispanic speech, as well as offering a possible model for the retention of post-*bozal* linguistic traits in other geographically and socially isolated Afro-Hispanic communities.

Highland Bolivia, known in colonial times as "Alto Perú", then the "Audiencia de Charcas", was the site of the earliest massive importation of African slaves to Spanish America. The use of such slaves had already been authorized for other

[5]   Lipski (1986e, 1987a), Schwegler (1994, 1999).

TABLE 1.1
Surviving post-*bozal* speech communities

COUNTRY	COMMUNITY	CRESEARCHERS	PRINCIPAL TRAITS
Colombia	Chocó	Ruiz García, Schwegler	Double negation, occlusive prevocalic /d/, occasional lapses of agreement
Colombia	El Palenque de San Basilio	Morton, Schwegler	Double or postposed negation, occasional lapses of agreement, postposed genetives
Cuba	Oriente, etc.	Ortiz López, Schwegler	*Elle* 's/he', *agüé* 'today', occasional double negation
Dominican Rep.	Villa Mella, etc.	Green, Lipski, Lorenzino, Megenney, Ortiz López, Schwegler	Double negation, occlusive /d/, occasional lapses of agreement, possible use of preverbal particle *a* (Green)
Ecuador	Chota Valley	Lipski, Maldonado Chalá, Schwegler	Lapses in S-V and N-Adj agreement, loss of prepositions, bare/invariant plurals, possible *ele* 's/he'
Mexico	Costa Chica (Guerrero, Oaxaca)	Aguirre Beltrán, Althoff, Lipski	Occasional lapses of agreement; paragogic vowels, loss of prepositions
Peru	Coast, Chincha, Sama-Las Yaras	Cuba, Lipski	Prevocalic occlusive /d/, occasional /ɾ / > [d], occasional /ɾ / > [l] in onset clusters, occasional lapses of agreement
Trinidad	various	Lipski, Moodie	Occasional lapses of agreement, loss of prepositions, loss of final consonants, possible use of preverbal *ta* (Moodie)
Venezuela	Barlovento	D. Domínguez, Megenney, Mosonyi et al.	Occasional lapses of agreement, neutralization /ɼ/-/ρ/, /ɼ/, /d/ > [d]

areas of Spanish America, mostly to replace dwindling indigenous workers. African slaves were thus brought to the highland mining areas of Bolivia and Peru.[6] Lists of slaves and comments on the nature of labor to be performed suggest that Africans taken to Bolivia were predominantly male (cp. Leons 1984c: 28), at least during the 16th century, when they worked in the Casa de la Moneda (the colonial mint) in Potosí and possibly also in the surrounding mines.[7] Many reports note the severe weather (cold and heavy snow) and harsh working conditions in Potosí and other highland areas, which together led to a high mortality rate (cp. Angola Maconde 2000: 29-36). In any event, the African slave population in Bolivia was never large, many mixed with indigenous or European residents, and the cultural, linguistic, and demographic profile of Afro-Bolivians declined steadily from a high point in the early 17th century, when Africans represented nearly 5% of the population (Crespo 1977: 28). A small collection of songs and indirect descriptions of Africans' dances and language survives as testimony of a much larger cultural patrimony. As occurred elsewhere (for instance in Mexico and central Colombia), the population of African descent eventually blended into the overwhelmingly mestizo population.

No documented permanent linguistic influence on developing Bolivian Spanish can be attributed to this earlier African population, but the data provided by the early language samples suggest what Afro-Hispanic speech in early 17th-century Bolivia might have sounded like to Spanish writers (cp. Lipski 1994, 1995a, 2005).

Despite the overwhelming adversities and the time span of more than four centuries, in this primarily indigenous and mestizo nation, a tiny but vibrant Afro-Bolivian community has survived to the present day. As we shall have occasion to see, the community has kept many Afro-Hispanic cultural and linguistic features. In the area of language, the speech of some of the oldest and most isolated Afro-Bolivians offers the biggest surprise of all: a fully intact restructured Afro-Hispanic language (spoken alongside highland Bolivian Spanish) that represents the only known survival of a grammatically complete restructured language arising from the acquisition of Spanish by some nine million *bozales* (African-born second language speakers of Spanish), forced into servitude far from their birthplace and unable to communicate with one another except in desperately acquired approximations to the colonists' language.[8]

---

[6]   Bowser (1974), Crespo (1977), Cuche (1981), Harth-Terré (1971, 1973), Millones Santagadea (1973), Pizarroso Cuenca (1977), Portugal Ortiz (1977).

[7]   In urban areas, male and female slave populations were more nearly equal, according to figures gleaned from Crespo (1977: 30-40).

[8]   There are tantalizing fragments of *bozal* language found elsewhere in Latin America, particularly in Cuba, where the *Palo Mayombe* ceremonies contain speech fragments in *bozal*

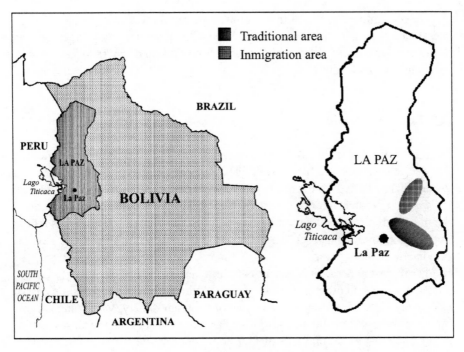

FIGURE 1.1
Areal map of Afro-Bolivian communities

Most contemporary Afro-Bolivians live in scattered communities in the provinces of Nor Yungas and Sud Yungas, in the department of La Paz, as shown in Figure 1.1.

A few Afro-Bolivians live in the neighboring province of Inquisivi; some have also migrated northward to the adjoining province of Caranavi. In past decades, many black Yungueños have left the region, some for La Paz, but most for the eastern lowlands, to Santa Cruz de la Sierra. The latter group no longer speaks the Afro-Yungueño dialect, but rather the *camba* dialect of eastern Bolivia.

Spanish (Fuentes Guerra and Schwegler 2005; Schwegler 2005). This is similar to the Afro-Brazilian speech of the *pretos velhos* "black elders", which also contains some *bozal* features (Bonvini 2000). Some practitioners of Afro-Cuban religions also use *bozal*-like Spanish when in trance (Castellanos 1990), providing suggestive but non-replicable supporting data. In Brazil, the restructured semi-creole Portuguese of Helvécia provides a case somewhat parallel to Afro-Bolivian Spanish (Baxter 1992, 1997; Baxter and Lucchesi 1993; Baxter et al. 1997; Mello et al. 1998; Ferreira 1985).

The remaining chapters of this book will present the key features of the afore-mentioned Afro-Bolivian Spanish, together with an interpretation of these data in the broader context of the contributions of the African diaspora to Latin American language and culture.

1.3. Life in the Yungas

Bolivia is divided into *departamentos* 'departments' and each department is divided into *provincias* 'provinces'. The *Yungas de la Paz* are located in the department of La Paz, to the northeast of the capital city. The Yungas are tropical valleys no more than a few thousand feet above sea level, surrounded by some of the most forbidding mountain terrain in all of South America, with peaks reaching more than 15,000 feet. These peaks cut a broad swath across several provinces, including Nor Yungas, Sud Yungas, Caranavi, Inquisivi, and parts of neighboring provinces. This torturous terrain, nearly vertical geography, lack of adequate roads and other infrastructure, and frequent mud and rock slides, have effectively cut off the Yungas from much of Bolivian society. Most Yungas communities are less than 100 miles from La Paz, but to reach even the closest settlements one must travel upwards of four hours in crowded and decrepit vehicles along a one-lane muddy mountain road with steep drop-offs and no guard rails (considered to be the world's most dangerous "highway" by travel agents and known as *la carretera de la muerte* 'death road' by Bolivians).[9]

The region is principally inhabited by an Aymara-speaking indigenous population, together with a considerable mestizo component; black Yungueños live both in villages with Aymara majorities and in *comunidades* (an officially recognized term in Bolivia) –scattered mountainside houses on lands once belonging to haciendas. The small towns have electricity and rudimentary telephone service, as well as some running water. In the *comunidades,* electricity has arrived only recently, and many houses still have either no electric service or just a single light bulb. Running water and indoor plumbing are all but nonexistent in the smaller *comunidades*. Most residents rarely if ever travel to La Paz or other highland areas, due to the bad road, the discomfort caused by the high altitude and cold temperatures of the *altiplano*, and the lack of funds to pay even the very modest cost of transportation.[10]

---

[9]   In late 2006, a new section of paved road was opened along the La Paz-Coroico route, which eliminates the necessity of traversing the dangerous stretch described above.

[10] Additional information on Afro-Bolivians in the Yungas can be found in Garrison (1999), Léons (1998), Medina (2004), Rossbach de Olmos (2007), and Templeman (1994, 1998).

Although the region produces excellent coffee, oranges, and other tropical products, the prohibitive cost of bringing these to urban markets precludes the development of a significant cash-crop agriculture. Most residents have devoted all arable land to growing coca, once the principal product of the old haciendas and now the only commercial viable crop in the Yungas The *cocales* 'coca plots' are made by cutting terraces into the steep slopes; a less labor-intensive but short-lived technique is the *zanjío,* consisting of furrows cut into the mountainside. The coca leaves are traditionally dried on slabs of local slate, known as *cachis.* Many coca growers now spread large plastic tarpaulins on available flat spaces for a more portable drying process. Harvesting and drying are highly dependent on the weather. Drying must take place within two days of harvest or the leaves turn black and are worthless for sale. Given the frequent and often unpredictable rains, this results in many lost work days and wasted product. Although nominally a mature coca plant can be harvested four times a year, in reality no more than two strong harvests plus one or two small yields are the norm. The coca is purchased at low prices by brokers, ostensibly for the legal Bolivian tradition of chewing coca leaves and brewing *mate de coca* herb tea, and for use in the many "cola" drinks produced around the world. Local production exceeds the needs of these markets, and an undetermined amount of the coca finds its way to the clandestine cocaine laboratories of eastern Bolivia.

1.4. Afro-Bolivian communities in the Yungas

Angola Maconde (2000), the most thorough scholar of contemporary Afro-Bolivian culture and himself a member of the community (from Dorado Chico, municipality of Coripata, Coroico, in Nor Yungas), lists the most important Nor Yungas black communities (population figures come from the 2001 census[11]):

Coscoma	(pop. 402)	Chijchipa	(pop. 126)
Mururata	(pop. 236)	Dorado Chico	(pop. 34)
Tocaña	(pop. 171)		

The same communities are mentioned by Binyán Carmona (1990: 135-141) in his account of the black "kings" of Mururata. Other communities contain more Aymara-Afro-Bolivian mixture. In Sud Yungas, the principal black community is

---

The rather optimistic predictions offered by Garrison and Templeman have not yet come to pass.

[11] Available at <www.ine.gov.bo>.

Chicaloma (pop. 634; now less than 50% black, but once the principal Afro-Bolivian community in the region), with black Bolivians scattered in many neighboring settlements. Angola Maconde states that "[e]n todas las comunidades afroaimaras de los Yungas, los descendientes africanos han asumido rasgos de la cultura indígena local como las técnicas agrícolas, vestimenta, pautas de organización social y, en casos, el manejo bilingüe del idioma aimará" (2003: 8-9) [in all of the Afro-Aymara communities in the Yungas, the descendents of Africans have adopted indigenous cultural traits, autochthonous agricultural techniques and social structures, and in some cases the bilingual use of Aymara (and Spanish)].

As a result of the social and geographic isolation, residents of the Yungas communities have retained cultural and linguistic traits that have faded from more populated urban areas. Black Yungueños in Sud Yungas are in a minority except in Chicaloma, where until the last generation, the Afro-Bolivian population was predominant. Black Bolivians living away from Afro-Bolivian communities have intermarried with Aymaras; they often speak Aymara fluently, and may identify culturally with the Aymara population at least as much as with the *afrodescendientes*. Even in communities where the black population is predominant, the women wear traditional Aymara clothing, including the *pollera* 'full skirt', derby hat, and they braid their hair in the Aymara fashion. Both Aymara and Afro-Bolivian men typically dress in western-style work attire, with less visibly apparent cultural syncretism.

In the Nor Yungas communities, where Afro-Bolivian speech still survives and where most of the present research was conducted (see Figure 1.1), black Bolivians remain linguistically and culturally separate from Aymaras; they learn enough Aymara to function efficiently in the Aymara-dominant local markets, but maintain a separate life style through networks of extended families. In his studies of the town of Chicaloma in Sud Yungas, Leons notes that "[...] Negros are culturally close to Hispanic patterns and [...] Spanish is their primary language [...]" (1984b: 23). Two pages later, he further explains:

> The non-agricultural occupations which Negros seek are those in which they utilize their fluency in Spanish and familiarity with Hispanic culture and which will likely lead to intersectional mobility. However, the Negro finds it difficult to merge into a general mestizo culture because of his physical distinctiveness, hence the current emphasis on cross-ethnic marriage "to make the race disappear". [...] [W]hile cultural distance between Negros and Hispanics in Bolivia lessen, physical distinctiveness remains. These physical distinctiveness [*sic*] may eventually assume social significance as a boundary marker that will continue to define limits of usual social familiarity [...] the Negro section of Chicaloma has been transformed from one that is culturally, racially, and socially distinct to a section that is racially and socially distinct. Thus it is understandable that Negros have turned to intermarriage in order to elimi-

nate the racial barrier. Many young Negros are also anxious to eliminate occupational criteria in the cultural aspect of their sectional membership, although, job shortage in towns and cities limits such attempts.

(Leons 1984b: 24-25).

These observations, made more than a quarter century ago, are not strictly true of the contemporary Nor Yungas Afro-Bolivian communities, and they are probably no longer accurate for today's Sud Yungas either. Leons' observations do, however, provide a useful glimpse into the complex social reality surrounding this nearly invisible minority within Bolivia.

Bridikhina (1995: 100-101) states that many black women from the Yungas region have migrated to La Paz and maintain more contacts outside of the region; she further asserts that, as a consequence, the women of this group have greater opportunities for racial and cultural mixture than the men, who largely remain in the region to work. Years prior, Newman had indicated that in Mururata, Nor Yungas, "the [Afro-Yungueño] is strictly endogamous" (1966: 48); significantly, Mururata is one of the villages in which the Afro-Yungueño dialect has been maintained to this day by older residents. The same patterns of dialect retention can be observed in the predominantly Afro-Bolivian Tocaña and in the small communities of Chijchipa (near Mururata) and Dorado Chico (near Arapata).

Although there are some differences among the Afro-Bolivian communities, the basic life style and daily activities are virtually uniform throughout the region. The typical communities, derived from former haciendas, consist of scattered family dwellings perched on the steep hillsides. These settlements normally consist of anywhere between 25 and 50 families, many of which are genetically related. Some communities have only a dozen or so families, and one also finds a scattering of larger communities with a significant Afro-Bolivian presence, such as Mururata and Tocaña. Typical houses are of adobe or a mixture of adobe and wood, with metal roofs or occasionally traditional thatching.

1.5. Demographic profile: how many Afro-Bolivians are there?

Tracing the demographic profile of Afro-Bolivians entails a considerable amount of extrapolation, since neither colonial nor post-colonial governments took pains to achieve accurate counts, and for more than a century official census data did not include Afro-Bolivians as a separate category. During the colonial period, by 1650 there were some 30,000 Africans (the majority *bozales*) in the Audiencia de Charcas out of a total population of 850,000. Of the latter figure, some 700,000 were considered indigenous, and presumably spoke little or no Spanish, so that

Africans represented about 20% of the Spanish colonial population. By the time of the official post-colonial census of 1846, 27,941 "black" residents were counted in a total population of nearly 1,400,000 (as is logical, the accuracy of any 19th-century census in Bolivia is open to question). After the abolition of slavery in 1851, blacks were no longer officially acknowledged. This naturally complicates the reconstruction of Afro-Bolivian history, language, and culture.

The last census to differentiate a black population was carried out in 1900: 3,945 Afro-Bolivians were officially counted, out of a total population of just over 1.8 million (some 0.2% of the total population). Of this total, 2,056 were in La Paz department (mostly in the Yungas), and another 930 were in Santa Cruz, with the remainder distributed throughout the nation. A description of the Yungas from the 1940s –that is, before land reforms following the 1952 revolution resulted in black families occupying former haciendas in the Yungas–estimated the black population of Bolivia as "6.700 individuos de *raza negra*, que cultivan productos tropicales en los pocos valles donde habitan" [6,700 individuals of the black race, who grow tropical products in the few valleys in which they live]; for the Yungas region, there were some 8,800 "blancos y mestizos" [whites and mixed-race] (i.e., native Spanish speakers), 16,700 Aymaras, 600 members of indigenous groups from the Amazonian region of Bolivia, and some 900 Afro-Bolivians (Meneses 1945: 67-8).

According to the sources summarized in Powe (1998: 815), by 1883 there were between 5,500 and 6,000 black residents of the Yungas. Half a century ago, Zelinsky (1949: 175) estimated the number of Afro-Bolivians at 6,000, while Leons (1984c) cites a figure of only around 2,000. As for the current Afro-Bolivian population, Spedding (1995: 320) suggests, based on personal observations, that there may be between 10,000 and 15,000 Bolivians with at least some visible African ancestry in the Yungas region. Another article (Anon. 2002) asserts that some 30,000 Afro-Bolivians live throughout the country (no documentation accompanies this figure, since no recent census has included this category).

In recent decades, many Afro-Bolivians have migrated from the Yungas to Santa Cruz, eastern Bolivia's lowland boom-town. At least 3,000 Afro-Bolivians are estimated to live in or around Santa Cruz (Anon. 2003). There is no indication that any unique Yungas speech forms have been maintained in Santa Cruz or anywhere else outside of the Yungas. Angola Maconde (MS) offers the breakdown given in Table 1.2 (estimates based on personal experience).

1.6. Afro-Bolivians' arrival in the Yungas

The origin of the black population in the Bolivian Yungas is not known with certainty, and tracing their arrival in the Yungas is hampered by the almost total

TABLE 1.2
Estimated Afro-Bolivian population
(from Angola Maconde, forthcoming)

Traditional Afro-Bolivian communities:	
Municipio de Coroico:	2,500
Municipio de Coripata:	1,000
Municipio de Chulumani (Sud Yungas):	1,000
Municipio de Irupana (Sud Yungas):	2,000
Municipio de la Provincia Inquisivi:	1,000
Afro-Bolivian communities resulting from internal migration:	
Municipio de Caranavi:	1,200
Municipio de Alto Beni:	1,800
La Paz (urban):	2,000
Cochabamba (urban):	2,800
Santa Cruz:	
Estimated total:	**15,800**
	(approx. 0.18% of Bolivia's population)

absence of historical documentation. Although some Afro-Yungueños believe that their ancestors arrived via Brazil, they were probably only in transit. There is no indication that (Brazilian) Portuguese was ever spoken in this area.

Afro-Bolivians appear to be the descendents of Africa-born *bozales* who arrived in this region. As such, these early arrivals must have spoken neither Spanish nor Portuguese. According to Leons (1984c), historical accounts date the presence of blacks in the Yungas at least since 1600, but the first official records (deaths, marriages, and other accounts) date from only just after 1700. By the end of the 18th century, the historical record is more substantial as regards black slaves on the haciendas of the Yungas and other central Bolivian regions.

It is likely that some Afro-Bolivians in the Yungas descend not from the initial African slave population in Potosí, but rather from the agricultural holdings in eastern Bolivia, such as Mizque, in the department of Cochabamba. Research by Brockington (2006: 145-156) provides extensive documentation of African slavery during the colonial period, including many natives of Angola and the Portuguese Congo. This is consistent with the retention of the surname *Angola* in the Yungas and with possible Kikongo linguistic survivals, discussed in Chapter 6.

By the end of the colonial period (early 19th century), Afro-Bolivians were already well established as *peones* on large haciendas owned by usually absentee landholders. Already then the main cash crop was coca; coffee and sugar cane were grown on some estates, and there is occasional mention of oranges and other tropical fruits and vegetables being grown for sale. At least until the second half of the 19th century, Afro-Bolivians were chattel slaves,[12] held under the same working conditions as black slaves in other Spanish American colonies. The first Bolivian constitution, of 1826, officially abolished new slavery, and provided a means by which existing slaves could purchase their freedom –at prices that very few would ever attain. Following protests by large landowners, an 1830 law effectively reinstated slavery, although new slavery was again officially denounced in the new 1831 constitution. Once more landowners protested; it was felt that only black laborers could work effectively in the Yungas, by then an area closely identified with Bolivia's black population (Llanos Moscoso and Soruco Arroyo 2004: 66). The situation remained largely unchanged until the agrarian reform process begun in 1952. Additional facts described by Lema (2005) and Aillón Soria (2005) situate black Bolivians in the Yungas and other agricultural regions by the end of the 18th century, but there still remain considerable gaps in Afro-Bolivian history, including routes of migration and the chronology of settlement in the various communities.

Until the second half of the 20th century, black Bolivians in the Yungas toiled as virtual slaves on the haciendas. All adults were required to work (without compensation) three days a week for the benefit of the landowner; the remaining four days produced food for the family. There were no rest periods. Children began laboring on the hacienda from around the age of 12-15 years. When their parents were temporarily incapacitated, children could partially offset the debt created by the adults' inability to perform the obligatory service. All work was conducted under the supervision of a *mayordomo* or overseer, often an Aymara speaker, who was the landowner's trusted employee. The *mayordomos* would then appoint a *jilacata* 'assistant' from among the peons. Both the overseers and the *jilacatas* used physical punishment to enforce working hours. Whipping with leather bullwhips and lashes was the usual punishment, which could result in receiving an *arroba* (25 lashes) or more. Particularly cruel were the corporal punishments inflicted by the *jilacatas* on members of their own suffering Afro-Bolivian compatriots. Women and elderly peons were also whipped, a punishment that occasionally extended to children.

In addition to the aforementioned requirement to work three days out of seven for the benefit of the landowner, peons on the hacienda were also required to par-

---

[12] Meaning that slave owners had absolute legal rights over the slaves, including the right to buy or sell them as any other piece of property.

ticipate in the systems of *pongo* (for men) and *mitani* (for women, this entailed work in the plantation house, such as cooking, cleaning, and other household chores). In most haciendas, peons were forbidden to attend school or study; most older Afro-Bolivians are therefore nearly or entirely illiterate. On some haciendas, Aymara was the only language allowed when peons wished to address their overseers.

The hacienda system was abolished soon after the agrarian reform of 1952. Most Afro-Bolivians remained on the parcels of land that had once belonged to the haciendas. They did not obtain land titles, but were free from the requirement to work for a landlord. Many of the Afro-Bolivian communities retain the names of the former haciendas: Dorado Grande, Dorado Chico, Chijchipa, Khala Khala, Coscoma, etc.

Shortly after 1952, public education gradually arrived in the Afro-Yungueño communities, although to this day some communities only have schools that cover the first two or three grades. To finish elementary school, children often must walk for several hours to reach the nearest community with a more comprehensive school. Today, educational reform and the ready availability of more and better schooling remains one of the most pressing necessities of Afro-Bolivians (and most other residents of the Yungas).

Few traditions of demonstrably African (or at least non-indigenous and non-Spanish) origin are found in the Afro-Bolivian communities. The two most obviously Afro-Bolivian cultural manifestations are the *saya* dance and drum music, and the *mauchi* funeral tradition.[13] The traditional Afro-Bolivian funeral ceremony includes singing the *mauchi* funeral chant, upon return from the cemetery after the burial. Centro Cultural Simón I. Patiño (1998) and Angola Maconde (2000: 89-91) offer the lyrics to this chant, which contains some words that are not in Spanish.

Montaño Aragón (1992: 265-268) draws many parallels between Afro-Bolivian and Yoruba culture. There is, however, no evidence that Yoruba speakers ever arrived in Bolivia. He asserts that ceremonial words like *opatalá* (Obatalá), *yamanyá* (Yemayá), and *olarún* (Olorún) have been used among Afro-Yungueños. My own interviews in the region, including those with members of the same families visited by Montaño Aragón, have failed to confirm any of these words. It is possible that some Afro-Bolivian intellectuals have studied

---

[13]   The word *mauchi* is of unknown origin (see Chapter 6 for additional references). A few older Afro-Bolivians recall that *mauchi* was once used as a verb, apparently of the form *mauchi(r)*, as in *ya mauchí* "he / she is dead" or *¿quién mauchió?* "who died?" The word is no longer used in this fashion, and the *mauchi* ceremony has all but disappeared from the Afro-Bolivian communities.

Afro-Hispanic religious practices from other countries, but there are no other demonstrably "modern" Afro-American practices or beliefs in the traditional Afro-Bolivian communities. This situation thus differs from that of the "neo-Africanized" cultural awareness found in more internationally integrated Afro-Hispanic groups, e.g., in Peru, Chile, Paraguay, Uruguay and Cuba (Santería).

1.7. National awareness of Afro-Bolivians

The relative remoteness of the Yungas (currently visited only by mostly foreign "eco-tourists", most of whom speak little Spanish and have no interaction with Afro-Bolivians) and the traditional marginality of black Bolivians have resulted in a nearly total lack of documentation of their speech and culture. Most Bolivians are passively aware of the nation's *afrodescendientes,* but few have accurate information, and negative stereotypes continue to lurk just below the surface of apparently cordial relations. To this day, residents of La Paz recall the greeting *¡suerte, negrito!,* literally "a black; good luck" said when encountering a black person in the street. This greeting –still occasionally heard but no longer socially acceptable in public– converted a black face into an amulet to be touched verbally for good luck. This may be a remnant of the *estornudo* or feigned sneeze practiced by white residents of Spain during the 16th–17th centuries whenever a black person passed by (cp. Pike 1967: 357).

The Bolivian government and many tourism companies have produced posters and postcards with smiling Afro-Bolivian faces (Figures 1.9-1.10), all the while that the official censuses and ethnic classifications ignore the presence and contributions of black Bolivians (Ceaser 2000).

The many government-sponsored and private tourist bureaus throughout the country contain abundant information on indigenous and mestizo cultures, but offer no written documentation on Afro-Bolivians. When queried on the topic, sketchy and inaccurate verbal information is generally offered. The Casa de la Cultura in La Paz makes no mention of Afro-Bolivians, nor does the otherwise well-presented Museo Nacional de Etnografía y Folklore, (the Museo did produce a short video on Afro-Bolivian dance culture (Figure 1.11), but it is not part of the exhibitions).

The Museo de Instrumentos Musicales de Bolivia in La Paz contains an extensive collection of Bolivian musical instruments. But none is from the Afro-Bolivians area. When asked, a museum guide pointed to some drums in the midst of a large and unlabeled collection. The Museo Costumbrista "Juan de Vargas" contains a single racially demeaning drawing of the *Zambo Salvito,* a sort of Bolivian "little black Sambo" racist icon immortalized by the novel of the same

FIGURE 1.2
Juan Angola Maconde and Manuel Barra in the village of Tocaña (2005).
Both were contributors to the present project, and Juan Angola Maconde in
particular was John Lipski's constant companion and colleague.

FIGURE 1.3
Fidel Salinas, Coscoma (2005), contributor to the present project.

name by Paredes Candia (1988b); in the museum, this drawing carries no explanation other than the title.

When Afro-Bolivian culture is mentioned in public discourse, it is usually in reference to the *saya,* an Afro-American dance and drum expression that is frequently presented at cultural events (held in various Bolivian cities) where tourists generally abound. However, as the Afro-Bolivian writer Fernando Cajías warns (Anon. 2002): "No hay que musicalizar la cuestión afro" [one should not reduce the Afro issue to music]. As an example of the tendency to reduce the serious plight of Afro-Bolivians to a colorful musical pageant, an article about an elderly former *saya* practitioner from Mururata shows him dressed in an elegant (borrowed) outfit (Figure 1.12).

The article fails to mention that this individual, who was interviewed as part of the present investigation, is nearly destitute, and normally wears ragged clothing that is ill suited to the capricious climate of Mururata's hilltop location.

Despite the relative popularity of the *saya,* there exists only a single comprehensive recording of traditional Afro-Bolivian music, produced by a Swiss-based private foundation. The recording is sold only at the foundation's office in La Paz (Figure 1.13).

When Afro-Bolivians are mentioned in the press in contexts other than music and dance, reference is usually made to folklore such as traditional medicine. Seldom is their desperate economic plight brought up. As an anecdote, the illustrations of an elderly *curandera* from Tocaña in Figure 1.14 (p. 53), also interviewed as part of the present project, appeared on the front page of the Sunday supplement in a chain of syndicated newspapers nationwide. The title of the section is "AFROS: la alegría silenciosa" [Afros, silent joy], but Angélica Pinedo, born in 1920 and 85 years old at the time of the interviews, confessed to me that she is utterly worn out from years of hard work, and must continue to receive "patients" all day long in order to support herself in a society that provides no social security or retirement benefits to rural Yungueños. The newspaper article also incorrectly reported her name and age, and blithely described her working "como si fuera una joven" [as though she were a young woman]. Doña Angélica received no acknowledgment of her participation, and was not even aware that her photo had appeared across the country until the present writer, accompanied by Juan Angola Maconde, brought her a copy of the newspaper. None of the other individuals interviewed and photographed for this article –including the aforementioned Pedro Rey dressed in the *saya* costume– had received the newspaper, and the same individuals were equally surprised and gratified to receive copies from us. This unfortunately not atypical incident underscores the fact that Afro-Bolivians still struggle to be taken seriously in a nation that prides itself on its multicultural population.

FIGURE 1.4
Angélica Pinedo, her brother, and the author John Lipski
(village of Tocaña 2005).

Until recently, only the occasional article by Afro-Bolivian writers appeared in the press. As of this writing (Sept. 2007), Juan Angola Maconde has begun a monthly column in the major daily *La Prensa,* in which he describes the plight of Afro-Bolivians.[14] How long this series will last, and what reception it will garner remains to be seen.

Few monographs written in Bolivia mention its black population, and this despite the fact that many are by writers who, traveling extensively throughout the country, offer detailed descriptions of indigenous groups. Cortés (1875: 26), for example, declares that "Bolivia está poblada de tres razas principales: la española, los aboríjenes i la que resulta de la mezcla en estas dos" [Bolivia is populated by three main races, the Spanish, the indigenous, and the race resulting from the mixture of these two]; when speaking of the Yungas (pp. 87-88), he mentions only the indigenous population. In a recent panoramic study that incorporates several official organisms, Plaza Martínez and Carvajal Carvajal (1985) omit mentioning Afro-Bolivians as an ethnic group, but instead concentrate on several small(er) indigenous communities. Nor are Afro-Bolivians mentioned in any of the previous ethnolinguistic surveys reviewed by the above-mentioned authors. Hudson and Hanratty note only that "African slaves [...] became an Aymara-speaking subculture in the Yungas, which they colonized for coca cultivation" (1991: xxvii, see also p. 62). Meneses' (1948a) unusually detailed account of the province of Nor Yungas mentions only indigenous inhabitants, including the sharecroppers under the control of *mayordomos*; the lack of mention of a black population in the Yungas is surprising in light of the fact that many Afro-Yungueños still alive vividly recall working for these same *mayordomos* during the time period in question, just over 50 years ago. In describing Sud Yungas, Meneses (1948b: 196-197) does mention the small black populations in both Nor Yungas and Sud Yungas. When speaking of Afro-Yungueños' purported disdain for indigenous inhabitants, Meneses quotes the phrase *eyos son di otro Dios; andan cayaos siempre, mascando su coca* [they have another God, they are always silent, chewing their coca] (1985b: 198). This phrase is unremarkable except for the apparent use of [j] instead of the palatal lateral [x], found in all Bolivian Spanish dialects. The premier Bolivian folklorist Paredes Candia asserts that blacks have disappeared from Bolivia "excepto en ciertas parcelas de los yungas cordilleranos" [except in a few parts of the Yungas] (1967: v. 2, 129);[15]

---

[14]   The first article in the "Afrociudadanizando" series is "¿Dónde está mi pueblo?" (Angola Maconde 2006).

[15]   Paredes Candia (1967: v. 1, 306-307) mentions other Bolivian folk traditions attributed to the former presence of black slaves.

FIGURE 1.5
Antonia Pinedo Zalles and Juana Barra Zalles, Chijchipa (2005),
contributors to the present project.

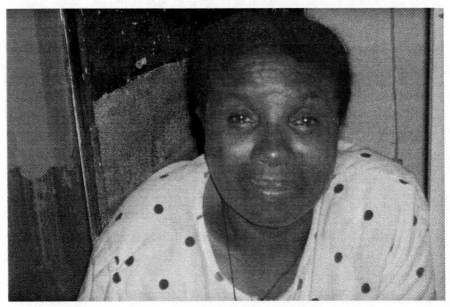

FIGURE 1.6
Juana Barra, Mururata (2007), contributor to the present project.

but vestiges of folklore remain, such as the *negrito* songs and dances, one of which, recovered in Sucre, contains the verse: *re re ré / Tata Romingo / E re re ré / Tata Facico*. This brief fragment exhibits (1) the conversion of prevocalic /d/ to [r] in *Romingo* < *Domingo*, common in all Afro-Hispanic language from the 15th century onward, and (2) the pronunciation of *Francisco* as *Facico*, containing both onset cluster reduction and loss of syllable-final /s/ –both traits of earlier and well-attested Afro-Hispanic *bozal* language (Lipski 1986b, 1988, 1992b, 1995a).

Despite centuries of neglect and official non-recognition, Afro-Yungueños are clearly aware of their separate status as *negros* (the term preferred by Afro-Bolivians), and they have recently begun systematic attempts to draw national attention in an attempt to obtain the legal and social recognition as a long-standing (and long-suffering) Bolivian ethnic minority.

1.8. Who speaks Afro-Yungueño Spanish?

Several thousand Afro-Bolivians scattered throughout the Yungas, but only a tiny fraction of this population maintains any fluency in the traditional Afro-Yungueño dialect, with a somewhat larger group possessing some passive competence. With the arrival of schooling in Spanish, Afro-Bolivians in the Yungas were exposed to national varieties of the language, as well as to standard written language. To this day, fragments of the traditional dialect can be heard in all of the predominantly Afro-Bolivian communities as well as in more mixed communities, though there it appears to be limited to Afro-Bolivians. But this traditional dialect has been reduced to a few stereotyped expressions, such as *jay*[16] and *cho*,[17] as well as unconscious carryovers from the older dialect, such as the occasional invariant plural or lack of noun-adjective concordance.

According to all the individuals interviewed, there were never explicit comments from teachers against the unique Afro-Bolivian dialect. The process of hearing and studying more normative "outside" Spanish caused most Afro-Yungueños to begin avoiding the traditional dialect, and to assume that their local speech was inferior. Many elderly Afro-Yungueños refer to themselves as having become *civilizaos* 'civilized' as a result of education and literacy. And when pressed, they also equate the traditional dialect with "uncivilized" behavior.

---

[16] An Aymara word meaning roughly "what?"; see Chapter 6.
[17] From the Aymara vocative *cchuy!*, meaning roughly "hey!".

FIGURE 1.7
Pablo Barra, Chijchipa (2007), contributor to the present project..

FIGURE 1.8
Mururata, the old cemetery.

Invariably the most fluent speakers are found among the communities' oldest
residents, age 65 and up. A few Afro-Bolivians in their 50's and even 40's are
able to speak the traditional dialect with reasonable fluency. Passive awareness
extends to some community members in their 20's and occasionally even adoles-
cents and smaller children.[18] In the twin communities of Mururata and Chijchipa
(described below), a higher percentage of residents have active competence in
the traditional dialect. Although community oral histories do not provide a firm
chronology for the gradual abandonment of the traditional dialect, extrapolation
from numerous interviews and personal testimonials yields the conclusion that,
by the late 1960's, use of the Afro-Yungueño dialect had diminished considerably as the vehicle for spontaneous communication in the Afro-Bolivian communities. It should be noted here that not all older Afro-Bolivians were raised speaking the Afro-Yungueño dialect exclusively or even fluently. Highland Bolivian
Spanish was often present, as it was commonly used by *mestizos* or Aymaras
who had married Afro-Bolivians, as well as by Afro-Bolivians who had lived or
worked outside of the traditional zones. One Afro-Bolivian born around 1885
and interviewed at the (self-proclaimed) age of 110 by Juan Angola Maconde
spoke non-Afro-Spanish, and had done so for most of his adult life, thus con-
firming the long-standing presence of non-Afro Spanish in at least some Afro-
Bolivian communities. Once the traditional dialect began to decline in daily
speech, certain stereotyped expressions survived as iconic reminders of the past.
In time, only these expressions remained in the memories of Afro-Bolivian community members. Today, when pressed for examples of the traditional dialect,
most Afro-Bolivians (except for the small number of fluent speakers) can only
offer the quintessential expression *cho, ande pueh ta(h) yendo?* 'hey, where are
you going?' This is one of the examples collected by Powe (1998: 850-851), and
is also embedded in the brief dialect sample given by Angola Maconde (2000:
13-14), himself a fluent Afro-Yungueño speaker. Other expressions readily
recalled by Afro-Bolivians are the traditional greetings *buen día de Dios, buenas
tardes de Dios* 'good morning from God, good afternoon from God', and the use
of *tío* 'uncle' and *tía* 'aunt' to refer to adults, terms used frequently even today.
    Many older community members who received no formal education make
occasional grammatical and phonetic slips into the traditional dialect without being
aware of doing so; this typically takes the form of invariant plurals and lapses of
noun-adjective gender agreement. Only rarely is subject-verb agreement suspended when Afro-Bolivians attempt to speak modern Spanish. Frequent among some

---

[18] Passive awareness refers to the fact that such speakers immediately recognize dialect-spe-
      cific words and expressions when presented with them, and also easily follow conversa-
      tions held in the dialect, a feat which is considerably more difficult for outsiders.

FIGURE 1.9
Postcard of an Afro-Bolivian child

older speakers is a weak articulation of word-final /s/ and loss of word-final /r/ in infinitives. These two traits of the Afro-Yungueño dialect stand in sharp contrast to the contemporary speech of the Yungas and surrounding highlands.

The precise geographic extension of the traditional Afro-Yungueño dialect in its most restructured form has yet to be determined. This is no easy task given widely scattered nature of homesteads and communities, and the lack of reliable testimony from neighbors and family members. Fieldwork conducted to date has documented the presence of this dialect only in the following Nor Yungas communities: Dorado Chico, Coscoma, Mururata, Tocaña, Chijchipa, and the immediate environs of these communities. Elderly speakers born in Santa Bárbara, near Tocaña, can also speak the dialect, but apparently they no longer use it in their tiny community. San José, near Dorado Chico, was also once home to a more attenuated form of traditional Afro-Bolivian Spanish (as evidenced by an interview with an elderly Afro-Bolivian, now living in La Paz), of which no remains can be found in this predominantly Aymara community.[19] Outside of this region Afro-Bolivians explicitly indicate

---

[19] Figure 8.1 (p. 187) shows the approximate location of these communities, most of which do not appear on readily available maps of Bolivia.

that they are neither familiar with nor employ the deepest form of Afro-Bolivian speech, although a few of its traits, such as invariant plurals and some lapses in noun-adjective agreement, are found as far away as Chicaloma (Sud Yungas).

Within the region where the traditional Afro-Bolivian dialect is spoken, the most restructured variety is found in Mururata and Chijchipa. Some residents of Mururata affirm that their own variety is a little "deeper" than that of nearby Chijchipa (a 15-minute walk away), but there is no empirical evidence to support this assertion. Most Afro-Bolivians in Mururata believe that the speech of Chijchipa is identical to their own. Only in these two communities are some of the following features found: (1) analogical preterits (e.g., *ponió* 's/he put') from *poner* 'to put', *hació* 's/he did' from *hacer* 'to do', *vinió* 's/he came' from *venir* 'to come', *dició* 's/he said' from *decir* 'to say'); (2) consistent use of the invariant 3rd person singular verb even with the first person *yo* (e.g., *yo eh* 'I am'); (3) use of *nuay* for 'I don't have'; and (4) complete suspension of grammatical gender marking.

In Tocaña, the other predominantly Afro-Bolivian community in this region, also known for its Afro-Bolivian sense of identity, little remains of the traditional dialect, even among the oldest residents. When pressed for dialect samples, more Spanish-like constructions emerge, a fact also noted by residents of Mururata.

Although speakers of the traditional dialect are found in all of the aforementioned communities and in some others as well, only in Mururata and Chijchipa does this vernacular continue to be used spontaneously and on a daily basis. Visits to Mururata and Chijchipa confirm that in conversations among Afro-Bolivians, the traditional dialect is used frequently, mixed unconsciously with non-Afro-Spanish. This Afro-Bolivian dialect is observed more frequently among women, who use it even when addressing small children. The latter typically respond in non-Afro-Spanish, but some active use of the traditional dialect occurs by the children, and passive competence is complete. In both Mururata and Chijchipa there are still some young adults (in their 20's) and even a few children who have active competence in the traditional dialect (mixing in of modern Spanish).

1.9. Why has Afro-Bolivian Spanish survived?

In Mexico, Chile, Paraguay, and Ecuador, there are numerous small Afro-Hispanic enclaves, including some surrounded by indigenous or mestizo populations with widely divergent histories and cultural practices.[20] In other countries,

---

[20]   For Mexico, see Aguirre Beltrán (1958); for Chile, Canto Larios (2003); for Paraguay, Machado (2000); for Ecuador, Lipski (1986e, 1987a), Peñaherrera de Costales and Costales Samaniego (1959), Schwegler (1994).

FIGURE 1.10
Postcard of scenes from the Yungas, with an Afro-Bolivian woman and child
identified only as from Chicaloma

for example Peru, Venezuela, Colombia, and Cuba,[21] there are isolated Afro-Hispanic communities within a larger society with considerable African cultural history. Several of these communities are descended from original maroon villages.
In El Palenque de San Basilio (Colombia), a complete creole language, possibly
formed at least partially in Africa before arriving in Colombia, continues to be
spoken (Friedemann and Patiño Rosselli 1983, Schwegler 1996a). Only in the
Bolivian Yungas, however, does what will be shown to be a complete restructured Afro-Hispanic language exist, evidently without maroon antecedents or ritual function, and apparently formed *in situ* over four centuries ago.

There are several reasons for the survival of Afro-Bolivian Spanish. Some of
these are:

- **GEOGRAPHIC ISOLATION.** Although today the Yungas are no more than half
  a day's drive from La Paz, prior to the ready availability of motorized

---

[21] For Cuba, Ortiz López (1998); for Venezuela, Mosonyi, Hernández and Alvarado (1983);
for Peru, Cuba (1996); for Colombia, Granda (1977) and Schwegler (1991a).

transport, only very few Yungueños ever traveled to other regions of the country. The mountainous terrain precludes travel by horseback, and even mules struggle along the narrow footpaths that until recently provided the only access to some communities. Travel on foot required several days of hiking. This fact and the unavailability of appropriate nighttime shelter deterred all but the most determined voyagers.

- **FORCED LABOR ON THE HACIENDAS.** Until the land reform of 1952, black Yungueños were forcibly concentrated on the haciendas, where they worked as peons or serfs. As such, they were not allowed to travel or change haciendas without the owners' permission. And although black Yungueños lived in their own dwellings rather than in barracks, the social and linguistic concentration was not unlike that found in the 19th-century Afro-Cuban *barracones* on the *ingenios* or sugar plantations, where African languages were commonly spoken. There is no evidence that Afro-Bolivians spoke African languages when they arrived in the Yungas. Not only is there no mention of African languages in Afro-Bolivian oral history, but no demonstrably African words survive in contemporary speech. Afro-Bolivians brought with them a partially restructured Spanish as a carryover from the period when *bozal* speakers of African languages worked in the highland mining areas.

- **PROLONGED ISOLATION FROM BOLIVIAN SPANISH.** Although nowadays almost all indigenous residents of the Yungas speak Spanish with reasonable fluency, until the second half of the 20th century this region was essentially a monolingual Aymara community. Older Afro-Bolivians who worked on haciendas under Aymara-speaking overseers were often forced to speak Aymara, presumably because of the overseers' limited competence in Spanish, as well as the contempt these same overseers exhibited towards the language of the landowners. Even today, Afro-Bolivians tend to know some Aymara, (most claim not to be fully bilingual); fluency in Aymara is more prevalent among the oldest residents, who recall times when Aymara was the lingua franca for non-black residents of the Yungas Black Bolivians arrived in the Yungas speaking an evidently partially restructured variety of Spanish, which they used for in-group communication against the backdrop of a very different surrounding language, much as Sephardic (Judeo) Spanish survived for centuries while surrounded by Balkan languages, Turkish, and Greek (Bürki, Schmid and Schwegler 2006). This configuration made Afro-Yungueño Spanish much more of an linguistic enclave prior to 1952 than it is today, and contributed to the retention of their local Spanish variety as a means of communication among Afro-Bolivians. Despite at least two centuries

FIGURE 1.11
Video of Afro-Bolivian dances.

of coexistence in the Yungas, few Afro-Bolivians have intermarried with indigenous residents. And although daily contacts are cordial and unproblematic, there is relatively little cultural mixing. It is noteworthy than while the non-Afro-Spanish used by contemporary Afro-Bolivians in the Yungas shows evidence of Aymara-influenced word order (witness, for instance, the preference for object-verb order, discussed further in Chapter 8), the traditional Afro-Bolivian dialect bears no demonstrable Aymara imprint.

- **STRONG ETHNIC IDENTITY AS *NEGROS*.** Despite the existence of the patently Central African surname *Angola* and the surname *Maconde* (probably referring to the Makonde people of Mozambique and the neighboring region of Tanzania) in the Afro-Bolivian communities, awareness of an African past was all but non-existent until small numbers of residents obtained higher education, beginning in the 1970s. Even today, few rural Afro-Bolivians have any knowledge of Africa, the Atlantic slave trade, or of the existence of communities of African descent elsewhere in the Americas. I have, for instance, been asked by numerous Afro-Yungueños young and old, whether there are black people in the United States. They also wondered if there are indeed black people in Africa and parts of Latin America. Despite the general lack of knowledge about things African, Afro-Bolivians have always had a strong sense of being *negros* (their preferred term), and of possessing cultural and linguistic values that set them apart from the remainder of their indigenous and mestizo compatriots. This sense of a close-knit ethnic community has immediate repercussions for language use, as all Afro-Bolivians are at least passively aware that the traditional dialect is spoken only by (a subset of) black residents. Even in communities with a high percentage of Afro-Bolivians, such as Mururata and Tocaña, some residents confessed to not using the traditional dialect in the presence of non-Afro-Bolivians. This behavior is apparently not linked to potential difficulties with understanding the dialect; rather it seems to have a purely social explanation, as speakers only feel comfortable using the dialect freely *entre puros negritos* 'only among black people' (in the words of one community member). Thus while a number of outside observers have commented on the "accent" of Afro-Bolivians in the Yungas, few scholars have actually heard the truly unique traditional dialect, which accounts for its absence both in treatises on Bolivian Spanish and in documents regarding Afro-Hispanic communities. This situation is similar to what occurred in El Palenque de San Basilio, Colombia, where the creole –known locally as *lengua*– is spoken alongside a regional vernacular variety of Spanish (Schwegler and Morton 2003) that was long misidenti-

PEDRO REY. *Un riachuelo desconsolado asoma a los ojos de este anciano cuando recuerda a sus hijos, que lo abandonaron en Mururata al enviudar hace cinco años. Desempolvó su viejo traje de saya, agradeció las fotografías y pidió que no se olviden de él*

FIGURE 1.12
Clipping about an Afro-Bolivian *saya* dancer.

fied as simply a curious (and presumably deformed) local Spanish dialect.[22]

For these and other reasons, a truly distinct Afro-Hispanic language survived until quite recently in central Bolivia, and it did so unbeknownst to the rest of the world –even to most other Bolivians. As with many minority languages and dialects in isolated societies that experience sudden insertion into the "modern" world through educational reform and improved transportation and communication, the traditional Afro-Bolivian dialect shows signs of disappearing within less than two generations of its intensified contact with the outside world. As is natural, this increases the urgency of documenting the speech of the last remaining generation of fluent speakers.

1.10. Afro-Bolivian "folk revival" and its implications for language usage

After centuries of marginality, discrimination, racism, forced servitude, and total neglect by the Bolivian government and the rest of the world, some contemporary Afro-Bolivians are achieving a measure of recognition through commercial diffusion of their music and dance (especially the *saya*), which constitute the core of Afro-Bolivian folk tradition. The *saya* is the one facet of Afro-Bolivian culture that is widely known throughout the country, and it has considerable potential for commercial success. The "Movimiento Cultural Saya Afroboliviana" is the major exponent of this Afro-Bolivian cultural dissemination. Most members of the group reside in La Paz. They participate actively in musical and cultural events in Bolivia and in neighboring coun-

---

[22] This town was visited during the collection of data for the comprehensive linguistic atlas of Colombia, but even the experienced fieldworkers heard (or at least noticed) the use of Spanish (Montes Giraldo 1962). It was not until the creolist Derek Bickerton teamed up with the Colombian ethnographer Aquiles Escalante, who had written an extensive but obscurely published and little-known study of Palenque many years earlier (Escalante 1954) that the true nature of the Palenquero language became known. Escalante (1954) had given numerous specimens of fairly authentic Palenquero speech, but described them as though they were archaic dialectal curiosities rather than a language distinct from Spanish. Together, Bickerton and Escalante (1970) demonstrated both the vitality of the Palenquero language and its status as a true creole language virtually unintelligible to Spanish speakers. These observations were later confirmed by Friedemann and Patiño Roselli (1983), Megenney (1986), Schwegler (1996a), and others.

FIGURE 1.13
Cover of recording of traditional Afro-Bolivian music.

tries. As the most politically and socially visible Afro-Bolivian group, the leaders of the Movimiento Cultural Saya Afroboliviana frequently act as spokespersons for all black Bolivians; their names often appear in interviews, newspaper and magazine articles about Afro-Bolivians. The focus on music and dance to the exclusion of the urgent plight of rural Afro-Bolivians is the source of some ambivalent feelings, but this same cultural manifestation is a magnet for attention from entities that would otherwise show no interest in black Bolivians.

1.11. Previous publications about Afro-Bolivians and their language

There is no mention of traits peculiar to Afro-Bolivians in any linguistic study of
Bolivian Spanish. In fact, the presence of a black population in contemporary
Bolivia is never even mentioned in such works. Bolivia is always cast as a multilingual mestizo nation, with Quechua and Aymara being the two indigenous languages that have the greatest contact with Spanish nationwide. Thus Coello Vila
divides Bolivia into three dialect regions, "determinados, en gran medida, por la
influencia del sustrato, por el bilingüismo y por las consecuencias emergentes de
las lenguas en contacto" [determined in large measure by substratum influences,
by bilingualism, and by the emergent consequences of language contact]. The
speech of the Yungas is a "variedad del castellano paceño [...] influencia del
aimara" [a variety of La Paz Spanish [...] [with] Aymara influence] (1996: 172-
173). This viewpoint is echoed by Templeman (1994: 8) that "The Spanish spoken by rural Black agriculturalists is a dialect, and Afro-Bolivians maintain a
small vocabulary of words of African origin" and Templeman (1998: 430) that
"Tocañans speak a dialect of Spanish. Their vocabulary consists of a mixture of
Spanish, Aymara, and African-derived words." In fact, no Afro-Bolivian lexical
items are of demonstrable African origin.

Spedding, who has spent considerable time in the Afro-Yungueños community, declares –accurately so– that "they speak a dialect of local Spanish with an
accent and styles of expression different from those used by Aymara-Spanish
bilingual speakers" (1995: 324). This assertion is true even of the "modern"
Spanish of Afro-Yungueños, which contain little of the Aymara interference traits
found among indigenous speakers. In a description of the largely Afro-Bolivian
village of Chicaloma (Sud Yungas), it is said that "[e]l idioma de varias familias
negras actualmente es el aymara y el castellano con ciertas variantes fonológi-
cas" [the language of many black families is currently Aymara and Spanish with
certain phonetic variants] (Gobierno Municipal de La Paz 1993: n.p.). It is true
that, in Sud Yungas, the Afro-Yungueño dialect has little presence: there, most
speakers are bilingual Aymara speakers, but there are no empirically verifiable
"phonological variants" separating black and non-black speakers in this region.
Costa Ardúz observes neutrally that in Nor Yungas "[h]ay también en la región
una minoría negra que si bien han adoptado muchos rasgos de su economía y
cultura aymaras, mantienen en lo fundamental su lengua materna como el castellano" [in this region, there is also a black minority that while having adopted
many Aymara cultural and economic practices, maintains Spanish as the mother
tongue] (1997: 76).

Powe, who traveled through the region and visited most of the small Afro-
Bolivian settlements, comments that "a curious aspect of Black (and Aymara)

FIGURE 1.14
Press coverage of an Afro-Bolivian *curandera*.

speech in this region is the pronunciation of the Spanish "rr" as an English "z" (1998: 816); this pronunciation in fact stems from indigenous influence, and characterizes the entire Andean region, from southern Colombia to northwestern Argentina. At another point, Powe gives a reasonably accurate transcription of some fragments of Afro-Yungas dialect (in this case from Chijchipa), written in non-Spanish fashion and inaccurately described as Aymara code-mixing:

> [...] Blacks sometimes use Aymara words or grammar when speaking. For instance instead of saying "*¿Dónde estás yendo?*" ("Where are you going?") they say "*¿Andi po teta ondo?*" and for "*¿Qué estás haciendo aquí?*" ("What are you doing here?"), they say "*ke po teta asi aki*" (Powe 1998: 850-851).

In fact, both iexpressions contain only patrimonial Spanish words, although with considerable phonological and morphosyntactic restructuring:

andi	[< *onde* < *dónde*]	'where (to)'
po(h)	[< *pos* < *pues*]	'oh well'
oté	[< *usted*]	'you'

ta	[< *está*]	'are'
ondo	[< yendo]	'going'

qué		'what'	
po(h)	[< *pos*] (std. *pues*)	'well, then'	
oté	[< *usted*]	'you'	
ta	[< *está*]	'are'	
así		[< *haciendo*]	'doing'
akí		[< *aquí*]	'here'

The use of *ande* 'where' for *onde* (the archaic form of *donde*) is found in many rustic Spanish dialects, including the Canary Islands, northern New Mexico, and parts of Central America, among others. It is also documented for rural Bolivia. Similarly, *pos* (the archaic form of *pues* 'well then') survives in all of rural Mexico, much of Central America, and sporadically elsewhere in the Spanish-speaking world. Non-Afro-Bolivians sometimes use this variant, which transforms into *pu(h)* in northern Chile and southern Peru. Neither *ande* nor *pos* is typically used by contemporary indigenous or mestizo speakers in the Yungas; this suggests that the words in question come from much earlier periods, in which Afro-Bolivians acquired Spanish from uneducated speakers of non-standard dialects. Whereas today's Afro-Bolivians may incorporate Aymara words and expressions into their Spanish, they derive their vernacular Spanish features not from contact with indigenous speakers but from earlier colonial sources.

Montaño Aragón notes that "[e]n cuanto al habla típica de los negros, el castellano pronunciado por ellos recuerda al empleado en el Río de la Plata y también en otras áreas de Latinoamérica" [as for the typical speech of black people, they pronounce Spanish in a fashion reminiscent of the Rio de la Plata and also of other parts of Latin America] (1992: 268). No examples accompany Montaño Aragón's statement, which probably refers to the combination of aspirated /s/ and *yeísmo* (lack of phoneme /ʎ/, although Afro-Yungueños do not pronounce /j/ as [ʒ] or [ʃ] as in the Río de la Plata region). He then gives a list of words of purported African origin, some of which are used elsewhere in Latin America. Another description of Afro-Yungueño speech is: "un castellano deformado en la pronunciación y a veces en lo semántico" [a phonetically and sometimes semantically deformed Spanish] (Montaño Aragón 1992: 272). His examples include:

Arroz	>	*aró, aló*	'rice'; in fact, the change /r/ > [l] has not been observed by anyone else in Afro-Yungueño speech or any other Bolivian dialect.
lo he	>	*loi*	3rd person singular clitic + 1st person singular of *haber* 'to have'

Usted	>	oté	'you'
madre	>	mai	'mother'
padre	>	pai	'father'
¿qué dice?	>	¿insé?	'what are you saying?'
eres	>	sois	'you are'
regalar	>	rigalar	'to give'
Estar	>	istar	'to be'

(Montaño Aragón 1992: 272)

Most of these items have nothing "Afro" about them, but rather represent the partial merger of unstressed /e/ and /i/, /o/ and /u/, especially in word-final position. *Mai* and *pai* are similar to the Portuguese forms, but are more likely derived from *comai* < *comadre* and *compai* < *compadre*, heard in vernacular Spanish dialects throughout the world. The form *sois* has not been observed or confirmed by any Afro-Bolivians consulted for the present project. The *voseo* verb form *sos* is passively known in this region, but is used actively only in the dialects of Bolivia's eastern lowlands and neighboring areas of Paraguay and Argentina. Some Chileans use the form *soi(s)* but this is unlikely to have made its way to the Bolivian Yungas. The item *¿insé?* is indeed used in Mururata and Chijchipa and occasionally in Tocaña, but is employed interchangeably with *¿acaso?,* said with rapidly rising intonation; its meaning is "really?", and as such functions as an expression of incredulity. It is unlikely to have come from *¿qué dice?*; a more plausible source for this as yet unstudied word may be *¿en serio?* 'really?'.

A newspaper article (Anon. 2004) describes Afro-Bolivian culture in traditional terms of dance and clothing, funeral rites, and handicrafts. One interesting allusion to speech is this:

> Hasta la manera de expresarse es diferente. Su lengua es el español, mas lleva modismos que sólo los negros comprenden. Los jóvenes investigan y creen que su acento es una herencia de los primeros hombres llegados de otro continente para ser sometidos como esclavos.

> [Even the way of speaking is different. Their language is Spanish, but with expressions that only Black people understand. Some young people have researched this and believe that their accent is a heritage of the first people brought from another continent as slaves].

I encountered few Afro-Bolivians who actively comment on the history of their speech modes. A black resident of Mururata (Nor Yungas) lamented:

> Hemos ido cambiando muchas costumbres de nuestros abuelos, nosotros mismos ya tenemos vergüenza hasta de hablar nuestro modismo que es tan bonito. Por ejemplo

jay, era una palabra que enriquecía nuestro hablar. La juventud actual, ya no quiere seguir practicando nuestra cultura que es muy rica.

[We've changed many of the customs of our grandparents; we are now ashamed to speak our dialect, which is so beautiful. For example the word *jay* [an Aymara interjection meaning roughly "what?"] used to enrich our speech. Young people now don't want to continue our culture, which is very rich.]

(Anon. n.d.)

1.12. Early Afro-Bolivian literary examples

Although Africans and their descendents have been living in Bolivia continuously since the 16th century, their representation in literary and folkloric texts is sparse, and is limited to a couple of 17th-century songs and a few 20th-century stories. The songs follow the *habla de negro* literary stereotypes established in Golden Age Spain by such writers as Lope de Rueda, Lope de Vega, Góngora, Simón Aguado, Sánchez de Badajoz, and later imitated in Spanish America by Sor Juana Inés de la Cruz (Lipski 1995b, 2005).

The first song is the anonymous "Esa noche yo baila". It begins as follows:

Esa noche yo baila.	'Tonight I dance.'
con Maria lucume	'with María Lucumí'
asta sol que amanece	'until dawn'
Plo mi Dios que sa acuya	'for my God who is there'
esa gente comensa	'the people begin'
aunque pe la buena fe	'even in good faith'
su hichito ya nace	'his son is born'

(Claro 1974: lxxv-lxxvii)

Another anonymous text from Alto Peru, apparently written in the late 17th or early 18th century, contains the *estornudo* that has metamorphosed into the *¡suerte negrito!* shout of modern Bolivia is the *villancico* "Afuela apalta (Negros al portal)". It opens this way:

Afuela, afuela apalta apalta	'Stand back, get away'
que entlamo la tlopa Gazpala	'king Caspar's troops are entering'
apalta, afuela	'stand back get away'
que entlamo la gualda re reye Guineya	'we the Guinea king's guards are entering'
e lo pífalo soplal	'blowing our pipes'
e mandamo echal plegon	'and shouting slogans'
respetamo ro branco	'we respect white people'
tenemo atención	'we are careful'

(Fortún de Ponce 1957: 122f.)

FIGURE 1.15
Cover of the novel *Zambo Salvito*

These texts contain numerous phonetic deformations, all of which probably occurred to a certain extent in early Afro-Hispanic language; these include substitution of *r* for *l* (a trait typical of Bantu languages), pronunciation of *d* as *r*, addition of final vowels to words ending in a consonant, elimination of final consonants, especially -*s* and -*r*, and intrusive nasal consonants (e.g., *nenglo* < *negro*). Some of the traits are common to most second-language learners of Spanish, others suggest areal traits of specific African language families, and some are idiosyncratic and possible pure inventions by the white racist authors of these *negrillo* songs. Grammatical modifications are more typical of second-language learners, and include lapses in noun-adjective and subject-verb agreement, use of disjunctive object pronouns instead of clitics, and a generally simplified syntax, with few subordinate clauses. These texts could have been produced anywhere, and do not reflect the inevitable three-way linguistic and cultural contacts involving Spanish, African languages, and Andean languages. Indeed, there is no confirmation that the songs were actually composed in Bolivia (or even in America), although they were presumably performed there.

Of potentially more relevance to contemporary Afro-Bolivian Spanish is the humorous skit "Entremés gracioso para la festividad de Nuestra Señora, año 1799", recently discovered in the archives of Potosí, Bolivia (Arellano and Eichmann 2005: 163-217). The text of this short play contains numerous examples of stereotyped Afro-Hispanic language that differ significantly from Golden Age texts produced in Spain and colonial Latin America. In addition to containing numerous examples of *bozales'* L2 use of Quechua words and expressions, this play exhibits several features found in contemporary Afro-Bolivian speech. These include:

(a)   loss of final /ɾ/ in verbal infinitives and in *mujer* 'woman, wife';
(b)   pronunciation of *pues* 'well, then' as *pue*;
(c)   realization of the palatal lateral /ʎ/ as an approximant or glide [j]; a genderless third-person subject pronoun *eye* (identical in form to *elle*, found in Afro-Cuban and Afro-Panamanian *congo* speech); and
(d)   consistent use of the 3rd person singular as invariant verb form.

Although the language of this skit is considerably different from contemporary Afro-Bolivian speech, it does suggest that some colonial literary imitations of Afro-Hispanic language were based on actual observation of *bozal* language, and not on mere repetition of time-worn stereotypes brought over from Spain. In the following examples from the "Entremés gracioso" (Arellano and Eichmann 2005), the aforementioned points (a) – (d) are given in bold-face are:

*Yo no **tiene** sino rientes.* (p. 165)	'I only have teeth.'
*Amiguito sacritana bata ya, **pué**, de **reñí**.* (p. 173)	'Sacristan, my friend, enough quarreling.'
*Y **plegunta** yo una cosa.* (p. 175)	'And I ask one thing.'
eye me rom pagará (p. 176)	'(s)he will pay me [for this offense]'
*dejame, **mujé**, po Rioso* (p. 191)	'leave me [alone], woman, for God's sake'
*y si tanto me provoca ute también **yevará*** (p. 197)	'and if you provoke me so, [I will] also carry you off'

1.13. Afro-Bolivian literary representations in the 20th century

Despite the relatively small size of the Afro-Bolivian population, a few 20th-century folktales and regionalist novels offer imitations of what is presumed to be the speech of Bolivians of African ancestry. Paredes Candia provides fragments such as:

Mile patloncito, costal lleno no puede doblalse.	'Look, boss, a full sack can't be folded.'
Me voy pa el pueblo, vas a vigilar bien a tu comagre porque el Pedrito está por acá. Si li pego en el poto, mi lo meto más adentro, si li pego en la cabeza mi lo besa mijor dejaré que terminen.	'I'm going to town. Look after your comadre because Pedrito is hanging around here. If I kick his ass, I'll get my foot stuck; if I hit him in the head, I'll get kissed; I'll just leave them alone.'
Mañana mismo, negrito flegado, compra una frazada. Calentate perno con el sol bendito, qué frazada ni que merda.	'Tomorrow, damn black man, buy a blanket. Warm up in the sun, to hell with the blanket.'

(Paredes Candia 1988a: 366-367)

These texts bear the characteristics of the Bolivian *Oriente* (e.g., the region around Santa Cruz), where a number of Afro-Bolivians have resettled from the Yungas in the past half century. Linguistic traits of these texts include aspiration of syllable-final -*s* and the diminutive suffix –*ingo*, not found elsewhere in Bolivia but typical of the Santa Cruz dialect. The most prominent non-Bolivian feature –implicitly associated with "black" Spanish– is the pronunciation of *r* as *l* (cp. *fregado* > *flegado* 'damned'), a pronunciation not found anywhere in Bolivia, not even among Afro-Yungas speakers. The formulaic use of the change of *r* to *l* to represent "black" speech, in the absence of other phonetic, grammatical, or lexical traits, has been a mainstay of the literary parodies of the *habla de negro* since the Spanish Golden Age. Quevedo (1988) remarked that in order to speak *guineo* –as he called *bozal* Spanish– it sufficed to change all instances of *r* to *l*: "sabrás guineo en volviendo las rr ll, y al contrario: como Francisco, *Flancico*; primo, *plimo"* [you can speak Guinea by turning every R into L and vice versa: *Francisco* to *Flancico, primo* to *plimo*]. Although some African language families (most notably the Bantu group) do produce this type of pattern, other African languages consistently distinguish *l* from *r*. Even speakers of African languages that do not distinguish *l* and *r* normally acquire Spanish and Portuguese with little confusion of these sounds (cp. the Spanish of Equatorial Guinea and the Portuguese of Angola and Mozambique [Lipski 1985a]), although early borrowings into these Bantu languages, based on the briefest contact with Romance languages, did embody this change. That this stereotype can persist through the end of the 20th century in a country where this sound change has probably not been heard for 400 years attests to the strength of racist parodies and their transmission in popular culture. The substitution of *r* for *l* in the absence of any other second-language traits is also found in Paredes-Candia's own novel *Zambo Salvito* (Fig. 1.8), set in colonial times and in the highlands, where this phonetic change has never prevailed:

¡Salvadol!, vení a vel lo que han hecho con tu padle el malvado del patlón, y el tigle de Pompeyo	'Salvador, come see what the damned boss has done to your father' (p. 14)
Ya no puele hijito, t'amos muy lejos, mejol que descansemos un rato y comamos estas racachitas que tlaigo.	'It can't be done, son, we're far away, we'd better rest and eat this food I've brought.' (p. 17)

(Paredes Candia 1988b)

It may be that the shift /r/ > [l] is identified with infantile speech; in the novel *Coca* (Botelho Gonsálvez 1941: 47), a very young girl says *Mamita, ¿papá tlaelá nalanjas?* 'Mommy, will daddy bring oranges?

Pizarroso Cuenca provides a story in which Afro-Bolivians speak in a dialect more reminiscent of Aymara speakers, a rather realistic portrayal for some areas of Sud Yungas, where Afro-Bolivians have married Aymaras, speak their language, and consider themselves to be Aymaras. Some examples are:

Gueno, ti lo voi hacer–il tal es, quil promesa lo cumplas. Il ternerito prieto ... mi lo darás in cuanto il obra ti lo haga.	'Okay, I'll do it if you keep your promise. The black calf ... you give it to me and I'll cast the spell.'

Mamita, el obra te loi cumpliu. Loi matau con macheti, a cumpadre in chumi, nada minus. Istá bien matau. No es quién velva! El ternero prieto lo llivaré. Loi hecho feliz al cumpadre.

'Baby, I've done it. I killed my *compadre* with a machete, just like that. He's good and dead. He won't come back. I'll take the black calf. I've made my *compadre* happy.'

(Pizarroso Cuenca 1977: 111-115)

These fragments contain the confusion of *i-e* and *o-u*, which is typical of Aymara-influenced Spanish, as well as occasional loss of definite articles. The text is perhaps a reasonable approximation to Afro-Bolivian speech in areas where the residents speak Aymara and identify with the Aymara culture, but it does not coincide with the unique Afro-Bolivian language found in Nor Yungas.

Botelho Gonsálvez's novel *Coca* (1941), set in the Yungas, contains black characters who speak unmarked Spanish, except for these two examples:

¡Mierrdas, indios, hay que apurar el trabajo!

'Damn Indians, get to work!'

¡Ignorantes, ignorantes de mierrda; apuren a los majo!

'Damn fools, work faster!' (p. 155)

(Botelho Gonsálvez 1941)

The first example may reflect the frequent trait of replacing the single tap [ɾ] with the trill [r]. The second appears to offer a case of an invariant or bare plural (*los majo* instead of *los majos*). There are no other indications in the novel that the author was familiar with the traditional Afro-Yungueño dialect, although his imitations of Aymara-influenced Spanish are quite realistic.

1.14. Data collection for the present study

Data for the present study were collected during several field trips, conducted in June 2004, August and October 2005, August 2006, and June 2007. The following communities were visited: Dorado Chico, Coscoma, Khala Khala, Coripata, Arapata, Coroico, Tocaña, Mururata, Chijchipa, Negrillani, and Chicaloma (Fig. 1.1, p. 25). Some Afro-Bolivians from the Yungas were also interviewed in La Paz, where they were residing temporarily. All visits were made with Juan Angola Maconde, to whom I owe a tremendous debt of gratitude. In Mururata and Chijchipa Antonia Pinedo Zalles provided expert guidance and introduction to the communities. In total, more than 100 Afro-Bolivians were interviewed and recorded, and the data from these interviews provide the primary basis for this study.

CHAPTER 2

PHONETICS AND PHONOLOGY

2.1. The phonetics of Afro-Yungueño Spanish

Although the most striking features of the traditional Afro-Bolivian dialect are found in the realm of grammar, the phonetic patterns also contrast with the neighboring Andean dialects of Bolivia. When switching between the traditional Afro-Yungueño dialect and modern Bolivian Spanish, Afro-Bolivians also shift certain phonetic patterns. For some speakers, traditional phonetic patterns also carry over partially to their contemporary Spanish. Unlike the grammatical features of the Afro-Bolivian dialect, which are not found in any other natively spoken variety of Spanish past or present, the phonetic features of this dialect are all found in other Spanish dialects, albeit in differing proportions. Many of the Afro-Bolivian phonetic traits are common denominators of attested and reconstructed Afro-Hispanic language, and whereas none can be attributed exclusively to contact with African languages, they coincide with the phonotactic patterns of a broad cross-section of West and Central African languages known to have come into contact with Spanish and Portuguese. In order to properly situate Afro-Bolivian phonetic patterns, I shall first describe the surrounding highland dialect, as spoken in La Paz and neighboring provinces. Nearly all Afro-Bolivians in the Yungas employ this regional Spanish as their second dialect.

2.2. Phonetic overview of highland Bolivian Spanish

The unique phonetic traits of the Afro-Yungueño dialect are set against the regional varieties of Spanish spoken in Nor Yungas, Sud Yungas, Caranavi, Inquisivi, and neighboring dialects of the department of La Paz (Figure 1.1). These regional features are essentially those of highland Bolivia, with overlays of Aymara phonotactic influence. Bolivian dialectological studies do not distinguish between the speech varieties of the Yungas (technically not highlands but rather tropical valleys) and the surrounding mountain highlands. Thus Coello Vila (1996: 172-173) divides Bolivia into three dialect regions, "determinados, en gran medida, por la influencia del sustrato, por el bilingüismo y por las conse-

64   John Lipski

cuencias emergentes de las lenguas en contacto" [determined in large measure
by substratum influences, by bilingualism, and by the emergent consequences of
language contact]. The Yungas subdialect is simply described as a "variedad del
castellano paceño [...] influencia del aimara" [a variety of La Paz Spanish [...]
[with] Aymara influence]. The maps in Figure 2.1 (from Canfield 1981: 29) show
the broad divisions of Bolivian Spanish, between the Andean highlands and the
eastern / northern lowlands. The central valleys, typified by Cochabamba, are
often considered to be a third dialect zone, although from the point of view of
pronunciation there is greater similarity to the highland dialect than to the eastern variety. The same is true of Tarija, often considered to be a separate dialect
(based on grammar, vocabulary, and intonation), but belonging substantially to
the highland dialect cluster.

2.3. Detailed phonetic traits of highland Bolivian Spanish

Highland Bolivian Spanish has the following characteristic phonetic traits:

(1) Syllable- or word-final /s/ is almost always a sibilant; aspiration or efface-
    ment is vanishingly rare. In comparative terms, the rate of retention of final
    /s/ as [s] in the Andean region ranks among the highest of all the Spanish
    dialects worldwide (Lipski 1983, 1984, 1986e). Occasionally, word-final /s/
    is voiced to [z], although not to the extent found in Ecuador and other
    regions that exhibit this feature (Lipski 1989b).
(2) The trill /r/ is given a groove fricative pronunciation approximately [ʒ] as in
    English *measure*. Among bilingual speakers, the realization of /r/ is more
    frequently the sibilant [z]. In the most popular varieties, a new phonological
    opposition based on voicing has been formed: /s/ and /r/ differ only in voic-
    ing, i.e., [s] vs. [z], thus sharing all other articulatory traits: *sazón* [sa'son]
    'season', *razón* [za'zon] 'reason'.
(3) Monolingual Bolivian Spanish speakers articulate the five vowels of Span-
    ish without confusion, but there is some instability of the oppositions /i/ vs.
    /e/ and /o/ vs. /u/, inversely correlated with fluency in Spanish among
    Aymara- and Quechua-speaking bilinguals. Although popular literature
    often portrays the Spanish of Aymara-dominant speakers as randomly mix-
    ing these vowel pairs, in fact for most speakers vocalic confusion is limited
    to a few lexical items. This form of speech is often referred to as *hablar
    moteroso,* roughly 'to speak wrong' (cp. the term *motoso / motosidad* used
    in Peru to describe the same vocalic mergers). Literary stereotypes are typi-
    fied by:

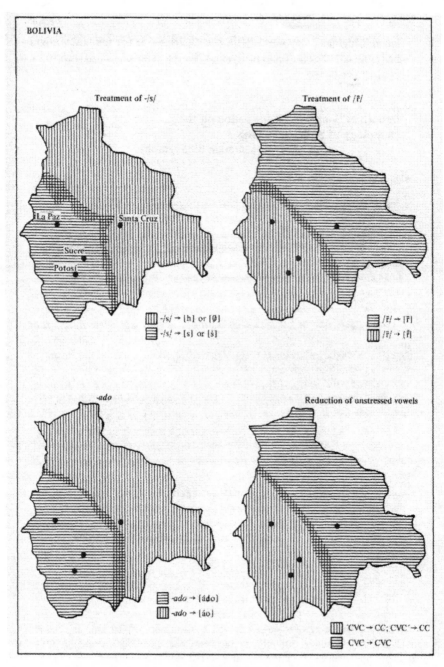

FIGURE 2.1
Bolivian dialect zones (from Canfield 1981: 29)

A la pocha, chi, criyu qui mi he equevucado di mircadu [...] u al consiju me he veneru, pur isu me istan merandu cumu para murdirmi? (Barrera Gutiérrez 2000a: 25)

'Damn, I think I've come to the wrong market, or to the town council; is that why they are looking at me like they want to bite me?'

Ahura tinis qui hablar con rispitamintos, chis. Trabajo in el Transeto. Wareta y mochachos win entosiasmos. Si te vas contra rotas, si ti pasas il simáforos en lo rojas, ti toco to pito. (Salmón 1999a: 27)

'Now you have to talk respectfully. I work in the Transit department. Enthusiastic boys. If you run stop signs or red lights, I'll blow my whistle at you.'

No poides, tata. Yo tener que regresar al tambo para coidar mis borritos. (Botelho Gonsálvez 1957: 20)

'I can't, sir. I have to return to my farm to take care of my donkeys.'

Nara sempre mama, nara, sultera jay suy. (Barrera Gutiérrez 2000b: 98)

'Nothing, mother, I'm a single girl.'

Chau "ahuichito", y dipindi di vus para salvarti, e si nu puidis, mi lo salodas a dun San Pidru, é si pur casoalidad ti mandan dundi dun "SATA", me lu deces qui il pruximu añu voy bailar la deablada in so comparsa. (Barrera Gutiérrez 2001b: 75)

'Good bye, grampa, it's up to you to save yourself, and if you can't, say hello to Saint Peter for me, and if you end up in the other place, let me know and I'll dance the "devil dance" in next year's carnival.'

Ti loy traydo un poquito di discados y requesón pa que comas [...] Juancho, istás meletar tris años, en tris años no has trabajadu. Por qui no te reteras y guelves a nuestro ayllu? (Botelho Gonsálvez 1945: 75)

'I've brought you some bread and cheese to eat [...] Juan, you've been in the army for three years, you haven't worked for three years. Why don't you quit and return to our lands?'

De esa si nu podria decir nada. La otra vez dicen qui ha quirido entrar en su tienda el hijo del Manuchu, que siempre estaba enamorado de ella. Piro mitió tal escánda-lo en Ismicha, que, el Sub le había ayudadu, haciéndolo meter a la policia al tipu. (Blym 1940: 36)

'I can't say anything about that. They say that last time that Manocho's son entered the store, he was always in love with her. But Esmicha was so upset that she got the assistant police chief to get the police after the guy.'

Examples observed in everyday speech include:

El choño dejamos [...] De ahí cuando está bien, está bien, está degamos que tienen el además en Junio sacamos el choño [...] y le metemos aguas y onos quince días. (Mendoza 1991: 249-250)

'We leave the *chuño* [desiccated potatoes] [...] then when it's ready, so to speak, then in June we get the *chuño*.'

Primerito así es, me he venido, no conocía, ya me ha traído me tía y después he dentrao en [...] (Mendoza 1991: 254)

'The first time, yes, I came, I didn't know, my aunt brought me, and then I got started [...]'

(4) The phoneme /ʎ/ (written *ll*) is always distinct from /ʝ/, and receives a palatal lateral pronunciation: *calle* ['kaᶒe] 'street', *playa* ['plaʝa] 'beach'. This is true of all Bolivian dialects, including eastern lowland and Amazonian regions, and in all sociolects. Bolivia is arguably the most *lleísta* nation in the entire Spanish-speaking world, together perhaps with neighboring Paraguay, where the distinction /ʎ/-/ʝ/ is found in all dialects. Unlike in Paraguay, where there is some shift of /ʎ/ to [ʝ] in the speech of the youngest generations,[1] Bolivian /ʎ/ is always realized as a palatal lateral, and does not merge with realizations of the palatal phoneme /ʝ/.

(5) The phoneme /ʝ/ is a palatal approximant. It does not acquire the prepalatal variants [ʒ] and [dʒ] found in the Río de la Plata dialects. In Aymara-influenced highland dialects, hypercorrect hiatus-breaking [j] may occur, similar to popular Central American speech: *creyo* < *creyo* 'I believe', *diya* < *día* 'day'. The feature in question is frequently represented in popular literature, for example:

¿Otro diya ya? Ahurita tengo que hacer. (Salmón 2000a: 23)

'Tomorrow already? I have things to do.'

Creyo que me estás llamando vieja. (Wilder Cervantes 2001: 14)

'I believe you're calling me old.'

An example from spontaneous speech is: *Sí, para ropa, traye ropas, fletan, trayen y nosotros pagamos* 'yes, for clothing, they bring clothes, they hire vehicles, we pay them' (Mendoza 1991: 249).

---

[1] Although in Paraguay the resultant [j] does not merge phonologically with /ʝ/, since the latter phoneme is usually realized as an affricate [dʝ].

(6) Phrase-final /r/ is often assibilated to [ɹ]; final /r/ never disappears in the highland dialect.

(7) The group /tr/ receives an alveolar pronunciation similar to [tʃ].

(8) As in other Andean dialects, unstressed vowels are usually devoiced (Lipski 1990c provides comparative data). Many word-final atonic vowels are devoiced. Figure 2.2 shows a spectrogram of the word *respuesta* 'response' as pronounced by an Aymara-Spanish bilingual speaker from La Paz, in the context *es una respuesta* 'it is a response'.

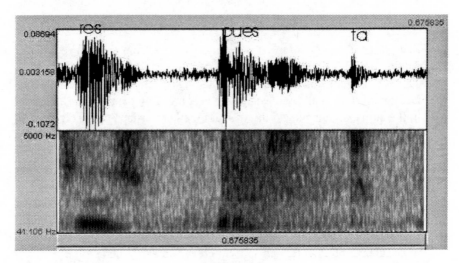

FIGURE 2.2
Pronunciation of respuesta 'answer' by a Bolivian Aymara-Spanish bilingual speaker

Word-internally in contact with /s/, unstressed vowels shorten and weaken to the point of disappearing, as shown in Figure 2.3, representing the pronunciation *ocurre eso sí* 'that happens'.

This weakening process has become lexicalized in the frequent *ps* from *pues*, in combinations such as *nops < no pues* 'well, no' and *sips < sí pues* 'well, yes', both frequent in popular literature:

Dentrenseps a sus cuarrtos. (Salmón 1999b: 15)
'Get in your rooms.'

Todo esops nos ocurre por causa de vos, choy [...] tieneps derecho. Por algo es mi magre. (Salmón 1999b: 15)

'It's all your fault [...] she has the right; after all she's my mother.'

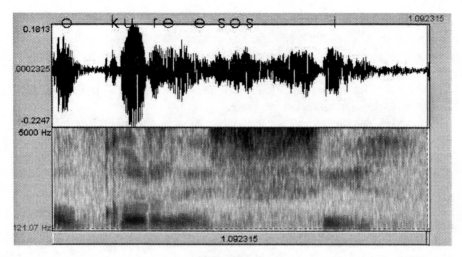

FIGURE 2.3
**Pronunciation of *ocurre eso sí* 'that really happens' by a Bolivian speaker
from La Paz**

(9) Velarization of phrase-final /n/ and word-final prevocalic /n/ to [ŋ] is fre-
     quent. It is not, however, as systematic as in Caribbean and Central Ameri-
     can dialects.

2.4. Phonetic characteristics of Afro-Yungueño Spanish

Afro-Yungueño speech bears similarities to other Afro-Hispanic speech manifestations, both as imitated in literary texts from previous centuries, and as currently existing in Latin America. These characteristics come from a combination of general second-language acquisition of Spanish, broad-based African
phonotactic commonalities (e.g., a preference for open syllables and lack of
onset clusters), and contact with Andalusian / Canary Island Spanish dialects or
their congeners in coastal regions of Latin America. However, given since the
phonetic traits in question appear in Afro-Bolivian enclaves surrounded by substantially different varieties of Spanish, it is not unreasonable to assume that
most of these traits are inherited from earlier second-language varieties of Spanish originally acquired by speakers of various African languages. Among the
Afro-Bolivian phonetic traits –most of which are also present in other Afro-Hispanic dialects, but not in surrounding highland Bolivian dialects– are the following:

(1) **Aspiration / loss of syllable-final /s/:** The switch from highland Bolivian
    Spanish to Afro-Yungueño speech is immediately noticeable, since in the
    latter dialect syllable- and word-final /s/ is weakly aspirated to [h], or omit-
    ted altogether (zero realization). The juxtaposition of the two dialects in the
    speech of the same individual is striking; true bidialectal speakers of non-
    Afro-Bolivian dialects are very rare.
       Afro-Yungueños rarely "slip" when speaking highland Bolivian Span-
    ish, thereby separating themselves from speakers who strive to eliminate
    features of their native dialect in favor of a prestige norm. Afro-Yungueños
    often speak *castellano* for extended periods of time without producing
    weakened /s/; the same cannot, for instance, be said of most Andalusians
    when they strive –typically outside of Andalusia– to pronounce final [s].
    When asked to describe their own dialect, some Afro-Yungueños say it is
    "como el dialecto *camba*" [like the *camba* dialect], located in the eastern
    lowlands of Bolivia. There, syllable- and word-final /s/ is strongly aspirated.
    There are, however, qualitative and quantitative differences: in the Afro-
    Yungueño dialect, word-final /s/ is more often lost than aspirated, and there
    is little aspiration of word-final /s/ when the following word begins with a
    vowel (e.g., *los amigos* 'the friends'), as occurs in the eastern dialects. The
    Afro-Bolivian communities in the Yungas are no more than 150 miles in a
    straight line from the lowland dialects of neighboring Beni department and
    in the Alto Beni region in the north of La Paz department. However, due to
    the mountainous terrain and lack of adequate roads, few Afro-Bolivians
    travel to these regions (with the exception of the considerable number of
    Afro-Yungueños who have permanently emigrated to eastern Bolivia in
    Santa Cruz de la Sierra). There are no other lowland phonetic or grammati-
    cal traits in the Spanish of the Yungas. I should also note that there is no evi-
    dence to suggest that the weakening of final consonants in Afro-Yungueño
    Spanish is a carryover from eastern and northern Bolivia.
       The same weakening of word-final /s/ is probably the basis for Montaño
    Aragón's comment (1992: 268) that "[e]n cuanto al habla típica de los
    negros, el castellano pronunciado por ellos recuerda al empleado en el Río
    de la Plata y también en otras áreas de Latinoamérica" [as for the typical
    speech of black people, they pronounce Spanish in a fashion reminiscent of
    the Rio de la Plata and also in other parts of Latin America]. In reality, there
    are almost no similarities between the Afro-Yungueño dialect and the speech
    of Buenos Aires / Montevideo; even patterns of /s/-weakening are different,
    since in the Rio de la Plata /s/ is strongly aspirated before word-internal
    consonants (cp. *hasta* ['aḥta] 'until'), a feature that rarely occurs in Afro-
    Bolivian speech.

(2) **Loss of word-final /r/:** Loss of word-final /r/ is common, especially in verbal infinitives: *nojotro va trabajá* 'we're going to work'; *si vua tené tiempo vua í con oté* 'if I have time I'll go with you'; *yo va recogé mi leña* 'I'm going to get firewood'. In Afro-Yungueño Spanish all verbal infinitives lack final /r/; this consonant is also lost at the end of some frequent nouns such as *mujé < mujer* 'woman', suggesting that the process was originally phonetic in nature. The contemporary Afro-Yungueño dialect gives a variable pronunciation to final /r/ in other words. There is no loss or modification of /r/ in word-internal preconsonantal position. It may be that verb stems lacking final /r/ were inherited from earlier Afro-Hispanic language in which the verb stems were on the way to being restructured.

(3) **Real and pseudo-*yeísmo*** *(familia > juamia* 'family'): In Spanish, *yeísmo* refers to the neutralization of the phonemes /ʎ/ and /j/ in favor of a non-lateral approximant, typically [ʒ] or [dʒ]. This process began in Spain in the 16th century, and now covers most of central and southern parts of the Canary Islands, and much of Latin America, except for the Andean highlands, Paraguay and surrounding Bolivian and Argentine dialects, and some parts of highland Colombia. In contrast to all other Bolivian Spanish dialects, the Afro-Yungueño dialect has merged the phoneme /ʎ/ with /j/, following the pattern of *yeísmo* begun in Spain by the early 16th century.

The combination /li/ in hiatus with a following vowel, most particularly *familia > juamía*, was apparently also reanalyzed as /ʎ/, and this reanalyzed /j/ then changed to [ɟ] as the result of the *yeísmo* in the Afro-Yungueño dialect. The disappearance of /ʎ/ as a separate phoneme is in itself unremarkable in Spanish, but the presence of an Afro-Hispanic *yeísta* enclave surrounded by a dialect that maintains /ʎ/ bears a striking similarity to vernacular Brazilian Portuguese, where dialects with a strong Afro-Brazilian presence routinely merge /ʎ/ with /j/ (e.g., *mulher* [muˈʎeɾ] > *muié* [muˈje] 'woman').

(4) **Conversion /f/ > [hʷ] before unrounded vowels** *(juamia < familia* 'family', *juiscal < fiscal* 'work gang leader', *cajué < café* 'coffee', *injuermu < enfermo* 'ill', *disjuili < desfile* 'parade', *juelismenti < felizmente* 'happily', *jualda < falda* 'skirt'). The change /f/ > [hʷ] is common in rustic varieties of Spanish before the diphthong [u] (e.g., *fuerte > juerte* 'strong'); however this change only occurs before unrounded vowels in some rural varieties of Spanish characterized by contact with substrate languages lacking either labiodental [f] or the bilabial fricative [ɸ] that apparently instantiated the phoneme /f/ in early colonial Spanish (Lipski 1995b).[2] Among Afro-

[2] The shift /f/ > [hʷ] before unrounded vowels is found among Afro-mestizo communities in southeastern coastal Mexico, in Esmeraldas province in northwestern coastal Ecuador, and

Yungueños, the change /f/ > [h] also occurs in onset clusters: *fruta* > *jruta* ['hɾuta] 'fruit', *flor* > *jlor* [hloɾ] 'flower'.

(5) **Realization of prevocalic /d/ as stop [d] or flap [ɾ].** Frequent in Afro-His-panic (and Afro-Lusitanian) literary texts, from the 16th to the 19th cen-turies, is the conversion of intervocalic /d/ to [ɾ], as in *toḏo* > *toṟo* 'all' (Lip-ski 1995a, 2005). Judging by the pronunciation of intervocalic /d/ in contemporary Afro-Hispanic dialects, it is likely that the sound that emerged was not always a flap but, sometimes an occlusive intervocalic [d]. Spanish writers accustomed to the usual fricative variant may have erroneously tran-scribed it as /ɾ/. Literary Latin American *bozal* Spanish imitations from the late 17th to the 19th centuries follow identical patterns. Currently, the pro-nunciation of intervocalic /d/ as an occlusive or flap is common in bilingual areas of Latin America where the indigenous language has no fricative real-ization of /d/, and is found in Afro-Hispanic speech of Equatorial Guinea, in parts of the Dominican Republic, Venezuela, Ecuador, Peru, and Colombia. This same feature (i.e., /d/ > [ɾ]) also typifies the speech of West Africans who learn Spanish (Lipski (1985a, 1985b, 1986a, 1986c, 1986f, 2005).[3] Among Afro-Yungueños, the occlusive pronunciation of prevocalic /d/ is variable, alternating with the usual Spanish fricative. Among Aymara-domi-nant bilinguals, pronunciation of /d/ as a stop is more frequent, and it is pos-sible that contact with Aymara speakers has reinforced the occlusive pronun-ciation of /d/ among Afro-Bolivians. Some Bolivian literary examples are:

Nu voy podir tingu qui vendir, ocuparu vuy a istar. (Barrera Gutiérrez 2000a: 62)
'I can't do it, I have to sell, I am going to be busy.'

El interos de la Lotereyas había costaro 30 mel. Vos señoretas Esmechas mi has daro diciseis mel y vos señoretas Marecas me has daro 14 mel. (Salmón 1999a: 30)
'A complete lottery ticket costs 30,000. You Miss Ismicha have given me 16,000 and you Miss Marica have given me 14,000.'

---

in the Colombian Chocó, where the African presence was especially strong, and where other linguistic vestiges of earlier Afro-Hispanic language may still be found. Examples can be found in Aguirre Beltrán (1958), García (1982: 29), Flórez (1950), Montes Giraldo (1974); Flórez (1951: 182) for other Afro-Hispanic regions of Colombia. In all these zones, Native American languages have also come into contact with Spanish, thus potentially adding a fur-ther variable to the mix. In the Amazonian region of Peru, where the impact of Native Ameri-can languages is extensive, the changes in question also occur frequently (Castonguay 1987; Erickson 1986; Escobar 1978; Mendoza 1976, 1978). They are also found in highland areas of Peru (e.g., Domínguez Condezo 1990: 44, 53; Mendoza 1976: 81-6), Ecuador (Moya 1981: 286-287; Toscano Mateus 1953: 83-84), among Quechua-Spanish bilinguals.
[3] Alleyne (1980: 62) gives examples from African-influenced creoles in the Americas.

(6) **Neutralization of flap /ɾ/ and trill /r/.** The flap /ɾ/ and trill /r/ are generally distinguished in Afro-Yungueño speech, but there are occasional examples of prevocalic /r/ realized as [ɾ] or vice versa: *horra* < *hora* 'hour', *ahorra* < *ahora* 'now', *careta* < *carreta* 'cart'. This same neutralization is characteristic of most vestigial varieties of Spanish, as well as of Sephardic (Judeo) Spanish, and the Spanish of Equatorial Guinea. Neutralization occasionally occurs in Spanish-Aymara interlanguage: *La Joya es cerro de la en ahí hay orro ahurra y hay empresas en ahí* 'La Joya is a mountain, there is gold now and there are [mining] companies there' (Mendoza 1991: 251).

(7) **Paragogic vowels:** *ele* 'he / she' < *él, ayere* < *ayer* 'yesterday'. The addition of final (paragogic) vowels to Spanish and Portuguese consonant-final words ending in a stressed syllable was a common feature of early *bozal* language, as well as of borrowings into African languages.[4] The scattered appearance of paragogic vowels in Afro-Yungas Spanish suggests that this process was once more widespread, affecting numerous consonant-final words ending in tonic syllables. In addition to the two aforementioned words, which are used by all speakers of the traditional Afro-Yungueño dialect, some older speakers pronounce *mujer* 'woman' as *mujere*, especially phrase-finally, rather than the usual *mujé*. In another juxtaposition of possibly older forms with the contemporary Afro-Yungueño dialect, one older speaker said *lo hacieron PEGARE, lu han hecho PEGÁ* 'they had him beaten, they had him beaten'; the first instance Spanish *pegar* 'to hit' contains a paragogic vowel, while the second occurrence typifies the Afro-Yungueño dialect, in which the final /ɾ/ of Spanish infinitives is lost.

The use of paragogic vowels is the one phonetic feature found in Afro-Yungueño speech that cannot be attributed either to regional dialects of Spanish or to contact with Aymara-influenced Spanish, since it occurs in neither. Of all the African languages known to have come into contact with Spanish during the colonial period, few have word-final consonants, and none has word-final liquids or /s/. When borrowing Spanish or Portuguese words containing syllable-final consonants into African languages, a fre-

---

[4] See Bal (1968, 1974), Martins (1958a, 1958b), Mendonça (1935: 116-118), and Lipski (2002b). Leite de Vasconcellos (1901: 158) and Schuchardt (1888: 250) noted that Kimbundu speakers in Angola still added the paragogic vowels in their L2 Portuguese as late as the end of the 19th century. Similar developments are found in Afro-Lusitanian creoles, particularly those of the Gulf of Guinea (São Tomé, Principe, Annobon). Alleyne (1980: 45-48) documents the extensive use of paragogic vowels in other African-influenced creoles. Althoff (1994) and Lipski (forthcoming) encountered a few cases of paragogic vowels in vestigial Afro-Mexican speech, along the Costa Chica (states of Guerrero and Oaxaca).

quent strategy was the addition of a paragogic vowel. The final paragogic
vowel (whose quality was normally dictated by processes of vowel harmo-
ny), was almost invariably added after a *stressed* syllable; when the final
syllable was unstressed, the Portuguese final consonant was most frequently
lost, as in Kikongo *kilapi* < *lápis* 'pencil'; *vokolo/ukolo* < *óculos* 'eyeglass-
es'; *woolo* < *ouros* 'a suit in cards'; *zikopu* < *copas* 'a suit in cards'.[5] A number of instances of paragogic vowels are also found in Afro-Brazilian Portuguese, where the Kikongo and Kimbundu input was substantial. Some of
the modified forms have become fixed in nonstandard rural varieties, especially in place names and nicknames.[6]

(8) **Raising of final unstressed mid vowels.** In vernacular Afro-Yungueño
Spanish, final unstressed /o/ is usually raised to [u], and final unstressed /e/
becomes [i]: *viejo* > *vieju* 'old', *noche* > *nochi* 'night'. The same occurs
with unstressed clitics and articles: *tanto qui ti [te] conoce* 'as much as [I]
know you', *ele mi [me] ha disió* 'he told me', *eje lus [los] hombre* 'those
men'. Aymara-Spanish bilinguals often reduce Spanish phonetics to the
three-vowel system of Aymara; thus an Aymara influence is always suspect.
However, in Aymara-Spanish interlanguage, stressed vowels are affected
even more than unstressed vowels, and shifts go in either direction, with /u/
> [o] and /i/ > [e] being at least as common as the opposite changes. From a
typological standpoint, the Afro-Bolivian vowel modifications bear little
similarity to Aymara-influenced Spanish, although recent contact with
Aymaras' Spanish may have reinforced already existing tendencies. Colonial literary texts, e.g., from Argentina and Uruguay (Lipski 2001) attributed raising of unstressed vowels to *bozal* speakers of Spanish, but this was
occasional and unsystematic. In some cases, this may have been due to

---

[5] Similar developments are found in Afro-Lusitanian creoles, particularly those of the
Gulf of Guinea. To cite only a few examples, from São Tomense {ST} (Ferraz 1979),
Principense {P} (Günther 1973), Angolar {A} (Maurer 1995, Lorenzino 1998), Annobonese
{Ann} (Barrena 1957, Ferraz 1984):

arroz > ST *loso*, Ann. *aloso*, P. *urosu*; *azul* > ST *zulu*; *barril* > ST *balili*; *Deus* > ST *desu*;
doutor > ST *dotolo*; *flor* > Ann. *foli*; *garfo* > ST *galufu*; *mais* > ST, P, A *mashi*; *óculos* >
ST *oklo*; *paz* > ST *pazi*; *Pedro* > Ann. *Pédulu*; *sabedor* > Ann. *sabedolo*; *senhor* > Ann.
sholo; *sol* > Ann. *solo*; *três* > ST *tleshi*; *voz* > ST *vozu*.

[6] Machado Filho (1964: 71, 84, 109-110), Raimundo (1933: 69-71), Ramos (1935: 248).
A sample includes: *baranco* < *branco; baravo* < *bravo; buruto* < *bruto; faraco* < *fraco; Fir-
imino* < *Firmino; Fulugenço* > *Fulgêncio; Puludenço* < *Prudêncio; purugunta* < *pergunta;
Quelemente* < *Clemente; suporeta* < *espoleta*. Alleyne (1980: 45-48) documents the extensive
use of paragogic vowels in other African-influenced creoles.

residual contact with Portuguese; for example, the shift of final atonic /e/ > [i] and /o/ > [u] occurs in several Afro-Argentine and Afro-Uruguayan texts:

"BATUQUE": Compañeru. Ya qui turu vusotro acabamu ri bairá, ri batuqui cun nuestra ningrita, para rase a cunnseé a ese Siñore branquillo, rumieru qui tinemu; ya qui hemu tumaru un pocu ri cachuri, y vamu a impezá ri nuevu nuetro bairi, mi parece mijuri, qui entre musotro memu, si fumase una caucioni, un renguarí ri brancu, para cantase cu primiso ri nuetro Generá [...] (Carvalho Neto 1965 [1843]: 295-296)

'Comrades; now that we have all danced the *batuque* with our women, so show this white man, and now that we have had some drinks and we're going to start dancing again, it seems to me to be better for us to compose a song for our General [...]'

"CARTA A LA NEGRA CATALINA A PANCHO LUGARES":

hacemi favol, ño Pancho — 'do me a favor Pancho'
de aplical mi tu papeli — 'to get my papers for me'
polque yo soy bosalona — 'because I'm a *bozal*'
y no lo puedo entendeli — 'and can't understand them'
yo quisiela uté me diga — 'I want you to tell me'
lo que ti queli decí, — 'what they say'
porque tio Juan, mi malido, — 'because Uncle John, my husband'
quieli también esclibí — 'wants to write also'

(Becco n.d.: 18-19) [1830])

COPLA AFROURUGUAYA:

Semo nenglu lindu — 'we are pretty black people'
Semo Vetelanu — 'we are veterans'
Y cum Milicianu — 'and with militiamen'
Quiliemi piliá. — 'We want to fight.'

(Pereda Valdés 1965: 135-136)

The same vocalic neutralizations are found in some 20th-century Bolivian stories in speech attributed to black individuals. In reality, the feature demonstrates merely Aymara influence:

Buenas noche, cumadre [...] qui tiene? (Pizarroso Cuenca 1977: 111-115)
'Good night comadre. What's happening?'

Cayá, cumadre, no yoris. Todo arreglari yo. Pero tienes qe darme tu ternero. (Pizarroso Cuenca 1977: 111-115)
'Be quiet *comadre*, don't cry. I'll take care of everything. But you'll have to give me your calf.'

Among contemporary Afro-Hispanic groups, raising of unstressed /e/ and /u/ is also found in the highland Afro-Ecuadoran community of Caldera, in Carchi province on a tributary of the Chota River. Field recordings made in August 2007 provide numerous examples, such as:

Ahora nusotru, ya usamo zapatu.
'Now we use shoes.'

No tenimu padri ni madri.
'We have neither a father nor a mother.'

Sólo a lus hombri nus pegaban.
'They only beat the men.'

(9) **Possible prenasalized consonants.** Word-initial prenasalized obstruents such as *mb-, nd-, ng-, mp-* are a common feature of many West African language families, particularly the Bantu group, well represented in Afro-Hispanic language contacts. Prenasalized consonants are found in the Afro-Colombian creole Palenquero (Friedemann and Patiño Roselli 1983: 98-103, Schwegler 1996: 51-55, 159, 234-236), and in ritualized Afro-Cuban language (Fuentes Guerra and Schwegler 2005: 49, 51, 62-63, 96-97, 135, 188, 193-194).

Prenasalized consonants have traditionally caused difficulties of interpretation and pronunciation for speakers of European languages, and when found word-initially they are often perceived and transcribed as preceded by a prothetic vowel. For instance, Spanish authors would interpret a combination such as *juro a ndioso* 'I swear to God' as *juro an Dioso*, mentally and graphically detaching the nasal element from word-initial position, reflecting familiar Spanish phonotactic patterns. Although most Afro-Hispanic texts reflect no particular linguistic sophistication as regards transcription of non-Spanish sounds, there are a few fragments that are suggestive of prenasalization (Lipski 1992c):

si cabeza m'enduele (< duele) bamo la casa Mundo.
'if my head hurts, let's go to Mundo's house.'

(Cabrera 1971: 517) [Cuba, early 20th century]

Bailar como un andimoños.
'Dance like a demon.'

(Lope de Vega 1893: 368; "La madre de la mejor")
[Spain, 17th century]

*Pues como samo lindo hoy, **en** samo (< samos / somos) malo de ojo.*

'Since we're pretty today, we're not fit to be seen.'

> (Lope de Vega 1893: 363; "El santo negro
> Rosambuco") [Spain, 17th century]

*Ya **liandoro** (< le adoro), ya **linquiero** (< le quiero).*

'I adore him, I love him.'

> (Lope de Vega 1893: 370; "El santo negro
> Rosambuco") [Spain, 17th century]

    Given the presence of the surnames *Angola* and *Maconde*, suggestive of Bantu languages, particularly from Central and Southeastern Africa, it is useful to search for evidence of prenasalized consonants. In contemporary Afro-Yungueño speech, only the Aymara lexical item *anchancho*, referring to a spirit manifested by a sinister echo, and –apparently through association with Spanish *chancho* 'pig'– also a mythical creature that appears at night to frighten wayfarers, suggests the former presence of prenasalized consonants.[7]

(10) **Possible vestigial neutralization of /l/ and /r/.** The neutralization of the liquid consonants /l/ and /r/, usually in favor of [l], is a frequently recurring stereotype of Afro-Hispanic language, both in syllable-final position (e.g., *puerta* > *puelta* 'door') and in previous centuries, when African-born second-language speakers were being described (cp. the prevocalic context in *negro* > *neglo*). Although many literary stereotypes are simple racist parodies, the lack of phonological distinction between /l/ and /r/ in the large Bantu family and in some other West African languages in contact with Spanish provided ample opportunity for such shifts in the Spanish and Portuguese acquired by African-born *bozales*. Currently, there are no Spanish or Portuguese dialects that regularly shift /r/ to [l] before vowels; the frequent shift /r/ > [l] in syllable-final position, e.g., in the Caribbean, seems to have immediate roots in Andalusia and the Canary Islands, although an African contribution cannot be discounted. There is independent evidence that *bozales* previously changed /r/ to [l] before vowels, for

---

[7] For an archaic Brazilian Portuguese dialect that bears other similarities to Afro-Bolivian speech, see Couto (1998: 382). There he gives examples such as *lá im vém ele / lenvém ele* for *lá vem ele* 'there he comes', *im des'de* for *desde* 'since'. In the case of *im antes de* for *antes de* 'before', *im* is clearly a variant of *em* 'in', and the expression corresponds to vernacular Spanish *en(den)antes* for *antes*. However, examples like *im vém* and *im vai* suggest reanalysis of a formerly prenasalized consonant.

example in Palenquero, and in the Portuguese-derived creoles of São Tomé, Principe, and Annobon.

The traditional Afro-Bolivian dialect does not systematically neutralize /l/ and /r/ in any position. As shown elsewhere, word-final /r/ usually disappears, while there is some neutralization between single /ɾ/ and trill /r/, but [l] never appears as the outcome of an underlying /r/, despite literary stereotypes suggesting otherwise, as shown in Chapter 1. Montaño Aragón (1992: 272) lists *aló* as a possible pronunciation for *arroz* 'rice', but my investigations in the Yungas have not confirmed this pronunciation, and when queried explicitly, all Yungueños indicated that they have never heard such a variant. In the traditional Afro-Yungueño dialect there are, however, a few nicknames that suggest an earlier period when some shifts of /r/ to [l] may have been prevalent: *Iḻica* from *Iṟene* (presumably beginning with the abbreviated *Ire* plus the diminutive suffix *-ica),* as well as *Nolberto* for *Norberto.* Spanish hypocoristic nicknames are often based on infantile pronunciation (Boyd-Bowman 1955, Lipski 1995d), but forms like *Noḻberto* are more suggestive of liquid neutralization in adult speech. The change of /ɾ/ > [l] in prevocalic position is rare, but occurs occasionally: *queḻe* < *quieṟe* '[I] want', *flotá* < *fṟotar* 'to rub'.

(11) **Onset cluster reduction.** Of the African languages that came into contact with Spanish and Portuguese during the Atlantic slave trade, consonant clusters in syllable onsets are all but nonexistent. When acquiring Spanish and Portuguese words with onset clusters, Africans at first employed their own phonotactic patterns, typically eliminating the second element of the onset cluster (always a liquid [l] or [ɾ]) or adding an epenthetic vowel between the two consonants (Lipski 2002b). Epenthesis was more common in stressed syllables, as still heard in vernacular Brazilian Portuguese, e.g., *fulô* < *flor* 'flower'. In unstressed syllables, cluster reduction was the preferred option: *nego* < *negro* 'black'. Examples of consonant cluster reduction persist in various Afro-Hispanic speech communities, e.g., the use of *ombe* < *hombre* 'man' in the Dominican Republic and in much Caribbean popular music (Lipski 2004); isolated examples are found in Afro-Venezuelan communities (Mosonyi, Hernández and Alvarado 1983) and in some Afro-Peruvian villages (Cuba 1996). Among Afro-Bolivians in the Yungas, most onset clusters are pronounced without modification. Vocalic epenthesis never occurs, although Aymara uses epenthesis when assimilating Spanish borrowings with onset clusters (Deza Galindo 1989: 279): *balanco* < *blanco* 'white', *palata* < *plata* 'silver, money', *phelecha* < *flecha* 'arrow', etc. In rapid speech, Afro-Yungueños sometimes reduce onset clusters, particularly in *nojotro* 'we', realized as [no'hotu] or ['notu],

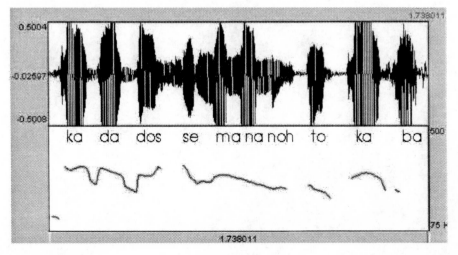

FIGURE 2.4
Afro-Bolivian pronunciation of *cada dos semana nos tocaba* 'we had
to [do it] every week'

nustru 'our' ['nustu], *costumbre* 'custom' [kus'tumbi]. It is possible that
onset cluster reduction was once more frequent in Afro-Yungueño Spanish, although when questioned explicitly, speakers do not acknowledge
this pronunciation.

(12) **Multiple high intonational peaks.** The suprasegmental patterns of Afro-
Bolivian Spanish are quite different from those of surrounding highland
Bolivian dialects. One distinctive characteristic is a series of early-aligned
H* tones and minimal downstep across non-exclamatory non-focused
declaratives. The example in Figure 2.4 of an Afro-Bolivian's pronunciation of *cada semana nos tocaba* 'every week it was our turn' illustrates this
phenomenon.

The presence of a series of non-downstepped high tones is not found in
the speech of the same Afro-Bolivian speakers when they use contemporary non-Afro Spanish. This intonational pattern is atypical of most
dialects of Spanish, but can be found in other Afro-Hispanic varieties. In a
recent study of the Afro-Iberian creole language Palenquero, Hualde and
Schwegler (2008) also demonstrate intonational contours that are atypical
of any Latin American Spanish dialects. In particular, all prenuclear
stressed syllables receive a uniformly high tone, as opposed to the more
usual downdrift and alignment of prenuclear high tones with the immediately post-tonic syllable. They note (p. 25) that contemporary Palenquero

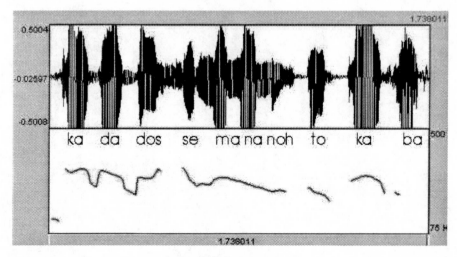

FIGURE 2.5
Afro-Bolivian pronunciation of *¿cómo estás pues?* **'well, how are you?'**

is a pitch-accent language like Spanish, and not a tone language. The creole thus sets itself apart from substratal Kikongo and similar Bantu languages. Hualde and Schwegler conclude that "at some point in the past Palenqueros reinterpreted Spanish stress as requiring an association with a lexical H tone" (2008: 26). Lipski (2007) offers examples of similar patterns from the Afro-Hispanic dialects of the Costa Chica of Oaxaca and Guerrero states in Mexico, from the Barlovento region of Venezuela, from the Chota Valley of Ecuador, from the speech of the *congos* of Panama, and from Afro-Cuban imitations of the speech of the last African-born *bozales*.

(13)   **Elongated main phrase stress vowels with circumflex intonation.** In Spanish, the main phrase-level accent falls on the last accented syllable of the phrase. In Afro-Bolivian Spanish, the final stressed syllable in the phrase is characterized by an extremely elongated vowel, with lengths ranging up to five times that of pre-final stressed syllables (see Figure 2.5).

The phrase-level main stressed vowel is also characterized by a sharply rising tone, which is followed by a rapidly descending tone, all within the confines of the stressed vowel. This "circumflex" intonation is not found in other Bolivian dialects of Spanish, but does bear some resemblance to the intonational patterns of Palenquero.

CHAPTER 3

THE NOUN PHRASE

3.1. The Afro-Yungueño noun phrase

Together with the restructured verb phrase, the Afro-Yungueño noun phrase represents one of the most significant departures from patrimonial Spanish syntax, and provides some of the most compelling evidence linking the traditional Afro-Bolivian dialect with other Afro-Hispanic speech communities, and with Afro-Iberian creole languages. As with the Afro-Yungueño verb phrase, the noun phrase is subject to considerable variation across the post-creole continuum, as Afro-Bolivian speakers slip in and out of the traditional dialect.

3.2. Indefinite articles

In the Afro-Yungueño dialect, the indefinite articles are *un* (masculine and feminine) and in the plural *uno(s)* or *unu(s)* (the two forms are in free variation). Recorded examples include:

Singular indefinite articles

(1)	*Nacían de **un** raíz.*	'They were born from a single root.'
(2)	***un** mariposa*	'a butterfly'
(3)	*Yo quiere ti preguntá **un** cosa.*	'I want to ask you something.'
(4)	***un** cruz grande*	'a large cross'
(5)	*si es **un** gaína o **un** conejo*	'if it is a chicken or a rabbit'
(6)	*gritá di**un** [di un] loma a otro loma*	'to shout from one hilltop to another'
(7)	*yo acorda **un** viaje mi abuelito ...*	'I remember one time my grandfather ...'
(8)	***un** mujé borracho*	'a drunken woman'
(9)	*Yo quisie ti hacé **un** pregunta.*	'I'd like to ask you a question.'
(10)	*tudu **un** semana*	'all week long'
(11)	*ni **un** vez*	'not even once'
(12)	*Juancito algún día va queré por lo menos í a chuparse **un** naranja.*	'Some day Juan will want to go and at least eat an orange.'
(13)	*Es **un** bandeja, ese bandeja disi que era di Bonifacio.*	'It's a tray, they say that tray belonged to Bonifacio.'

Plural indefinite articles

(14) *Ya pasó **uno(s)** cuanto mes.*   'A few months went by.'
(15) *Yo tiene que alistá **unoh** cinco*   'I have to prepare five sections of land.'
     corte.

In everyday speech, in which traditional elements combine with modern Spanish morphosyntax, the Spanish feminine articles *una / unas* often appear, at times in conjunction with non-agreeing adjectives (e.g., *una mujé alto* 'a tall woman'). The traditional form is, however, invariant, and is always derived from the Spanish masculine articles. Some examples illustrating the combination of traditional and modern Spanish elements are:

(16) ***una** letra totalmente tapado*   'totally illegible handwriting'
(17) *había **una** curva ancho*   'there was a broad curve'
(18) ***unos** bolsas*   'some bags'
(19) *con **unas** hierba yamado*   'with some herbs called'

The indefinite quantifiers are *algún* and *algunu(h)*; in partially modernized speech, gendered *alguna* and *algunas* may appear:

(20) *Juancito **algún** día va queré por*   'Some day Juan will want to go and at
     lo menos í a chuparse un naranja.   least eat an orange.'
(21) *Debes recordá jai **algunuh***   'You must remember some names.'
     nombre.   'some illnesses'
(22) ***algunuh** enfermedá*
(23) *Yo también tengo **algunos** foto.*   'I too have some photographs.'

3.3. Definite articles

The traditional forms are *el* and *la* in the singular, and *lu(h)* in the plural. Although in the traditional dialect only *lu* is heard for the plural, many speakers frequently pronounce the article with a final aspiration or even a sibilant [s], approximating modern Spanish. Afro-Yungueño *lu* is derived from *los*, combining the dialect-general loss of final /s/ and the raising of unstressed /o/ to [u] which permeates Afro-Bolivian Spanish.[1] The singular article *el* combines with *de* 'of, from' and *a* 'to' to form the contractions *del* and *al*, which parallels modern Spanish. Examples of *lu(h)* and the corresponding contractions include:

---

[1] Schwegler and Morton (2003) mention vowel raising in the Spanish dialect spoken in El Palenque de San Basilio, which at times produces similar results.

(24) *lu mujé*   'the women'
(25) *lu peón*   'the peasants'
(26) *lu negociante*   'the businessmen'
(27) *Yo ta vení jai del pueblo.*   'I'm coming from town'
(28) *Siempre buscaba padrino del pueblo.*   'They always look for a godfather from the (same)   village.'
(29) *nojotro lu doliente acompañá nomás*   'we mourners would accompany'
(30) *Lus patrón vivían La Paz.*   'The landowners lived in La Paz.'
(31) *Lo metían como lus camba*   'They [pronounced it] like the *cambas*.'
(32) *Ají lu juamía pobre, eyu hacía pueh valé.*   'Thus the poor families, they made the best of it.'
(33) *Lu casa como ustedeh bajó luh casa fue pos ambos, ambo lao frinte a frinte.*   'The houses were, like where you' walked down, the houses were on either side [of the trail], facing each other.'
(34) *Nojotro lu negro siempre hacía nustro baile.*   'We black people always had our dance.'
(35) *Yo lo hacía como hacía lus mayó.*   'I did it like the older people did.'
(36) *Luh patrón y luh mayorodomo no dejaba que venía polecía*   'The landowners and the overseers would not allow the police to come.'
(37) *Placenta cayó ultimo de luh do.*   'The placenta came out after the two [twins had been born].'
(38) *Lu profesó obligó.*   'The teachers required [it].'
(39) *todito lu mujé*   'all the women'
(40) *De lu primos debes recordá jai algunos nombre.*   'You should remember the names of some cousins.'
(41) *Lu profesor taba jai marchandu.*   'the teachers were marching'
(42) *Lu guagua taba desfilando.*   'The kids were in the parade.'
(43) *pa lu huahua ya no*   'not for the children any more'
(44) *Eje mortaja tenía que quitá lu padrinu.*   'The godparents had to take off the shroud.'
(45) *No era pa luh persona mayó.*   'It was not for the elderly.'

Lo(h)/lu(h) is sometimes used with singular reference, which suggests that in the formative stages of the Afro-Bolivian dialect, there may have been only a single definite article *lu* for both singular and plural reference; this often occurs with nouns such as *juamía* 'family' and *gente* 'people' when they have plural reference:

(46) *Era lu secretario generá.*   'He was the general secretary.'
(47) *lu juamía*   'the family'

(48) *ese lu taza di café*	'that cup of coffee'
(49) *ese lu ropa*	'that clothing'
(50) *Lu gente vivía puro abajo.*	'All the people lived downhill.'
(51) *pa lu gente mayó*	'for the elderly'

In general, the traditional Afro-Bolivian dialect maintains the singular definite articles *el* for nouns that are grammatically masculine in Spanish and *la* for grammatical feminine nouns; there are no gender distinctions in the plural, since only *lu(h)* is used, nor is gender marked elsewhere in the Afro-Bolivian noun phrase. There are no documented instances where *el* is used with nouns that are grammatically feminine in Spanish; however, in the traditional dialect, there are several cases in which *la* is used with nouns that are grammatically masculine in Spanish. Examples include:

(52) *eje taza qui ta la suelo*	'that cup that's on the ground'
(53) *Eyu lo llevó la pantión.*	'They carried him to the cemetery.'
(54) *Nojotro iba lavá ropa la río.*	'We would go to wash clothes in the river.'
(55) *volvendo la cementerio*	'returning from the cemetery'
(56) *la zanjio y la plantada*	'the cutting of terraces and the planting'
(57) *Mi mama mi mandaba por agua pueh la pozo.*	'My mother sent me for water [from] the well.'
(58) *Yo encontraba cun lu lu demá amigo la camino.*	'I met up with my other friends on the trail.'
(59) *Yo llegaba la patio.*	'I arrived at the doorway.'
(60) *Mi quita mi gorro pa poné aquí la pulmón.*	'[He] took off my hat to put it here over my chest.'
(61) *Cuando nojotro era chiquito no entraba a la cuarto escuro.*	'When we were little we didn't enter the dark room.'
(62) *disi duende nos va meté la barranco al chumi.*	'They said the *duende* [evil dwarf] would take us to the ravine, to the stand of trees.'

3.4. Null definite articles

Spanish syntax generally requires that a determiner accompany all nouns used in subject position. When definite reference is lacking, these NPs take on a generic reading: *las manzanas son sabrosas* 'apples are tasty'. In Afro-Bolivian speech, definite articles are not used for generic subjects, and may be absent even when clear definite reference is intended in both subject and object positions. As in

Palenquero (Schwegler 2007), null articles appear only with definite or generic nouns. Some examples from my corpus are:

(63) *Tiene su mujé;[la] **mujé** aprendió[a] tomá.*
'He had a wife; the wife learned to drink.'

(64) *Va acabá **mundo** [va a acabarse el mundo].'*
'The world is coming to an end.'

(65) ***Hombre** huasqueaba mujé [los hombres ... las mujeres].*
'Men would whip women.'

(66) *[La] **mujé** murió [el]año pasao.*
'The women died last year.'

(67) *[El mayordomo pegaba [la]**gente**, [el] **patrón** atrás de[l] **mayordomo**.*
'The overseer beat people, the boss was after the overseer.'

(68) ***Mujé** [las mujeres] no trabaja jai en eje pueblo.*
'Women don't work [haciendas] in that community.'

(69) ***nube**[las nubes ta bien rojo] están bien rojas.*
'The clouds are very red.'

(70) *Venía [el] **patrón**.*
'The landowner came.'

(71) *Ya no viene jai a **fiesta**[las fiestas] aquí ... ellu ya no viene.*
'[They] don't come to parties here any more, they don't come any more.'

(72) *[El] **negro** muy poco fue [a la guerra].*
'Blacks rarely went [to war].'

(73) ***Patrón** vivía La Paz [el patrón vivía en La Paz].*
'The owner of the hacienda lived in La Paz.'

(74) ***Perro** ta flojo [los perros son flojos].*
'Dogs are worthless.'

(75) *[Los] **Huahua** iba recogiendo esuh moneda.*
'The kids would pick up those coins.'

(76) *Ninguno ni[el] **doliente** tiene que dormí ni un poquitu.*
'No one –not even the mourners– could sleep even a little bit.'

(77) *Ahora[la] **custumbre** ya pierdió.*
'Now that custom has been lost.'

(78) *[El] **Negro** invita pue, hay que invitá pue.*
'Black people give invitations, it's necessary to invite.'

(79) *Si [el] **mayordomo** tiene ... ehtá criando conejo, gayina había qui ir a buhcá cachu pa [los] **conejo**.*
'If the overseer was ... raising rabbits or chickens, I had to go and find food for the rabbits.'

(80) *[El] **jilacata** tiene que ehtá masiendo.*
'The overseer's assistant has [had] to be weeding.'

(81) *[Los] **huahua** por jugá quebra uh, hahta pega di ese cántaru.*
'A child playing could hit or break a water jug.'

(82) *Entonce Pascua era pa [los] **negro**.*
'So then Easter was for black people.'

(83) *Yo subía un lao di [del] **pantalón**.*
'I rolled up one pant leg.'

3.5. Demonstratives

The Afro-Bolivian demonstratives are *eje* ['e-he] < *ese* (in Mururata and Chijchipa; pronounced *ese* in most other Afro-Bolivian sub-dialects) in singular and *ese/eje lu* in plural. Spanish *este, estos, esta, estas, aquel, aquella, aquellos, aquellas* are not used in the traditional dialect, although *este* occasionally appears in partially modernized speech (84).

(84)	en **este** semana	'this week'
(85)	**Ese** tía es mamá di fulano.	'That women is so-and-so's mother.'
(86)	**ese** lu taza di café	'that cup of coffee'
(87)	**ese** malditos patrones	'those damned landowners'
(88)	**ese** noche de todo santo	'that All Saints' Eve'
(89)	yo llegó **eje** día	'I arrived that day'
(90)	**ese** mujé que tengo	'that wife of mine'
(91)	**Eje** perro ta ladrá.	'That dog is barking.'
(92)	**Eje** mujé ta jay la cocina.	'That woman is in the kitchen.'
(93)	ya nojotro no conoce **ese** ritmo	'we don't know that [dance] rhythm'
(94)	Mujé no trabaja jai en **eje** pueblo.	'Women don't work in that village.'
(95)	**Eje** cholo jay llegó.	'That Indian arrived.'
(96)	¿Qué poh ta hací **eje** niña?	'What is that girl doing?'
(97)	**Eje** gringo quiere ehcuchá como nojotro habla.	'That white man wants to hear how we talk.'
(98)	**esos** albu	'those trees'
(99)	**esu** hierba	'those herbs'
(100)	**esus** mora	'those blackberries'
(101)	d'**esus** tiempo ya no	'no more about those times'
(102)	**esus** dos testigo	'those two witnesses'
(103)	**Esus** palo no sirvi.	'Those trees are no good.'

In the Coripata / Dorado Chicao variety, *esuh* is the typical plural form (ex. 98-103 above), while in Mururata and Chijchipa only *eje lu* is used in the plural (ex. 104-106 below):

(104)	**Eje lu** mujé ta jay la cocina.	'Those women are in the kitchen.'
(105)	**ese lu** taza di café	'those cups of coffee'
(106)	**ese lu** ropa	'those clothes'

As in modern Spanish, *ese/eje* can serve as demonstrative subject (ex. 107-111) and object pronoun (ex. 112), referring to 'that person / thing over there'. *Ese / eje* also takes the place of modern Spanish *eso* referring to a generic idea:

(107) *Eje qui ta allá no han di copiá porque no sirvi* 'Don't copy that [on the blackboard] because it's wrong.'

(108) *Eje taba mirá.* 'That person was looking.'

(109) *Si eje era mujé, tenía que llevá vestíu ropa viejo.* 'If that [person] person was a women, [she] had to wear old clothes.'

(110) *Ese taba bailando morenada.* 'That [person] was dancing the *morenada.*'

(111) *Ese es pa despachá casa siguiente día.* 'That is to send home the next day.'

(112) *Ese yo ta mirando.* 'I am looking at that [person].'

3.6. Possessives

The possessive determiners in the Afro-Yungueño dialect are *mi, mi(s), tu(s), su, su(s),* and *nuestru/di nojotro(s).*[2] Examples include:

(113) *Mi nacimiento es Chijchipa.* 'I was born in Chijchipa.'

(114) *cuando mis hermana vivía* 'while my sisters were alive'

(115) *¿Eyu va llevá sus producto a vendé?* 'Are they going to take their products to sell?'

(116) *Tenían sus depósito.* 'They had their deposits.'

(117) *Sus mujé lloraba; grave lloraban.* 'Their women cried; they cried a lot.'

(118) *¿Tu juamía ta bien no mah?* 'Is your family doing well?'

(119) *Yo eh tu compadre.* 'I am your compadre.'

(120) *Yo va recogé mi leña.* 'I'm going to gather my firewood.'

(121) *Yo ta tomá mi plato.* 'I'm eating my food.'

(122) *Yo quedó con mi mama.* 'I stayed with my mother.'

In Mururata and Chijchipa, plural possessives are formed by adding the plural article *lu* to the singular possessive:

(123) *Nojotro cun mi lu amigito nojotro ponía charlá fuerte.* 'We and my friends, we got to talking a lot.'

(124) *Arapata ya tiene su lu carro, tiene su lu bus.* 'Arapata now has its cars, its buses.'

(125) *cun tu lu visitante tu lu acompañante* 'with your visitors, your company'

[2] In Mururata and Chijchipa the most traditional form for the first person plural is *nostu.* The second person singular forms *tu / tu(s)* co-occur with the subject pronoun *oté,* derived from Spanish *usted.*

(126) **nostu lu** huahua   'our children'
(127) Yo peliaba cun **mi lu** hermano   'I fought with my brothers.'

The disjunctive possessives mío, tuyo, suyo are not used in the traditional Afro-Bolivian dialect. Occasionally di mí 'mine' is used (ex. 128-129), sometimes in conjunction with the Aymara-influence double possessive (ex. 130-131):

(128) Juanita ponió, era una idea **di**   'Juanita put [it], it was an idea of mine,
       mí, eje yuca.   that yucca.'
(129) **Di mí** también es.   'It's mine, too.'
(130) Ese es **di mi mi** primo hermano.   'He is my first cousin.'
(131) Ya es **mi** obligación **di mí.**   'Now it's my obligation.'

3.7. Indefinite and negative pronouns and adjectives

Afro-Yungueño Spanish maintains the Spanish indefinite pronoun algo 'something', and the indefinite adjectives algún 'some (sing.)' and algunu 'some (pl.)'. In partially modernized Spanish, the plural adjective algunuh/algunus can appear, even with nouns that are grammatically feminine in Spanish (ex. 135-136):

(132) **Algún** persona **algún** viudu   'Some person, some widower also.'
       també.
(133) cuando **algún** persona mayó   'when an older person died ...'
       muria ...
(134) Oté tiene qui hací hervi eje lu   'You have to boil these herbs,
       yerba **algún** cosa.   something.'
(135) **algunus** enfermedá   'some illnesses'
(136) **Algunuh** mujé siempre sacaban   'Some women always sang their verses
       sus coplia.   [coplas].'

In the traditional dialect, algún 'something' is used instead of alguien 'somebody' to refer to an indefinite individual:

(137) Como si **algún** mi empuya atrás.   'As though someone were pushing me
                                                   from behind.'

As in modern Spanish, algunus/algunuh is used as indefinite plural pronoun: (138-139):

(138) **Algunuh** tenía casa di hacienda   'Some had estate houses, then.'
       pues.

(139) **Algunus** *también tenia qui*   'Some only had to work two days.'
       trabajá doh día no mah.

The negative pronoun *nada* is used as in modern Spanish; in addition, *nada* may
be added phrase-finally to reinforce negation, as shown in Chapter 5 (p. 138).
The negative adjective *ningún* is used as in modern Spanish:

(140) *Ele nuay* **ningún** *marido nada.*   'She doesn't have any husband at all.'
(141) *Yo no va* **ningún** *misa nada.*   'I don't go to any mass at all.'
(142) *Nojotro no sabe* **ningún** *aymara*   'We don't know any Aymara at all.'
       nada.

Ninguno 'none' is used instead of modern Spanish *nadie* 'no one' in reference to
people:

(143) **Ningunu** *mi ayuda.*   'No one helps me.'
(144) **Ningunu** *pueh va ti viní mirá.*   'No one will come to see you.'
(145) **Ninguno** *jay no tendió.*   'No one spread [coca leaves to dry].'
(146) **Ningunu** *tiene qui í a su casa.*   'Nobody should go home.'

3.8. Suspension of gender agreement; masculine gender prevails

In Spanish, elements of a noun phrase generally agree in number; gender agreement with the head noun also occurs in the case of determiners and adjectives
ending in gender markers. Masculine gender is typically marked by the suffix
–o, and feminine gender with *–a,* although many nouns and adjectives end in *–e*
or a consonant, in which case gender marking is opaque. In the Afro-Yungueño
dialect, lack of gender concordance is always manifested by the masculine gender, as occurs in many Spanish- and Portuguese-derived creole languages. Even
in Afro-Bolivian varieties that mix traditional forms and modern Spanish configurations, the masculine gender prevails for adjectives, and usually for articles
and other determiners as well:

(147) *las mujeres* **altos** *[altas]*   'the tall women'
(148) *si esi es* **un** *gaína [una gallina]* 'whether it is a hen or a rabbit'
       o un conejo
(149) **nuestro** *cultura* **antiguo**   'our former culture'
       [nuestra cultura antigua]
(150) **ese** *[esa] mujé que tengo*   'that wife of mine'
(151) **otro** *[otra] cosa*   'another thing'

90 John Lipski

(152) **un**[a] *mariposa,* **un**[a] *mujé* 'a butterfly, a woman'
(153) **ningún**[ninguna] *misa nada,* 'no mass, no woman'
      ningún [ninguna] mujé
(154) **esos** *hierba [esas hierbas]* 'those herbs'
(155) *con la gente* **antigo** [antigua] 'with the old folks'
(156) *esa casa* **chico** [chica] 'that little house'
(157) **algunos** *enfermedá [algunas* 'some illnesses'
      enfermedades]
(158) *Siempre contaba* **algunos** *cosa* 'He always told some things.'
      [algunas cosas].
(159) **esos** *fiesta [esas fiestas]* 'those parties'
(160) *Yo tenía que poné agua* **todo los** 'I had to put water [to boil] every
      tarde [todas las tardes]. afternoon.'
(161) **tudu un** *semana* 'a full week'
(162) **ese**[esa] *tía es mamá di fulano* 'that woman is so-and-so's mother'
(163) **todito eso** *hierba,* **mezclao** 'all of those herbs mixed together'
      [toditas esas hierbas,
      mezcladas]
(164) *No era pa* **luh** *persona mayó* 'It wasn't for the adults.'
      [las personas mayores].
(165) *La sopa bien* **rico**[rica] *era.* 'The soup was very tasty.'
(166) **esos** *mora [esas moras]* 'those blackberries'
(167) **ese** *[esa]* **lu** *[la] taza di café* 'that cup of coffee'
(168) *tres jornada* **adelantao** 'three days' work in advance'
      [jornadas adelantadas]
(169) *Había una curva* **ancho** 'There was a wide curve.'
      [ancha].
(170) *Asimihmo la gente era* **vivo** 'Just the same the people were clever.'
      [viva].
(171) *[la] nochi* **entero** *[entera]* 'all night long'
(172) *noticias* **antiguo** *[antiguas]* 'old stories'
(173) **único** *foto [la única foto]* 'the only photograph'
(174) *esa gente era* **malo** *[malo]* 'those people were bad'
(175) *con la cabeza bien* **bañadito** 'with the head well-washed'
      [bañadito]
(176) *con sebo de vaca* **negro** *[negra]* 'with fat from a black cow'
(177) *No tengo muy* **buen** *casa [una* 'I don't have a well-built house.'
      casa muy buena].
(178) *los hombre con camisa* **blanco** 'the men in white shirts'
      [camisas blancas]
(179) *Han quedao* **hartos** *viuda* 'Many widows have remained.'
      [hartas viudas].

(180) **unos** *quince mula [unas quince*   'fifteen mules'
       mulas]
(181) *[La] comunidad **entero** [entera]*   'The entire community would go.'
       iba.
(182) **nuestru** *[nuestra] medicina di*   'our own medicine'
       nojotro
(183) **Eje** *[esa] sal ta matá*   'That salt is killing [you].'
(184) *mula **ensillao** [ensillada]; silla*   'a saddled mule, a white saddle, a white
       blanco[a], manta **blanco**[a]*   blanket'
(185) *obra **vendido**[a]*   'contracted labor'
(186) *Huahua iba recogiendo **esuh***   'The children would gather up those
       [esas] moneda.   coins.'
(187) *gritá **diun** [de una] loma a **otro***   'to yell from one hilltop to another'
       [otra] loma

These examples demonstrate that, when combining the traditional Afro-Bolivian dialect and modern Spanish, plural marking is more robust than gender marking. In the traditional Afro-Bolivian dialect, we recall, marking of plural and gender both are omitted.

3.9. Invariant plurals in Afro-Bolivian Spanish

Most varieties of Spanish maintain the morphophonetic distinction of singular vs. plural (e.g., *árbol* vs. *árboles* 'tree(s)', *casa* vs. *casas* 'house(s)'), although erosion of final and intervocalic consonants may lead to non-canonical combinations (cp. *casa < casas̠* = plural 'house̠s').[3] The widespread loss of word-final consonants, e.g., in rustic dialects of southern Spain, often leads to phonological restructuring in vernacular speech, resulting in the loss of canonical plural endings: *árbo < árbol [árboles]* 'trees'; *re < res [reses]* 'cows' etc.[4] In Afro-Iberian creole languages, nouns and adjectives usually remain invariable, in a form derived from the singular (and in the case of adjectives the masculine gender); when pluralization must be indicated, established plural markers are used.[5] For

---

[3] In rustic Andalusia Spanish examples, the common loss of word-final /l/ is accompanied by loss of intervocalic /l/; this may lead to a new type of plural formation: *arbo / árboe, perá < peral / perae, animá < animal / animae* (Moya Corral 1979: 81-84).

[4] Carrasco Cantos (1981: 99), Salvador Plans (1987b: 40).

[5] Papiamentu postposes *nan*, which is also the third person plural pronoun: *kasnan* 'houses', *bukinan* 'books'. There are exceptions, such as *animá-animale* 'animal(s)'; *mujé-mujere* 'woman-women'. Schwegler (2007) provides a detailed account of pluralization in Palenquero.

example, Palenquero preposes the plural particle *ma*, as in *ma hende* '(the) people', *ma kusa* '(the) things'. Most creole languages have exceptions, but invariant nouns are the general rule.

In the most traditional forms of Afro-Bolivian speech, nouns and adjectives remain invariant in the plural. The use of invariant plurals may have been aided by the frequent loss of final /s/ and /r/, but this usage is so systematic as to suggest that invariant plurals have been present since the emergence of the Afro-Bolivian dialect.

In the case of Spanish nouns and adjectives that add only [s] to form the plural, Afro-Yungueño invariant plurals sound like the result of eliding word-final /s/, as in eastern Bolivia. For those nominal and adjectival plurals that add [es] to the singular, the presence of invariant plurals is easily distinguishable from the erosion of final consonants. Invariant plurals are one of the most robust features of the Afro-Yungueño dialect, and often persist even in what speakers perceive as non-Afro-Bolivian Spanish. Typical examples include:

(188) *lu **peón*** < *los peones*   'the peasants'
(189) *lu **mujé*** < *las mujeres*   'the women'
(190) *con sus **tambó*** < *tambores*   'with their drums'
(191) ***persona mayó*** < *personas*   'older people'
       mayores
(192) *Lu **profesor** [los profesores]*   'The teachers were marching.'
       taba jai marchandu.
(193) *Íbamos a Coroico con tres **real***   'We would go to Coroico paying three
       [reales].   reales.'
(194) *No eran **peón** [peones].*   'They were not peons.'
(195) *Eso complica loh **riñón***   'That causes complications for the
       [riñones].   kidneys.'
(196) *Yo lo hacía como hacía los*   'I did it just like the older people 'used
       ***mayó** [mayores].*   to do it.'
(197) *los **cabezador** [cabezadores]*   'the work-team leaders'
(198) *tres **hombre** tres **mujé** [tres*   'three men and three women'
       hombres y tres mujeres]
(199) *todito lu **mujé** [toditas las*   'all the women'
       mujeres]
(200) *algunos **enfermedá** [algunas*   'some illnesses'
       enfermedades]
(201) *Los **patrón** [los patrones] y loh*   'The landowners and the overseers
       ***mayordomo** no dejaba que venía   wouldn't allow the police to come.'
       polecia.
(202) *Ese presión complica disi al*   'They say that high blood pressure
       *corazón, a loh **riñón** [los riñones].*   complicates the heart, the kidneys.'

(203) *los **juiscal** [los fiscales]*   'the dance leaders'

3.10. "Stripped plural" noun phrases

In the most traditional form of Afro-Bolivian Spanish, in plural noun phrases the plural article *lu* is combined with invariant nouns and adjectives. In partially modernized speech, an alternative construction appears, namely the marking of plural /s/ on only the *first* element of plural noun phrases –usually a determiner. Noun phrases in which plural is marked only on the first element are known as "stripped plurals". Stripped plurals are frequent in Afro-Hispanic and Afro-Portuguese dialects, past and present. Typical examples include the following (following earlier practice, omitted elements appear between brackets):

(204) *esos **fiesta** [esas fiestas]*   'those parties'
(205) *Huahua iba recogiendo esuh*   'The kids would pick up those coins.'
         ***moneda**.*
(206) *loh **dirigente***   'the leaders'
(207) *en idioma antigo di mis **abuelo***   'in the old language of my grandparents'
(208) *loh **guagua jóven***   'the young children'
(209) *unas **muñeca** de estuco*   'some stucco statues'
(210) *No hay catres **harto**.*   'There are not enough cots.'
(211) *nuestros **antepasado**, nuestros*   'our ancestors, our grandparents'
         abuelo
(212) *con personah **mayó** [mayores]*   'with older people, then'
         pueh
(213) *Siempre contaba algunos **cosa**.*   '[He] always told some things.'
(214) *Había que llevá personas*   'It was necessary to take along
         ***responsable**.*   responsible people.'
(215) *Los **invitao** tiene que i poh*   'The guests had to go dancing in front
         bailando delante mula.   of the mules.'
(216) *Tiene un señor aquí, acorda*   'There is a man here who remembers
         *pueh de loh **baile** de loh **negritu**.*   the black people's dances.'
(217) *Lindos **matrimonio**, pero esos*   'Beautiful weddings, but those men
         *tío di anteh, aura esos **joven** qui*   from before, these young people
         han quedao, ya no saben pueh.   now, they don't know any more.'
(218) *Algunuh **mujé** [algunas mujeres]*   'Some women would recite verses.'
         *siempre sacaban sus **coplia** [sic].*
(219) *¿Han venidu esus **médico** di*   'Have those Cuban doctors come?'
         Cuba?
(220) *esos **tortilla** nomah pueh*   'just those tortillas'

This type of "stripped plural" marking is not typical of any non-Afro Spanish dialect, past or present. A few similar configurations can be found in varieties of Spanish with an African connection. In the Colombian Chocó, for example, the primarily black population routinely aspirates and deletes word-final /s/. Popular poetry from this region, however, frequently depicts /s/ as remaining on the first element of plural noun phrases (Caicedo 1992); Schwegler (1991a) provides data from spontaneous speech. Some literary examples from Caicedo are given in examples (221a) to (221e):

(221)   a.   *Hoy leroy sus **coca** y lorejo jrito.* (p. 11)
             'Today I give out the coca and I leave them cold.'

        b.   *Despué quesas **cosa** le hacía jaltá.*
             'After these things that he needs.' (p. 12)

        c.   *Hace unos **regüelto** con goma e boboche.* (p. 12)
             'He mixes rubber and stuff.'

        d.   *Tengo seiscientos **navío**.* (p. 37)
             'I have 600 ships.'

        e.   *Se despiertan los **lucero**.* (p. 39)
             'The stars come out.'

Similar stripped plurals also crop up in the Afro-Ecuadoran dialect of the Chota Valley (Lipski 1986e, 1987a; Schwegler 1994), where just as in highland Bolivia, word-final /s/ is normally retained as a clear sibilant [s], but omitted on "stripped" nouns or adjectives (given in small caps); *niñas COLEGIAL* 'school girls'; *las CASITA eran de paja* 'the houses were made of straw'; *cogíamos nuestras PALA* 'we grabbed our shovels'.

In vernacular Brazilian Portuguese, stripped plurals are very frequent.[6] This form of plural-marking is not found in any European Portuguese dialect, and is one of the features invoked in theories that view vernacular Brazilian Portuguese as a semicreole, formed through contact with African languages during the colonial period (Holm 1987, 2004). There is considerable documentary and circumstantial evidence that marking plural /s/ on the first element of noun phrases has been a component of Afro-Iberian language at least since the late 16th century. A

---

[6] See Amaral (1955), Azevedo (1984), Guy (1981), Jeroslow (1974), Megenney (1989), Rodrigues (1974), and Sarró López (1988).

few questionable examples come from Spanish literature prior to the 17th century, but the first, truly unequivocal examples of stripped plural noun phrases are
not documented prior to the *villancicos* or Christmas carols written by the Spanish nun Sor Juana Inés de la Cruz in Mexico in the late 17th century. These songs
purport to represent the speech of African *bozal* slaves newly arrived in the
Americas. The poems contain several instances of stripped plural noun phrases,
such as: *las Leina [las reinas]* 'the queens'; *estos Parre Mercenaria [estos
padres mercenarios]* 'these mercenary priests'; *Los demoño [demonios]* 'the
demons'; *lus nenglu [los negros]* 'the blacks'; *los branco [blancos]* 'the white
people'; *turo las Negla [todas las negras]* 'all the black women' (Cruz 1952: 26,
40, 248, 257, 315).

In 17th-century Afro-Portuguese literary imitations, stripped plural NPs are
also frequent. In the anonymous song "Sã qui turo" (Anon. 1647), we find the
line*: Vamos o fazer huns fessa [vamos fazer umas festas]* 'we're going to have
some festivities'.

In a collection of anonymous 17th-century Afro-Portuguese poems, stripped
plural NPs abound. Examples from Hatherly (1990) include:

(222)   a.   *Vozo cus **coza** [com as coisas] di Apolo?* (p. 16)
             'You with your Apollo stuff?'

        b.   *en turus **parti** [todas partes] qui mi acho* (p. 21)
             'everywhere I find myself'

        c.   *para os **pletinho** [os pretinhos] fazero [...]* (p. 25)
             'for the black folks to do [...]'

        d.   *huma diesses **rapaliga** [dessas raparigas]* (p. 25)
             'one of those girls'

        e.   *A diozo levanta us **mão** [as mãos] [...]* (p. 28)
             '[We] raise our hands to God [...]'

These stripped plural NPs reappear in several key 18th-century Afro-Portuguese texts, suggesting that, by this time, such constructions had become com-
monplace in the emerging Afro-Portuguese vernacular that was to form the basis
for restructured Brazilian Portuguese semicreole. One example comes in a letter
purportedly written by the 'Rei Angola' to the 'Rei Minas' in Lisbon in 1730 (see
Tinhorão 1988: 191). The text was probably not written by an African, since it
was eventually published in a collection of vignettes to which black authors
would have little access. At the same time, the consistent use of recognized Afro-

Portuguese pidgin elements suggests that such a language was sufficiently familiar to non-African observers in Portugal as to enable a reasonably accurate imitation. This text contains numerous instances of plural marking only on the first
element of NPs: *os forgamenta [os folgamentos]* 'the celebrations'; *os fia [os fil-
hos]* 'the children'; *muitos ano[s]* 'many years'; *nossos festa [nossas festas]*
'our celebrations'.

Another institutionalized manifestation of Afro-Portuguese culture within
Portugal were the numerous religious processions in which the black community
participated every year. This tradition began at least as early as the beginning of
the 17th century, with Africanized *villancicos* being performed in chapels and
churches, including at the royal court. These ritualized events, and the black participation therein, lasted until the early 20th century in many parts of Portugal
(Tinhorão 1988: 158). During these processions, Blacks would increasingly
depict African practices, including dancing and mock combat. This practice was
already established by the early decades of the 18th century, when an Afro-Portuguese dancer at the celebration of Nossa Senhora do Cabo uttered an exclama-
tion containing several stripped plurals: *os pistola [as pistolas]* 'the pistols'; *os
bala [as balas]* 'the bullets'; *cos nosso frecha [com as nossas flechas]* 'with our
arrows' (Tinhorão 1988: 159).

Another interesting document, purporting to represent Afro-Portuguese as
used in the transition from Portugal to Brazil, is a fragment of "O preto, e o bugio
ambos no mato discorrendo sobre a arte de ter dinheiro sem ir ao Brazil", published in 1789 (Coelho 1967: 73-74). This example contains key elements identified in earlier Afro-Lusitanian texts, but most of the structural changes do not
appear to have ever occurred in vernacular Afro-Brazilian Portuguese. This fact
makes the text, and similar pamphlet parodies that apparently were printed in
great numbers, suspect as an indication of the language actually used by Africans
in the later colonial period of Brazil. There are, however, several stripped plural
NPs, including: *os pleto, e os blanco [os pretos e os brancos]* 'the blacks and the
whites'; *uns blanco [uns brancos]* 'some white people'; *os mavioso doutrina [as
maravilhosas doutrinas]* 'the wonderful doctrines'; *cos oreia aberto [com as
orelhas abertas]* 'with [our] ears open'.

Stripped plurals also appear frequently in the restructured Portuguese spoken
in the working-class neighborhoods or *musseques* of Luanda, Angola. In Angola,
the urban second-language varieties of Portuguese, especially as spoken in the
squatter communities of Luanda, have been referred to as *Musseque Portuguese*,
a name derived from the KiMbundu term used to designate the shantytowns
themselves. A number of prominent Angolan writers have used this language in
literary works. These are gaining international recognition, and a few linguists
have seen in Musseque Portuguese (MP) more than just another second-lan-

guage variety of a European language spoken in Africa. In fact, it has been suggested (Perl 1989) that MP bears more than a casual resemblance to established Afro-Iberian creoles, and that MP is genealogically related to such Latin American creoles as Papiamento and Palenquero. *Musseque* Portuguese shares with Afro-Yungueño Spanish and with vernacular Brazilian Portuguese the following deviations from monolingual varieties of the respective languages:

(i)   gravitation toward the 3rd singular verb form as invariant verb;
(ii) lapses in noun-adjective agreement;
(iii) some invariant plurals;
(iv) bare nouns, lacking the required definite articles;
(v)   *in situ* questions. *Musseque* Portuguese shares with rapid Afro-Yungueño speech the appearance of *ta* + INVARIANT VERB constructions, the result of morphophonetic erosion. In the case of Angolan Portuguese, this arises from the reduction of *estar* to *ta* as well as the continental Portuguese progressive construction based on *estar a* + INFINITIVE (*está a trabalhar* 'to be working'). Neither in *musseque* Portuguese nor in Afro-Yungueño Spanish is a true PARTICLE + VERB construction (similar, for instance, to *estar a*) in existence.
(vi) *Musseque* Portuguese has numerous stripped plurals, just like vernacular Brazilian Portuguese. In *Musseque* Portuguese, stripped plurals are more frequent that in Afro-Bolivian Spanish. Some literary examples are in (223a-d):

(223) a. *Falta os **home*** [Men are lacking] ... *Todos vai pràs **mina*** [Everyone is going to the mines] ... *Muitos morre nas **mina*** [Many die in the mines] ... *Feticeiro dos **guerra*** [A sorcerer from the wars] ... *os **home** tá servage* [the men are savages] ... *é os **selvage**, é porco* [it's the savages, they are filthy] ... *Pode levá eles nas **mina*** [You can take them to the mines] ... (Castro Soromenho 1979)

b. *Os **conversa** num é bom?* [Aren't the talks any good?] [...] *Juaquim não esquesse dar os **comprementu** nos outros **pessoa** qui me pregonta* [Joaquim doesn't forget to give his best regards to the other people that you're asking me about ...] (Ribas 1969)

c. *E os **minino** vai'mbora* ... [And the kids are leaving] {Cochat Osório, "Aiué" (Andrade 1961)}

d. *Eu vai na terra dos **branco**, ganhar muito dinheiro* [I'm going to the land of white people, to earn a lot of money] {Eduardo Teófilo, "O contrato" (Andrade 1961)}

John Lipski

3.11. Subject pronouns

The traditional Afro-Bolivian dialect has significantly restructured the Spanish
pronominal system, eliminating gender marking in the third person, as well as
the familiar-formal distinction in second-person pronouns (Fig. 3.1).

FIGURE 3.1
Afro-Bolivian subject pronouns

	singular	plural
1st person	*yo*	*nojotro*
2nd person	*oté*	*otene*
3rd person	*ele*	*eyu(h)*

In the most traditional speech, regional *tú* '2nd sing.' and *vos* '2nd sing.', both of
which are normally used in highland Bolivian Spanish, are not used. Afro-
Yungueño Spanish is the only restructured variety of Ibero-Romance in which
the second-person singular pronoun is not derived from Spanish / Portuguese *vos*
or *tú*. It is also the only natively spoken variety of Spanish in which the pronominal system does not distinguish gender in the third person, a trait shared by all
Romance-derived creole languages, but by no non-creole variety of any
Romance language.[7] A few fossilized combinations reflect the final /s/ associated
with the second person singular, for example the future / exhortative *asti* < *(tú)
has de*. In the third person, there is no inflection for grammatical gender in the
most traditional register; *ele* refers to both 'he' and 'she', while *eyu* combines the
function of Spanish *ellos* and *ellas*. The Spanish neuter pronoun *ello* 'it' is not
used either in the Afro-Yungueño dialect.

The Afro-Yungueño pronoun *ele* neutral in terms of gender, and the same is
true of plural *eyu(s)*. The singular form *ele* bears a superficial resemblance to the
Portuguese pronoun *êle* 'he', which appears to be the source of Palenquero *ele*
(also unmarked for gender). However, in Afro-Bolivian Spanish, *ele* appears to
be derived from Spanish *el* 'he', through the addition of a final paragogic vowel,
also found in words such as *ayere* < *ayer* 'yesterday'. In the traditional Afro-

---

[7] The same two traits are shared by the speech of the *congos* of Panama (Joly 1981, 1984;
Lipski 1986h, 1986i, 1989a, 1997); in this ritualized language, the second person subject pronoun is *utene* (used both for singular and plural), and the third person (singular and plural)
pronoun is *elle*. Since part of *congo* speech involves semantic inversion (speaking "back-
ward"), *elle* is often used to refer to the first person singular; *utene* is occasionally used in this
fashion. Góndola Solís (2005: 5) gives the variant *antene*.

Bolivian dialect, *ele* can only be used in the singular, unlike in Palenquero and Portuguese, where *ele* and *êles,* respectively, are plural pronouns (plural Pal. *ele* is sporadic and highly archaic [Schwegler 2002]).

There are no other demonstrably Portuguese or Luso-creole elements in Afro-Yungas Spanish; most non-patrimonial Spanish forms can be traced to Aymara, or to heavy phonetic distortion.[8] In the Afro-Yungueño dialect, paragoge appears to be confined to the words *ayere* and *ele*; this suggests that the items in question are remnants of an active process.

3.12. Use of overt subject pronouns

Spanish is classified as a null-subject language, meaning that, in general, non-focused subject pronouns can be eliminated, since the accompanying verb morphology is usually sufficient to identify the subject. This behavior stands in contrast to languages like English or French, in which subject pronouns are almost always obligatory. There is considerable dialectal variation in Spanish as regards the use of optional overt subject pronouns. In the Caribbean dialects, for example, use of overt pronouns is comparatively high (e.g., Hochberg 1986, Otheguy and Zentella 2007). This has frequently been attributed to the loss of word-final /s/, which distinguishes the second and third person singular forms (and in some tenses also the first person singular). On the other hand, dialects of Andalusia and the Canary Islands, where loss of final /s/ occurs at an even greater rate than in the Caribbean, show no enhanced use of overt subject pronouns.

---

[8] Schwegler (1994) has noted the use of *ele* as subject pronoun in the Afro-Ecuadoran communities of the Chota Valley. My own fieldwork in this region (Lipski 1986e, 1987a) did not register this usage. Subsequent fieldwork in May, 2007 confirmed only the common use of *ele* as an expression of surprise or alarm, a meaning that Schwegler had also noted. Powe (1998: 137) also noted the exclamatory use of *ele*. *Ele* used in this fashion alternates with *elaquí*. *Ele / elé* has been glossed as coming from *hele (aquí)* (e.g., in the glossary at the end of Icaza 1950: 124 and in Guevara 1968: 96), although in Ecuador *ele / elé* is not normally used in the demonstrative sense associated with Spanish *he(le) aquí,* which means roughly "here is ..." or "behold". The alternative form *elaquí* (sometimes spelt *elaqui* in the literature) is more clearly demonstrative in function. Córdova (1995: 432) defines *éle* as "exclamación voluble de sorpresa, admiración, disgusto" [interjection of surprise, admiration, displeasure]. Jaramillo de Lubensky (1992: 74) defines the variants *ele* and *elé* as a word that "enfatiza algo antes mencionado. Expresa sorpresa" [emphasizes something previously mentioned, expressing surprise]. On the other hand, *hele* and *helaquí* are defined simply as "forma demostrativa equivalente a 'he aquí'" [demonstratives equivalent to "here is"] (Jaramillo de Lubensky 1992: 101). This usage is well attested in Ecuadoran regionalist literature. The rare pronominal use of *ele* in the Chota dialect is yet another tantalizing demonstration of the comparative reconstruction that still remains to be done on of Afro-Hispanic language.

Highland Bolivian Spanish does not stand out in its use of overt subject pronouns; they are typically employed for emphasis or contrast, but not in cases
where the subject can be clearly identified by other means, including the preceding context as well as verb morphology. Creole languages, on the other hand,
typically require the use of overt subject pronouns, presumably because of the
absence of verb morphology signaling person and number. This behavior can be
found in all Afro-Iberian creoles, including Palenquero, Papiamentu, Cape Verde
and Guinea-Bissau creole Portuguese, and the Portuguese-derived creoles of São
Tomé, Príncipe, and Annobón. Afro-Bolivian Spanish stands in sharp contrast
with the surrounding non-Afro Hispanic dialect, in that it makes nearly categori-
cal use of overt subject pronouns. In the traditional dialect, in which verbs are
invariant for person and number, subject pronouns are almost always used. When
speaking contemporary Bolivian Spanish, the same speakers do not use overt
subject pronouns, except in the usual circumstances requiring contrastive emphasis or focus. For those speakers –a majority in the contemporary Afro-Bolivian
communities– who switch between the traditional dialect and more decreolized
forms in the same discourse, the appearance of overt subject pronouns correlates
with the use of traditional invariant verb forms. Examples of non-emphatic or
non-contrastive overt subject pronouns are given in (224) and (235):

(224) *Ta bien nomás **uhtede** tomó sus*   'Okay, you had your coffee, we already
       *cajuecito **nojotro** ya tomó.*   had some.'

(225) *Entonce **nojotro** fue la pantión;*   'Then we went to the cemetery; I went
       yo fue la panteón   to the cemetery'

(226) ***Eyu** pueh así hacía fiesta.*   'They had celebrations like that.'

(227) ***Yo** no acorda **yo** fue huahua eje   'I don't remember, I was a child then, I
       *tiempo; chico **yo** jue, algo **yo***   was small; I remember when they
       *acorda, **yo** acorda cuando lo*   were taking him to the cemetery.'
       ehtaba yevando la pantión.

(228) ***nojotro** vivía jay abajo.*   'We lived down there.'

(229) *Lu gente vivía puro ay abajo y*   'The people lived down there, and we
       ***nojotro** salió pa aquí.*   came up here.'

(230) ***Nojotro** ya no sigui ese ritmo*   'We don't have that rhythm any more,
       *como ante, y **nojotro** ya no, ya*   we don't practice that custom any
       no yeva pues ese costumbre,   more; now we're all mixed in with
       costumbre qui tenía ante; ya   the indigenous population; now
       ***nojotro** ya tiene como ya*   we're a bit ashamed to sing that
       ***nojotro** mezclao con lo tatito ya;*   *mauchi.'*
       *ya **nojotro** tiene peh vergüenza*
       ya un poco ya di cantá eje
       mauchi.

(231) *Yo quedó con mi mama, entonce* *yo no ma pue siguíu hacienda.* — 'I stayed with my mother, and then I just worked on the hacienda.'

(232) *yo cuando ta, yo tenía diez año a once* — 'when I was, when I was 10 or 11 years old'

(233) *Claro yo como fue chico yo no acorda vela.* — 'Of course since I was a child, I don't remember about candles.'

(234) *No hacía valé pueh nada eyo no hacía valé pueh era orguyoso no ve, eyu no hacía valé, eyu era orguyoso.* — '[They] didn't make the best of it, [they] were too proud, they didn't make the best of it, they were proud.'

(235) *Disi, eyu habla siempre así.* — 'They say, they always talk that way.'

As shown in example (236) below, in one case, a speaker of the traditional dialect responded to a question (couched in a mixture of the traditional dialect and modern Spanish) in which the subject pronoun *usted / oté* was absent; she used a null pronoun in her response, which under other circumstances could be expected to contain overt *yo* 'I', used further on in the same sentence:

(236) *Q: ¿Ya entró la huacho?* *A: [Yo] ya entró la huacho, entonces [yo] ehtá trabajando ahí, [yo] tenía que hacé minga pa la, pa la pongueaje yo tenía qui hacé pueh mi canasto.* — 'Q: Then you started to work the harvest plot? A: I started to work, then I was working there, I had to do the *minga* chores, for the peons, I had to carry my basket.'

Examples of the use of null pronouns with fully conjugated verbs and overt pronouns with invariant verbs in the same discourse are given in (237) to (245):

(237) *Según eyu habló disi no había; lo han velau con ... porque no había vela.* — 'According to what people say, there weren't any [candles]; they had the wake with ... because there were no candles.'

(238) *Mah abajito fue casa di Don Manuel según tengo entendido* — 'Further down was Don Manuel's house, as I understand it.'

(239) *Yo quisie ti hacé un pregunta, un ideaita tengo* — 'I want to ask you a question, I have the idea that ...'

(240) *Deben di recordá jay después cuando hacían otro día.* — '[You] must recall how [they] celebrated the day after [the funeral].'

(241) *Loh doh día tocaban campana.* — 'They tolled the bells for both days.'

(242) *De lu primos debes recordá jai algunos nombre.* — 'You must recall the name of some of the cousins.'

(243) *Así han abusado con nosotro.* — 'They abused us like that.'

(244) *Nos **curaban** con puro hierba
       así.*   'They cured us only with herbs.'

(245) *Ya recién **regalas** ese canasta,   'Then you give out food from the
       das ese cerveza.*   basket, you give out the beer.'

3.13. Object clitics

In Afro-Yungueño Spanish, direct and indirect object clitics are identical in form,
as shown in Figure 3.2:

FIGURE 3.2
Afro-Bolivian object clitics

	singular	plural
1st person	*mi*	*no(h)*
2nd person	*ti*	*lu(h)*
3rd person	*lu*	*lu(h)*

The second person singular clitic *ti* corresponds to the subject pronoun *oté*
(ex. 246-248). The object clitic corresponding to plural *otene* is *lu(h)* (ex.
251, 253-255):

(246) *yo va **ti** dicí ...*   'I'm going to tell you ...'
(247) *Yo **ti** va ayudá.*   'I'm going to help you.'
(248) *Oté tiene que tomá todo que   'you have to take everything that the
       dostor ta **ti** dando.*   doctor is giving you.'
(249) *ele **mi** ha disió ...*   'he / she told me ...'
(250) *Eyu **lu** llevó la pantión.*   'They took him to the cemetery.'
(251) *Lu planta **luh** deja plantando.* 'The plants, they plant them.'
(252) *... qui cumida **lu** gustaba*   '... what [kind of] food he liked'
(253) *A loh doh Juanito yo va **lus**   'I'm going to tell both Juanitos.'
       contá.*
(254) *Yo va **luh** da un poco de   'I'm going to give you a little food.'
       comidita.*
(255) *Yo va **luh** ayudá*   'I'm going to help you (pl.)'

As shown in (256), the use of *lu(s)* as indirect object clitic persists even when
mixing modern Spanish with the traditional dialect, e.g., with subject-verb
agreement:

(256) *yo voy a hablá mi nativo, yo no*   'I'm going to speak my native [dialect],
       lu tengo vergüenza ni lu tengo   I'm not ashamed of it or afraid of it
       miedo ni nada.   or anything.'

Disjunctive object pronouns are identical to subject pronouns (the disjunctive *sí*
'oneself' is never used).

3.14. Syntax of object clitics

In clauses with a single verb, object clitics in Afro-Yungueño Spanish follow
standard Spanish patterns. They occur in immediate preverbal position:

(257) *Mi ha dició.*   'He/she told me.'
(258) *Yo mi caíu.*   'I fell down.'

In combinations involving auxiliary or modal verbs plus infinitives or gerunds,
object clitics in the most traditional form of the dialect occur between the auxiliary verb and the infinitive or gerund, as in Portuguese:

(259) *Ello vivía, ello salía mi avisá*   'They were living, they came to tell me
       aquí.   here.'
(260) *Están mi charlando.*   'They are talking to me.'
(261) *Yo va ti avisá.*   'I'm going to tell you.'
(262) *¿Por qué no viene mi mirá?*   'Why don't you come see me?'
(263) *Yo quiere ti preguntá un cosa*   'I want to ask you something.'
(264) *Yo va ti llevá jay.*   'I'm going to take you.'
(265) *¡Va ti baña bien!*   'Go bathe yourself well!'
(266) *¿Quién va ti bañá?*   'Who is going to bathe you?'
(267) *Nojotro va ti visitá.*   'We're going to visit you.'
(268) *Yo quería ti llevá.*   'I wanted to take you.'
(269) *Iba ti dejá.*   '[I] was going to leave you.'
(270) *Yo taba ti disindo.*   'I was telling you.'
(271) *Lu gente ta sentao ti esperando.*   'The people are sitting and waiting for
                                                 you.'

(272) *Si es pa ti matá, yo ti mata*   'If it's about killing you, I'll kill you.'
(273) *Yo va ti disí si entiendi.*   'I'm going to tell you to see if you
                                                 understand.'

(274) *Yo quisie ti hacé un pregunta.*   'I'd like to ask you a question.'

When the progressive has been reduced to the form *ta* + INFINITIVE, object clitics
generally occur before *ta* rather than between *ta* and the infinitive:

(275) *¿Quién **ti ta** mentí?*   'Who is lying to you?'

However, the order CLITIC + *ta* occasionally occurs, as in

(276) *ese qui **ta ti** decí tu compadre*   'what your compadre is telling you'

In the traditional Afro-Bolivian dialect there are occasional examples of redundant doubled object clitics, very frequent in highland Andean Spanish but less common in Afro-Bolivian Spanish:

(277) *yo qui ti **lu** bautiza tu huahua*   'I who baptize your child'

CHAPTER 4

THE AFRO-BOLIVIAN VERB PHRASE

4.1. Introduction

The Afro-Bolivian verb phrase departs from other varieties of Spanish in striking ways, and it is here where the semi-creole nature of the traditional dialect is most readily apparent. Patrimonial Spanish worldwide maintains consistent subject-verb agreement, involving grammatical person and number. Such agreement extends to the full range of verb tenses and moods,[1] and while there is some regional and social variation in the selection of tenses and moods, subject-verb agreement is never suspended in natively spoken Spanish. It is in fact in the area of subject-verb agreement that second-language varieties of Spanish stand out most readily, and the teaching of agreement and tense/mood usage is one of the principal components of instructional programs for second-language learners.

Afro-Bolivian Spanish departs from these norms in several ways. As this chapter will show, these departures are consistent with earlier Afro-Hispanic *bozal* language as well as with Afro-Iberian creole languages. Together with the restructured noun phrase, the Afro-Yungueño verb phrase presents the most significant difference with respect to patrimonial Spanish patterns, and the strongest evidence for an earlier *bozal* contact variety not derived from a simple imperfect acquisition of received Spanish. Two key features of the Afro-Bolivian verb phrase are:

(1) In the traditional Afro-Yungueño dialect, verbs are invariant for person and number.
(2) Afro-Bolivian verbs do inflect for tenses, but use only a very reduced subset of the Spanish tense system. In the preterite tense –the repository of the greatest number of irregular verb forms in Spanish– all verb stems are regularized in Afro-Bolivian speech. The robust Spanish subjunctive mood disappears completely.

---

[1] The Spanish verb system is traditionally described as tense-based, and terms like "present", "past", and "future" are used as descriptors. Some Spanish verb paradigms also encode mode (e.g., subjunctive and conditional) and aspect (preterite, imperfect).

Given that nearly all Afro-Bolivians freely alternate between the traditional dialect and contemporary Spanish in their spontaneous speech, the presence of conjugated verbs and other verb tenses and moods can be found in many speakers. A careful study of conjugated vs. unconjugated verbs reveals an older layer, in which only a limited subset of Spanish tenses are in evidence. It is this older layer that will be a principal focus in the sections that follow.

4.2. Invariant verb forms: the 3rd person singular

Immediately noticeable in the traditional Afro-Bolivian dialect is the complete suspension of subject-verb agreement (e.g., *yo/nojotro/eyu* TIENE 'I/we/they HAVE'. No other variety of Spanish past or present so completely suspends the subject-verb agreement system.

Afro-Yungueño Spanish has thus restructured the verb phrase more fully than the recently studied Helvécia Portuguese semicreole of Brazil,[2] the only variety of Portuguese in which the first person singular verb is occasionally replaced by the third person singular. Afro-Bolivian Spanish has a much more radically restructured verb system than vernacular Brazilian Portuguese, where even in the most extreme varieties only the first person plural and third person plural are replaced by the third person singular: *nos/êles trabalha* 'we/they work'.

The Afro-Bolivian verb suspends all subject-verb agreement in favor of a single invariant form for each of the tenses used in the traditional dialect: present, preterite, and imperfect (e.g., *yo/nojotro/eyu* CRECIÓ 'I/we/they GREW UP', *nojotro/eyu* TENÍA 'we/they [USED TO] HAVE'). Only when speaking partially modernized combinations of Afro-Bolivian speech and modern Spanish are some verbs conjugated, but there remain many Afro-Bolivians who routinely produce speech segments in which verbs never exhibit agreement with their subjects, thus contrasting rather sharply with the situation in Helvécia, where only occasional lapses are found.

In nearly all cases, the Afro-Yungueño invariant verb is derived from the Spanish 3rd person singular indicative. Comparative evidence from historical reproductions of *bozal* Spanish, and from contemporary L2 varieties of Spanish, as well as from the first stages of Spanish child language, confirm the unmarked status of the 3 s. verb form (e.g., Bybee 1985: 50-51). This includes vestigial Spanish of such areas as the Philippines, Trinidad, the Isleños and Sabine River

[2] Baxter and Lucchesi (1993), Baxter, Lucchesi and Guimarães (1997), Ferreira (1985), Megenney (1993, 1994), Mello et al. (1998).

Spanish speakers of Louisiana, as well as transitional Spanish-English bilinguals throughout the United States (Lipski 1986d, 1990a, 1990b, 1996b). The Spanish of Equatorial Guinea –the only officially Spanish-speaking nation in sub-Saharan Africa and where Spanish is a widely spoken second language– also exhibits frequent gravitation to the third-person singular as the default unmarked verb form, and this despite the fact that Guineans routinely attempt to conjugate verbs correctly (Lipski 1985a).

In the case of the common stem-changing verbs *tener* 'to have,' *venir* 'to come,' and *poder* 'to be able', the invariant Afro-Yungueño forms retain the diphthong of the 3rd person singular form: *yo tiene/viene/puede, nojotro tiene/viene/puede*, etc. For less common originally stem-changing verbs, the invariant form often lacks the diphthong; from *acordar* 'to remember' comes *yo acorda* 'I remember'; from *perder* 'to lose' comes *nojotro perde* 'we are losing'; from *llover* 'to rain' comes *llove no má* 'it's [just] raining'. The range of invariant verbs in Afro-Yungueño Spanish is reflected in the following selection of examples, all from spontaneous speech:

(1) *Nojotro **tiene** [tenemos] jrutita.*
'We have fruit.'

(2) *Yo no **entiende** [entiendo] eso de vender jruta.*
'I don't understand that [business] about selling fruit.'

(3) *Esus palo no **sirvi** [sirven] porque se **va** [van] yená jai di poliya [esos palos no sirven porque se van a llenar de pollilas].*
'Those trees are worthless because they will be filled with termites.'

(4) *Yo **creció** [crecí] junto con Angelino.*
'I grew up with Angelino.'

(5) *Nojotro **creció** [crecimos] loh do.*
'The two of us grew up.'

(6) *Eyu **vivia** [vivían].*
'They were living.'

(7) *Eyu **salía** [salían] mi avisá aquí*
'They came to warn me here'

(8) *¿De qué nojotro pobre **va** [vamos] viví?*
'What are we poor folks going to live on?'

(9) *Nojotro **trabajaba** [trabajábamos] hacienda.*
'We worked on the haciendas.'

(10) *Lu patrón siempre **tenía** [tenían] partera.*
'The landowners always had midwives.'

(11) *Leña no cargaba como nojotro **cargaba** [cargábamos].*
'[Nobody] carried firewood like we carried firewood.'

(12) *Yo sí lo **carga** [cargo]... y si por una urgencia yo **va** [voy].*
'I really do load [the coca], and if it's urgent, I go.'

(13) *Lu negociante **lleva** [llevan]; **dice** [dicen] al volvé **va** [van] pagá.*
'The coca buyers carry [it] off; they say that they will pay when they come back.'

(14) *Aquí de los persona mayor, tío,*
     ¿quiene mah por ayá queda
     [quedan]?

'Uncle, who of the older people are still
left?'

(15) *Lo que nojotro ta [estamos]*
     hablando este rato.

'What we're talking about right now.'

(16) *Para ele e extraño como nojotro*
     habla [hablamos].

'For him it's strange the way we talk.'

(17) *Yo anda [ando] sin tiempo*
     siempre.

'I'm always out of time.'

(18) *Nojotro no sabía [sabíamos]*
     nada.

'We didn't know anything.'

(19) *Qué día yo va [voy] í.*

'What day I'm going to go.'

(20) *Yo y mi mamá iba [íbamos].*

'My mother and I went.'

(21) *Lus mujé tenía [tenían] que, en la*
     cocina al lado de mamá.

'The girls had to [cook], in the kitchen,
next to Mom.'

(22) *Nojotro bailaba [bailábamos]*
     ante.

'We used to dance back then.'

(23) *La pelea lu mujé trompeaba*
     [trompeaban] igual que el
     hombre.

'[In] fights, the women would hit [each
other] the same as the men.'

(24) *Si nojotro va [vamos a] querer, si*
     nojotro va [vamos]... nojotro vale
     [valemos].

'If we are going to want, if we are
going to … if we are worth [it].'

(25) *Nojotro é [somos]; nojotro habla*
     [hablamos] bien.

'We are; we speak well.'

(26) *Eyo va [van] leé, nojotro va*
     [vamos] leé.

'They are going to read, we are going to
read.'

(27) *Yo miró[miré] jay.*

'I saw it.'

(28) *Yo llegó [llegué] ese día.*

'I arrived that day.'

(29) *Cuando yo canta [canto].*

'When I sing.'

(30) *¿Ustede miró [miraron]?*

'Did you all see?'

(31) *Yo ta [estoy] medio mal.*

'I'm in bad shape.'

(32) *Yo no conoció [conocí] hacienda.*

'I never knew the haciendas.'

(33) *Igualmente nojotro tenía*
     [teníamos] que buscá.

'Just the same we had to look for [it].'

(34) *Nojotro cura [curamos]*
     enfermedad di nojotro.

'We cure our own ailments.'

(35) *Nojotro fue [fuimos] jay Coroico.*

'We went to Coroico.'

(36) *Ayere yo fue [fui] jay.*

'I went yesterday.'

(37) *Yo va [voy] ti ayudá.*

'I'm going to help you.'

(38) *Yo coyuntó [coyunté] juego.*

'I banked the fire.'

(39) *Yo disió [dije] jay.*

'I said [it].'

(40) *Nojotro **va** [vamos] hablá*   'We'll talk about anything.'
      cualquier cosa.

(41) *Yo **quiere**[quiero] ti preguntá un*   'I want to ask you something.'
      cosa.

(42) *Nojotro **sembraba** [sembrábamos]*   'We grew rice.'
      arroz.

(43) *Yo **acorda** [acuerdo].*   'I remember.'

(44) *Nojotro **bajaba** [bajábamos] con*   'We would go down with a gallon of
      galón de alcohol.   alcohol.'

(45) *Nojotro **va** [vamos] volvé otro*   'We'll come back another day.'
      día.

(46) *Yo **quedó** [quedé] con mi mama.*   'I remained with my mother.'

(47) *Nojotro lu negro siempre **hacía***   'We black people always had our
      [hacíamos] nuestru baile.   dances.'

(48) *Ya nojotro no **conoce***   'We don't know that rhythm any more.'
      [conocemos] ese ritmo.

(49) *Nojotro **iba** [íbamos] lavá ropa la*   'We would go to wash clothes in the
      río.   river.'

(50) *Yo **tiene** [tengo] que alistá unos*   'I have to prepare five *cortes* [sections
      cinco corte.   of a coca plantation].'

(51) *Nojotro **fue** [fuimos] siempre uno*   'We were always united.'
      nomá.

4.3. Verb tenses in Afro-Bolivian speech

In the traditional Afro-Yungueño dialect, only three verb tenses are used: the PRESENT, the PRETERITE, and the IMPERFECT, together with progressive forms in the present and imperfect. There are no subjunctive forms; in sentences that normally require a subjunctive in modern Spanish, forms derived from the indicative are used instead, (spontaneous Afro-Bolivian Spanish does not produce a high rate of complex sentences with subordinate clauses).

In the aforementioned PRESENT and PRETERITE tenses, *invariant* 3rd person singular verb forms are used without exception. Since all speakers of the traditional Afro-Bolivian dialect also use contemporary Spanish, they frequently mix in other Spanish verb tenses. When used, the "modern" Spanish verb tenses always exhibit full subject-verb agreement.

The Spanish synthetic future (e.g., *hablaré, comeré, iré*) is vanishingly rare throughout the Andean region, and when it does occur, it expresses probability rather than future. Occasional conditional forms are found in the speech of Afro-Bolivians who combine the traditional dialect with modern Spanish; in such instances the conditional forms express probability (e.g., *¿qué diría[n] pues ayere?* 'what could they have said yesterday?'). The present perfect indicative (e.g., *ha dicho* 'he/she has said'), a commonly used form in Andean Spanish, does occur from time to time in the Afro-Yungueño dialect, but nearly always with subject-verb agreement. This form is used more in the Coripata area (Dorado Chico and Coscoma, see the map in Figure 1.1), and is less commonly heard in Mururata, Chijchipa, and Tocaña. When present-perfect forms do appear, non-standard analogical past participles are often heard: *dició [dicho]* 'said,' *hacío [hecho]* 'done'. This suggests that the present perfect was not part of the original Afro-Bolivian dialect, but rather is an accretion from modern Andean Spanish. Examples of perfect tenses obtained from partially modernized speech are given in examples (52) to (60):[3]

(52) *A mí **me ha** llevao seis año Caranavi.*
'He's been taking me to Caranavi for six years.'

(53) *Ele mi **ha dició**.*
'He told me so.'

(54) *Así jay mi **ha dició**.*
'That's just how he told me.'

(55) *Me **han mandao** esta mañana Dorado Grande.*
'They've sent me to Dorado Grande this morning.'

(56) ***He ido** Caranavi seis año.*
'I've been going [to] Caranavi [for] six years.'

(57) *¿Ande pue se **han ido**?*
'Where have they gone?'

(58) ***Han quedao** hartos viuda.*
'Many widows have remained.'

(59) *Libra mi **han dao** precio di veinte.*
'They have given me a price of 20 [bolivianos] per pound.'

(60) *Así **han abusado** con nosotro.*
'That's how they have abused us.'

In the most traditional register, the Spanish third person singular form is the invariant stem for the present indicative, preterite, and imperfect tenses, as shown in examples (1) to (51). All evidence suggests that these tenses have been part of the Afro-Yungueño dialect since its inception.

The remaining tenses have been superimposed through contact with other varieties of Spanish, and subject-verb agreement is more frequent. Even in the three canonical Afro-Yungueño tenses, the most frequent verbs (usually irregular) are the first to exhibit subject-verb agreement in partially decreolized speech, suggesting that these forms were lexicalized early in the developmental stage of Afro-Yungueño Spanish: thus many Afro-Yungueño speakers who exhibit

---

[3] Only one non-agreeing example appears in the corpus: *cuando [los] soldao[s] ha[n] venido* 'when the soldiers came'.

numerous instances of non-agreeing verbs routinely produce the agreeing forms *(yo) sé* 'I know,' *soy* 'I am,' *tengo* 'I have,' etc. Only in the most traditional Afro-Bolivian speech communities such as Mururata and Chijchipa is the 3rd person singular employed invariably for these common verbs: *yo eh* 'I am' (< *yo es*), *yo sabe* 'I know,' *yo tiene* 'I have'.

(61) **Tengo** *un hermano allá [en] Coroico.*   'I have a brother there in Coroico.'

(62) *Yo no* **tengo** *carácter pa vender.*   'I'm not cut out for selling.'

(63) *Cuánto mujé* **éramos**   'There were a lot of us women.'

(64) **Era** *tres día y media.*   'It was three and a half days.'

(65) *No sé ustede cómo jai* **hacían** *en casa.*   'I don't know how you (pl.) managed at home.'

The verb *ir* 'to go' constitutes an exception in that the invariant 3 s. predominates, particularly in the periphrastic future *ir a* + INFINITIVE:

(66) *¿Di qué nojotro pobre* **va** *viví?*   'What are we poor folks going to live from?'

(67) *¿Qué día yo* **va** *í?*   'What day should I go?'

(68) *Si nojotro* **va** *querer.*   'If we should want.'

(69) *Eyu* **va** *leé.*   'They are going to read.'

(70) *Yo* **va** *andá caracayo.*   'I'm going barefoot.'

The table 4.1 summarizes verb tense usage and subject-verb agreement in Afro-Yungueño Spanish; AGR indicates that full subject-verb agreement occurs in these tenses.

4.4. Possible restructuring to an aspect-based verbal system

The Spanish verb system has inherited the tense-based patterns of Latin; "present" tense refers to the moment of the utterance, "future" refers to points subsequent to the moment of speaking, and so forth. There are also aspectual and modal distinctions: the preterite is among the perfective forms, indicating completed action, while the imperfect is, as the name indicates, an imperfective form, indicating ongoing action. The subjunctive and conditional forms in Spanish indicate a mood distinction, frequently associated with hypothetical or unreal situations. Most creoles with European lexifier languages have verbal systems in which aspectual distinctions predominate, albeit based on derivatives of the orig-

TABLE 4.1.
Afro-Yungueño verb paradigms; regular verbs

TENSE	*trabajar*	*comer*	*vivir*	
PRES.INDICATIVE	*trabaja*	*come*	*vive*	
PRETERITE	*trabajó*	*comió*	*vivió*	
IMPERFECT	*trabajaba*	*comía*	*vivía*	
PRES. SUBJUNCTIVE	AGR	AGR	AGR	
CONDITIONAL	AGR	AGR	AGR	AGR =
PLUPERFECT SUBJ.	AGR	AGR	AGR	full subject
PRESENT PERFECT	AGR	AGR	AGR	verb
PLUPERFECT INDIC.	AGR	AGR	AGR	agreement
FUTURE	AGR	AGR	AGR	
INFINITIVE	*trabajá*	*comé*	*viví*	
GERUND	*trabajandu*	*comendu*	*vivindu*	
PAST PARTICIPLE	*trabajau*	*comíu*	*vivíu*	

inal tense-based verb paradigms. The traditional Afro-Yungueño dialect only employs three verb paradigms that have been derived from patrimonial Spanish: present, imperfect, and preterite, as well as a periphrastic future based on *ir a* + INFINITIVE and a progressive based on *ta* + GERUND/INFINITIVE. This raises the question of whether there has been any modification of the general Spanish usage of these tenses toward a more creole-like system.

There are *some* indications of a partial shift to an aspectually-grounded verb system in Afro-Yungueño Spanish. For example, in Dorado Chico and neighboring communities, conditionals and contrafactuals are expressed by the periphrastic *ir a* + INFINITIVE future (e.g., *vua tené < voy a tener* 'I am going to have'), now acting as an irrealis marker:

(71) *Si **vua** (< voy a) tené tiempo, **vua***   'If I had time, I would go with you.'
     i con oté.
(72) *Si nojotro **va** querer.*   'If we [had] wanted.'

In Mururata and Chijchipa, counterfactuals are also expressed by means of *ojala* (< Sp. *ojalá* 'hopefully') plus present-tense verbs:

(73) **Ojala** *yo* **tiene**, *yo ti* **presta**.   'If I had [money], I would lend [it] to
you.'

In Mururata and Chijchipa, *aiga* < rustic Sp. *haiga* (3 s. present subjunctive of
the auxiliary verb *haber* 'to have') is used in fixed constructions to express probability in the past. This combination would be rendered by the conditional in
contemporary Spanish (ex. 74-75 below); sometimes both the conditional and
aiga are used in the same utterance (ex. 76):

(74) **Haiga** *sidu pueh di doh di la*   'It must have been 2:00 p.m.'
tarde.
(75) **Haiga** *síu doce di la noche.*   'It must have been 12:00.' midnight.'
(76) *Las dos de tarde, tres* **haiga** *sido;*   'It must have been 2:00 p.m., 3:00 p.m.;
cuatro **sería**.   4:00 p.m. it must have been.'

Sometimes, present tense is used when referring to past imperfective situations.
This is not the "historical present" found in narrations (which usually has perfective meaning), but rather "habitual past":

(77) *Ninguno ni doliente* **tiene** *que*   'No one, not even the mourners, could
dormí ni un poquitu; **tuditu** **tiene**   sleep; everyone had to meet the
que amanecé.   dawn.'
(78) *Ahí lu gente volvendo la*   'Upon returning from the cemetery, the
cementerio **tiene** *que cená.*   people had to eat.'
(79) **Ha** *qui llivá pueh oya.*   'It was necessary to take cooking pots.'
(80) *Si mayordomo* **tiene**, **ehtá** *criando*   'If the overseer was raising rabbits or
conejo, gayina.   chickens.'

These examples are consistent with an aspect-based verb system in which tem-
poral references are subordinated to considerations of perfectivity, punctuality,
and non-occurrence.

4.5. The infinitive in Afro-Bolivian Spanish

Afro-Yungueño, infinitives are formally identical to Spanish infinitives, minus
the final /r/ : *trabajá* < *trabajar* 'to work,' *comé* < *comer* 'to eat,' *i* < *ir* 'to go'.
The loss of final /r/ is one of the most characteristic phonetic traits of the Afro-
Bolivian dialect. It thus contrasts with contemporary Bolivian dialects, in which
word-final /r/ is always strongly articulated. As in other popular varieties of
Spanish, some Afro-Yungueño infinitives corresponding to stem-changing verbs

contain diphthongs derived from the present tense forms: *pierdé* < *pierde* from *perder* 'to lose,' *vuelvé* < *vuelve* from *volver* 'to return'.

The Afro-Yungueño infinitive is used in the same contexts as in contemporary Spanish, e.g., with modal verbs and in periphrastic future constructions:

(81)	*No asti de **sembrá**.*	'You shouldn't plant.'
(82)	*Nojotro va **trabajá**.*	'We're going to work.'
(83)	*Asti **recordá** jay.*	'You probably remember.'
(84)	*No hay jay pa **velá**.*	'There is nothing for the wake.'
(85)	*Nojotro no puede **civilizá**.*	'We can't become "civilized".'
(86)	*Había que **llevá** personas responsable.*	'It was necessary to take responsible people.'
(87)	*¡No qui mi **juastidiá**!*	'Don't bother me!'
(88)	*Nojotro va **hablá** cualquier cosa.*	'We're going to talk about anything.'
(89)	*Nojotro va **leé**.*	'We're going to read.'
(90)	*¡No asti **í**!*	'Don't go!'
(91)	*Yo va **salí** entero.*	'I'm going to come out alright.'

In early *bozal* Spanish texts, the bare infinitive (usually lacking final /r/) was frequently used as invariant verb. Given that the infinitive is relatively scarce in natively spoken Spanish and Portuguese, the frequent use of the infinitive in *bozal* imitations is evidently at least in part a reflection of "foreigner talk" deliberately contrived by from Spanish and Portuguese speakers (Lipski 2002d). Some literary examples are given (92a) to (92f):

(92) a. *A mí **llamar** Comba de terra Guinea, y en la mi tierra comer buen cangrejo.* {Reinosa, *Coplas* (Cossío 1950: 111-117)}
'My name is Comba, from Guinea, and in my land we eat good crabs.'

b. ***Andar** allá, por Xanta Mareya, por Xanta Mareya, a mí no **extar** tan buovo como tú **penxar**; tú **penxar** que no **entender**, a mí ruindadex.* {Silva, *Segunda Celestina* (Baranda 1988: 128)}
'Go there, by St. Mary, I am not as foolish as you think, you think I don't understand, foolishness.'

c. *¿Porque vos, mia Senora, **estar** tanto destemplada?* {Gil Vicente, *Floresta de enganos* (Vicente 1912: vol. 2: 196)}
'My lady, why are you so upset?'

d. *Yo **quedar guardar** qui hasta que siñor **salir** y negro nunca **fogir**.* {Pastor, *Lucrecia* (Sevcik 1999: vv. 593-595)}
'I will stay here until you leave, and this black man will never flee.'

e. *Ya yo lo **sabé** Cantal lo Mastine.* {Gabriel de Santillana, Villancico (Mansour 1973: 70)
'Now we can sing the matins.'

f. *¿Lo tiple **essá** tura junta?* {Anon. 'Flansiquiya' (Tejerizo Robles 1989: 178-179)}
'Are all the sopranos together?'

Most spontaneous L2 Spanish gravitates toward the 3rd person singular rather than the infinitive, although examples of the bare infinitive reappear in 19th-century Afro-Cuban *bozal* texts, as shown in (93a) to (93k):

(93)   a. *La vieja Asunción nunca **jablá**.* (A. Ruíz García 1957: 49)
'Old Asunción will never speak.'

b. *Yo también me **calentá** [...] y cuando **cuchá** campana, yo me va pa la Tamisa.* (Cabrera Paz 1973: 124)
'I also get hot […] and when I hear the bell, I'll go to mass.'

c. *No, siñó, yo no **matá** ninguno, yo **sentá** atrá quitrín pa yegá prisa, prisa, na panadería.* (Estrada y Zenea 1980: 72)
'No sir, I didn't kill anybody; I was sitting back there in the carriage to arrive quickly at the bakery.'

d. *Yo tindora, ya yo **jablá** mimo hoy don Ciriaco.* (Benítez del Cristo 1930: 132)
'I love you; I talked to Don Ciriaco today.'

e. *Ya yo no sé si lon gato **matá** la jutía o si la jutía **matá** lon gato.* (Cabrera 1983: 134)
'I don't know if the cat killed the pig, or the pig killed the cat.'

f. *Yo **llevá** ya mucho tiempo comiendo con mano, y **queré** dame guto comé con tenedó y cuchillo lo mimo que gente rica, porque viejo no **queré** morí sin meté pinchacito tenedó dentro carne sabroso.* (Conseguegra Guzmán "Yo queré meté pinchacito tenedó dentro carne sabroso" Feijóo 1979: 113)
'I have been eating with my hands for a long time and I want to have the pleasure of eating with a fork and knife like rich people, because this old man doesn't want to die without sticking a fork into some tender meat.'

g. *Cañón pañó no **sebí** pa ná. Cañón pañó tira tiro paf y se **cayá**.* (Zell 1953: 295)
'Spanish cannon are no good, Spanish cannon go "boom", and then are silent.'

h. *Yo **sabé** que ño Rafé son guardiero tu bují que ta namorá de ti y tú le **correspondé**.* (Cruz 1974: 35)
   'I know that Mr. Rafael is the guardian of your hut (*bohío*), that he's in love with you, and that you return his love.'

i. *En la guerra yo **peliá**.* (Feijóo 1980: 282)
   'I fought in the war.'

k. *Bueno, sumesé, siende como **disí** la niña.* (Gelabert 1875: 152)
   'Well, your honor, as the girl said.'

The traditional Afro-Yungueño dialect does not routinely use the infinitive as invariant (finite) verbs, but several instances appear in the corpus, including some with clear preterite reference:

(94)	*como nojotro **hablá**...*	'the way we talk...'
(95)	*Cuando no **llové**, es tiempo di seco.*	'When it doesn't rain, it's the dry season.'
(96)	*Ya **viní** temprano tía Francisca.*	'Francisca came early.'
(97)	*Ya **viní** pues.*	'[She] came.'
(98)	*Ya **vení***	'[He] came.'
(99)	*Pero dici que ele **subí**.*	'But I hear that he climbed up.'
(100)	*¿Ande pue oté **viví**?*	'Where do you live?'
(101)	*¿Así **disí**?*	'Is that what [they] say?'
(102)	*Ya **perdé**, awicha.*	'[He's] dropped out of sight, grandma.'

In some of these cases, momentary accentual displacement may be at stake,[4] but there are enough recurrent examples to suggest a more systematic use; for instance, *viní/vení* in examples (96)-(98) and *viví* in (100) above were produced by three different speakers on separate occasions.

Some other, more ambiguous possible uses of the infinitive as invariant verb are:

(103)	*Cuando persona ya **morí**.*	'When somebody died.'
(104)	*Hace tiempo que ya **murí** mi abuelo.*	'My grandfather died a long time ago.'
(105)	*Ta **vení** di a mi casa; yo ta **vení** di tal parte.*	'[I'm] coming from my home; I'm coming from such and such a place.'

---

[4] In emphatic speech, Afro-Yungueño speakers often pronounce final atonic syllables with a high tone, which is ordinarily associated with the tonic syllable in Spanish.

In the case of *morir* 'to die,' it is possible that the occurring form *morí/murí* is simply a rapid speech variant of the expected 3 s. preterite *murió*; the forms *murí* as found in (103)-(105) above were only observed during rapid unmonitored speech. The 3 s. preterite of *venir* 'to come' is the irregular *vino*, whereas a putative analogical form would be the non-occurring *venió*. In fact, the occurring form appears to derive from the Spanish infinitive from which the final /r/ has been dropped, as in all Afro-Yungueño infinitives. When queried, speakers of the Afro-Yungueño dialect explain that *ya murí* is an abbreviated version of *ya muriu*, the expected preterite form. A few other verbs ending in *–ir* allow for the same abbreviation; these include *subir* and, occasionally, *decir*.

It is noteworthy that in the semicreolized Portuguese dialect of Helvécia, Brazil, whose morphosyntactic features coincide to a large extent with those of traditional Afro-Yungueño Spanish, invariant verb forms –apparently derived from the infinitive– also appear occasionally with past reference (Baxter (1992: 14): *io COMPRÁ por mirré* 'I bought [it] for a thousand *reis*'; *eu COMÊ só uma vez* 'I only ate once'. Baxter (1992: 14-15) speculates that what appears to be an uninflected infinitive actually results from the appearance of the same sequence of sounds throughout the present indicative verb conjugation, to which the infinitive has been added as a contributing factor.

4.6. Gerunds and progressive forms

The Afro-Yungueño gerunds derive from the respective Spanish gerunds. Gerunds of verbs in the second and third conjugations usually lack the Spanish diphthong: *llovendu* < *lloviendo* 'raining,' *subindu* < *subiendo* 'rising,' *vivindo* < *viviendo* 'living'. Progressive tenses are frequently used; in these cases, the verb *estar* occurs in the invariant forms *ta/taba*. Some progressive forms exhibit what appears to be a phonetically reduced gerund, identical to the Afro-Yungueño infinitive, as shown in section 4.8.

4.7. Past participles

Afro-Yungueño past participles of Spanish regular verbs drop the /d/ of the suffix: *caminau* < *caminado* 'traveled,' *prendiu* < *prendido* 'lit, turned on,' *subiu* < *subido* 'climbed'. As the foregoing examples show, the final /o/ is usually realized as [u]. Spanish irregular past participles rarely occur, and, in a couple of cases, analogical leveling has occurred: *diciu* replaces *dicho* 'said,' and *haciu* replaces *hecho* 'done'.

4.8. Combinations of *ta* + INFINITIVE

One of the most controversial issues in the study of Afro-Iberian language is the possible monogenesis of Afro-Romance creoles (from a proto-creole based on a Portuguese-derived pidgin); as a corollary, assertions have been made that, in the Caribbean and perhaps elsewhere in Latin America, an Afro-Hispanic pidgin evolved into a creole language similar to Palenquero or Papiamentu. A key feature of such a putative creole would be a verb system based on preverbal TMA particles combined with invariant verb stems derived from the Spanish infinitive.[5] Ziegler (1976) and later Castellanos (1990) offered a grammatical sketch of what such a *bozal*-derived creole grammar would look like, based on Afro-Cuban examples taken from literary and folkloric texts. A key feature of this putative Spanish creole is a verb phrase based on the particles *ta* (presumably derived from Spanish/Portuguese *estar*) as imperfective/progressive; *ya* (the Spanish adverb meaning 'already') as perfective, and *va* (the 3 s. form of *ir* 'to go') as future/irrealis. All dialects of Spanish use periphrastic future constructions based on *ir a* + INFINITIVE with future reference. Since the preposition *a* is absorbed by the 3 s. verb form *va*, the suspension of normal subject-verb agreement (in favor of the 3 s. as invariant verb) produces invariant *va* plus some derivative of the Spanish infinitive. This is the putative *bozal* creole future/irrealis form.

From literary imitations of *bozal* speech it is impossible to tell whether *va* was a true particle, or simply as part of the normal periphrastic construction. Determining whether *ya* was used as a particle in *bozal* texts is equally difficult. Spanish *ya* normally precedes overt subject pronouns. Even in *bozal* attestations, it is rare to find *ya* between subject pronoun and verb, the expected position for a particle. In other Ibero-Romance derived creoles (e.g., Papiamentu, Palenquero, Philippine Creole Spanish, Cape Verdean creole, Asian Portuguese creoles), the perfective particle (either derived from Spanish *ya*, Portuguese *ja,* or from the auxiliary verb *ha*) always occurs in immediate preverbal position.[6] Moreover, many uses of *ya* in Spanish involve present-tense verbs, with *ya* retaining its meaning of "already". Only in those very rare cases when preverbal *ya* combined with an invariant verb can a strong case be made that *ya* is behaving as a particle.

---

[5] The various proposals are summarized and analyzed in Lipski (1986f, 1986g, 1987b, 1991, 1992a, 1993a, 1996a, 1998a, 1998b, 1999a, 2002a).

[6] The Papiamentu future/irrealis particle *lo* (from Portuguese *logo* 'later') occurs before overt subject pronouns, but after full subject DPs: *lo mi bai* 'I will go,' providing one possible exception to the assertion that TMA particles derived from sentential adverbs must occur in immediate preverbal position. In vernacular Papiamentu, there is a tendency to place *lo* between subject pronouns and verbs...

The fact that the Spanish- or Portuguese-derived particle *ta* is used in all contemporary creoles has lent considerable support to monogenetic theories that posit a pidginized Portuguese "reconnaissance language" as the forerunner of these creoles (cp. Naro 1978: 342).[7] However, in my view, major differences in the use of *ta* among these creoles suggest multiple routes of evolution.

In the pre-19th-century Spanish *bozal* corpus, there are no examples of *ta* or *está(r)* used with an invariable verb stem in a fashion suggestive of its use as a preverbal particle. However, the 19th-century Cuban *bozal* corpus provides a different panorama, with some apparent instances of *ta* as an aspectual particle. This has led to claims that Cuban *bozal* Spanish became a true creole, sharing with Palenquero and Papiamento (and with Cape Verdian) an earlier Afro-Lusitanian heritage (cp. Megenney 1984). Afro-Cuban literary examples include:

(106)   a.   *Como que yo **ta** cuchá la gente que habla tanto [...] yo **ta** mirá gente mucho.*
'Since I've heard that the people are talking a lot [...] I look at people a lot.'
(M. Cabrera Paz [1973: 124],
"Exclamaciones de un negro")

      b.   *Sí, páe, yo **ta** robá un gaína jabá, y dipué yo robá una yegua.*
'Yes father, I stole a spotted hen, then I stole a mare.'
(L. Cabrera [1976: 39], *Francisco y Francisca
(chascarrillos de negros viejos)*)

      c.   *Horita **ta** bení pa cá.*
'Now (she) is coming here.'
(Villa, " Drumi, Mobila"
[1938a: 183-186])

      d.   ***Ta** juí, **ta** pujá mí, siñó.*
'(He) flees, (he) pushes me, sir.'
(Suárez y Romero [1947: 69], *Francisco*)

---

[7] Indeed, a creole-like verb structure using the particle *ta* is not present in any Afro-Portuguese pidgin texts, from the 15th century to the 20th, although found in some fashion in all Afro-Portuguese creoles. Found in many texts is the portmanteau verbs *sar* (apparently a fusion of *ser* 'to be' and *estar* 'to be') and *santar,* possibly a fusion of *sentar* 'to sit down' and *estar* 'to be' (Lipski 1999c, 2002c).

e. *Primero **ta** llorá na má.*
    'First (she) cries no more.'

(Santa Cruz,
Historias campesinas [1908: 133])

In the Afro-Caribbean literary examples, *ta* typically combines with an invariant stem derived from the Spanish infinitive lacking final /r/, an established phonetic reduction which began as early as the 16th century (Lipski 1995a). A probable source for some instances of *ta* in Afro-Cuban texts is Papiamentu, which was present in 19th century Cuba and Puerto Rico as thousands of sugar cane cutters were taken from other Caribbean islands during the sugar plantation boom.[8] Small pockets of Papiamentu speakers are documented for Cuba and Puerto Rico, and other Papiamentu elements penetrated Afro-Cuban Spanish.[9] Adding to the plausibility that the Afro-Cuban instances of *ta* are due to language contact is the virtually complete absence of such constructions in the many other Afro-Hispanic corpora from Latin America.

One possible instance where verbal constructions involving *ta* appear in tandem with Afro-Cuban speakers in an even more complex language contact situation comes in some attributions of the pidginized Spanish spoken by Chinese laborers in 19th century Cuba (Lipski 1998c, 1999b). These indentured laborers were recruited from the Portuguese port of Macau, and in addition to their native Cantonese, some may have had at least passive knowledge of Macau Portuguese creole, which employs the particle *ta* in fashions similar to Afro-Iberian creoles.

The first Chinese laborers to arrive in Cuba worked as cane-cutters, alongside newly-freed Afro-Cubans, some of whom were African-born *bozales* speaking their own varieties of pidginized Spanish, as well as Papiamentu-speaking laborers recruited from Curaçao. In the Chinese-Cuban corpus, there are a few indications of *ta* used as a preverbal particle in a fashion similar to that found both in Macau creole Portuguese and in Caribbean *bozal* Spanish, as shown in (107):

(107) a. *Como que yo **ta** cuchá la gente que habla tanto [...] yo **ta***
           *Pa mi no sabe, **ta trabajá**, quema carbón.*
           'I don't know, (I) am working, burning charcoal.'

(Jiménez Pastrana 1983: 110)

---

[8] Lipski (1993a, 1996a, 1998a, 1998b, 1999a, 2002a).
[9] Fuentes Guerra and Schwegler (2005: 62) and Schwegler (2006) document examples of *ta* in Afro-Cuban *bozal* remnants from regions of Cuba for which there is no documentation of Papiamentu-speaking laborers.

b.   *Yo **tá peliá** ¡tú tá la casa!*
'I am fighting, [and] you are at home.'

(Jiménez Pastrana 1983: 128)

The presence of what appears to be a derivative of the Spanish infinitive in examples like (107) above cannot be readily explained through imperfect learning of native speaker models; although the reduction of *está* to *ta* is common in vernacular Cuban Spanish, the reduction of the gerund to a form similar to the Spanish infinitive minus the final /r/ is not attested for any other variety of Spanish. In fact these constructions are identical both to Macau creole Portuguese and to Afro-Iberian creoles, including some attestations of Cuban *bozal* Spanish.

Outside of Cuba and Puerto Rico, *ta* used as putative verbal particle in Afro-Hispanic speech makes only a few ghost appearances, none of which holds up robustly under closer scrutiny. Tompkins (1981: 311) cites an older Afro-Peruvian informant in Cañete, who recalled a line from an old song: "Lima ta hablar y Cañete ta pondé", meaning 'Lima speaks and Cañete responds'. My own fieldwork (conducted in 2003) in the same region failed to uncover any recollection of this line, or other attestations of *ta* used as particle in Afro-Peruvian speech or song (the informant who had provided the quotation to Tompkins was reported as deceased). This suggests that at least some creoloid verb forms may have occasionally surfaced in Afro-Peruvian speech, although apparently never coalescing into a consistent pattern. In her analysis of vestigial Spanish in Trinidad, Moodie (MS) uncovered one instance of what she believes to be a creoloid construction with *ta*: *La esposa cuasi ta olvidá el español.* 'His wife has almost forgotten Spanish.' According to Moodie, this combination is very infrequent in the speech of even the oldest community members. Moodie's putative *ta* example may be the result of phonetic erosion not only conjugated *estar* to *ta* (frequent in all colloquial varieties of Caribbean Spanish), but also of the gerund, which accompanies *estar* in progressive constructions: *está hablando > [es] tá hablá [ndo]*. Vestigial Trinidad Spanish has many other examples of the erosion of final syllables.

Another possible instance of the construction *ta* + INFINITIVE found outside of Cuba appears in an enigmatic *bozal* poem by the Panamanian writer Víctor Franceschi (108):

(108)   *Si te pica por allá,*   'If it bites you there'
         *cuando tu **tá** tlabajá*   'when you are working'
         yo te puee asegurá   'I can assure you'
         que tu vaj a recordá   'that you will remember'
         *lo que mama **tá** avertí.*   'what your mother warned you.'

(Franceschi 1956: 30)

The construction *tú tá tlabajá* 'you work' and *mama tá avertí* 'mother warns you' are the only documented literary examples of the construction *ta* + V$_{inf}$ outside of Cuba and Puerto Rico.

In Afro-Yungueño Spanish, the normal verb phrase contains an invariant verb derived from the Spanish 3rd person singular. Preverbal TMA particles are not a usual part of the VP. However, the traditional Afro-Yungueño dialect often allows, in rapid speech, for constructions based on the auxiliary verb *estar* (reduced to invariant *ta*), plus what has the superficial appearance of the Spanish infinitive (lacking the final /r/ as in all Afro-Yungueño speech), instead of the usual gerund ending in *–ando* or *–iendo*. Recorded examples from the Afro-Yungueño corpus include:

(109)	*Nojotro ta hablá bien.*	'We talk well.'
(110)	*¿Qué pueh ta tomá? ¿qué oté ta tomá?*	'What are you drinking?'
(111)	*Yo ta tomá mi plato.*	'I am eating my food.'
(112)	*¿Ande pue oté ta í?*	'Where are you going?'
(113)	*Eje perro ta ladrá.*	'That dog is barking.'
(114)	*¿Qué pue ta hací con nojotro?*	'What is [he] doing with us?'
(115)	*Ta manejá siempre.*	'[I] am always driving.'
(116)	*¿Qué poh ta hací eje niña?*	'What is that [landowner] woman doing?'
(117)	*Yo ta í jay.*	'I'm going.'
(118)	*¿Qué oté ta hacé?*	'What are you doing?'
(119)	*Yo ta subí pa hacé saya.*	'I am going up to dance the *saya*.'
(120)	*Eje taba mirá.*	'She was looking.'
(121)	*¿Andi pue tía ta í?*	'Where are you going, ma'am?'
(122)	*Eje sal ta matá.*	'That salt is killing [you].'
(123)	*¿Oté ta tomá [pastilla]?*	'Are you taking [pills]?'
(124)	*Yo ta tomá.*	'I am taking [them].'
(125)	*¿Quién ti ta mentí?*	'Who is lying to you?'
(126)	*¿Quién ta comprá?*	'Who is buying [coca]?'
(127)	*Oté ta pedí plata.*	'You are asking for money.'
(128)	*Yo ta jay comé.*	'I'm eating.'
(129)	*Elay ahora tiempo ta llové.*	'Wow! It's raining.'

In the Afro-Bolivian corpus, the appearance of *ta* + INVARIANT VERB is relatively infrequent, and I observed it only in Mururata and Chijchipa. When explicitly queried on this combination, speakers of the Afro-Yungueño dialect do not consider it a consistent feature of their speech, although when presented with specific examples extracted from the corpus, they all qualify the construction as "possible". At the same time, they always consider the second element as simply shortened forms of the gerund. Afro-Bolivian speakers effectively regard the use of *ta* + VERB as a performance phenomenon, and indeed a comparison with the remainder of the Afro-Yungueño corpus points to phonetic erosion in rapid and unguarded speech as the origin of this construction. As such, it cannot be considered an integral part of the verb system of their dialect. This is amply confirmed in the following fragment, from a man remembering how acquaintances used to traditionally greet one another during chance encounters on the road:

(130) *¿Di ande pue compa ta*   'Where are you going, *compadre*? I'm
       viniendo? Ta vení di a mi casa;   coming from my house, I'm coming
       yo ta vení di tal parte; ¿ande   from someplace. Where are you
       p(u)e compa ta indo?   going, compadre?'

In (130) above, *ta* combines with a rapidly pronounced gerund, which then erodes to a form similar to the infinitive, only to re-emerge as a full gerund a moment later.

The free alternation between progressive constructions (with a fully realized gerund) and eroded combinations that resemble the Spanish infinitive offers a possible route of evolution for the emergence of *ta* + INVARIANT VERB structures in Afro-Iberian creole languages. The transitory performance nature of such configurations in Afro-Yungueño speech precludes including the latter in a genealogy of creole languages based on the use of the particle *ta*, but the Afro-Bolivian dialect provides a plausible scenario for the coexistence of full progressive forms (albeit with an invariant form of *estar*) and reduced constructions of the superficial form *ta* + INFINITIVE for extended periods of time. If the presence of native varieties of Spanish or Portuguese were removed from the environment, as probably occurred in proto-creole scenarios in Curaçao, El Palenque de San Basilio and possibly in Cuban slave barracks, it is not difficult to see how the *ta* + INFINITIVE might eventually prevail, since this combination in effect represents a paradigmatic simplification, using the same verb form for progressive constructions and in infinitival contexts.[10]

---

[10] Armin Schwegler (personal communication) suggests that if Palenquero originally arose in Cartagena rather than in the maroon community of San Basilio, then contact with non-creole Portuguese was a plausible ingredient to be added to the mix, since, as shown by Arbell (2002), Portuguese speakers were relatively numerous in that city during the crucial time period (17th century).

4.9. Possible use of *ya* as perfective particle

Ziegler (1976) and later Castellanos (1990) offered a grammatical sketch of what
a creole language based on Afro-Cuban *bozal* speech would be like, based on
examples taken from literary and folkloric texts. A key feature of this putative
Spanish creole is a verb phrase based on the particles *ta* (presumably derived
from Spanish/Portuguese *estar*) as imperfective/progressive; *ya* (the Spanish
adverb meaning "already") as perfective, and *va* (the 3 s. form of *ir* 'to go') as
future/irrealis. Determining whether *ya* was in fact used as a particle in *bozal*
texts is problematic. Spanish *ya* normally precedes overt subject pronouns, and
even in *bozal* attestations it is rare to find *ya* between subject pronoun and verb,
the expected position for the particle. In other Ibero-Romance derived creoles
(e.g., Papiamentu, Palenquero, Philippine Creole Spanish, Cape Verdean creole,
Asian Portuguese creoles), the perfective particle (either derived from Spanish
ya/Portuguese *ja* or from the auxiliary verb *ha*) always occurs in immediate preverbal position. Moreover, many uses of *ya* in Spanish involve present-tense
verbs, with *ya* retaining its meaning of "already". Only in those very rare cases
when preverbal *ya* + INVARIANT VERB has a past/perfective meaning is it possible
to postulate particle status for *ya*. Some *bozal* texts in which *ya* may have func-
tioned as an aspectual particle are given in (131):

(131) a. ***Ya*** *mi llegá la bují.* (Cabrera Paz 1973: 128)
           'I arrived at the hut.'

       b. *Yo ta yorá poque Calota **ya** ta morí.*(Ignacio Villa 1938a [Guirao 1938:
           185])
           'I am crying because Carlota died.'

       c. ***Ya*** *yo jablá mimo hoy don Ciriaco [...] ya yo cuchá a usté.* (Benítez del
           Cristo 1930: 132)
           'I spoke today with Don Ciriaco [...] I heard you.'

       d. ***Ya*** *yo brubí.* (Villaverde 1981: 24)
           'I returned'.

       e. ***Ya*** *yo no puedi aguantá má un sofocació de ese.* (Mellado y Montaña
           1975: 287)
           'I couldn't stand any more suffocation.'

       f. ***Ya*** *yo te jabrá notro casione.* (Creto Gangá 1975: 50)
           'I told you on other occasions.'

The traditional Afro-Bolivian dialect offers a few ambiguous examples such as *ya murí* '(he) died'. These constructions resemble an infinitive preceded by a perfective particle, rather than a phonetically simplified form of the preterite. With the verb *murí,* the particle *ya* can occur between the subject and the following invariant verb; my recorded examples include:

(132) *Fulano ya murí.*   'So and so just died.'
(133) *Ele ya mirá que ya sentá.*   'She saw that she was sitting down.'

The corpus contains several examples of *ya viní* 'came' with perfective meaning, but when an overt subject occurs it is postverbal, corresponding to the status of *venir/llegar* as unaccusative verbs in Spanish, in which postverbal position is preferred for non-focused subjects:

(134) *Ya viní temprano tía Francisca.*   'Francisca came early.'

4.10. Possible use of *va* as future/irrealis particle

Since all dialects of Spanish use periphrastic future constructions based on *ir a +* INFINITIVE with future reference, and since the preposition *a* is absorbed phonetically by the 3 s. verb form *va* (< *va a*), only the suspension of normal subject-verb agreement in favor of the 3 s. as invariant verb yields the putative *bozal* creole future/irrealis. It is impossible to tell from literary examples whether *va* was behaving as a true particle, or simply as part of the normal periphrastic construction. Some literary examples are given in (135):

(135) a. *¿Quiene va pagá la pato? [...] luego me va drumí.* (Cabrera Paz 1973: 127)
'Who will pay the piper? [...] then I'll go to sleep.'

b. *Aguora tú lo va pagá.* (Estrada y Zenea 1980: 73)
Now you're going to pay for it.'

c. *¿Y nélle lo muchachito va pendé su Paña de nuté?* (Morúa Delgado 1975: 41)
'And those boys will depend on that Spain of yours?'

d. *Yo te va matá [...] Engancha aquí la colmillo y yo va dí.* (Cabrera 1989: 24)
'I'm going to kill you [...] Sink your teeth into this, and I'll tell you.'

e. *Así yo no va murí.* (Cabrera 1971: 254)
    'That way I won't die.'

f. *Yo va consultá la fuersa.* (Berenguer y Sed 1929: 119)
    'I'm going to consult the force [military detachment].'

g. *Yo va caminá.* (Suárez y Romero 1947: 67)
    'I'm going to walk.'

h. *Yo va vé.* (Bacardí Moreau 1916-1917: v. 2, p. 193)
    'I'm going to see.'

i. *Yo va preguntá a too la gente si conoce a mi yijo Eulogio.* (Sánchez Mal-
    donado 1961: 240)
    'I'm going to ask everybody if they know my son Eulogio.'

k. *Yo me va cuplá billete.* (José Florencio López [Jacan] 1879: 20)
    'I'm going to buy a ticket.'

In the traditional Afro-Bolivian dialect, the verb *ir* 'go' remains invariant as *va*
(examples 136-148; *va* at times even has past or conditional meaning (137-139):

(136)	*Nojotro va trabajá.*	'We are going to work.'
(137)	*Si va tené tiempo, va trabajá.*	'If I have time I will work.'
(138)	*Si nojotro va queré.*	'If we (would) want.'
(139)	*Eyo va leé, nojotro va leé.*	'They are going to read, we are going to read.'
(140)	*Yo va recogé mi leña.*	'I'm going to get my firewood.'
(141)	*Yo va andá caracayo.*	'I'm going to walk barefoot.'
(142)	*Yo va llegá.*	'I'm going to arrive.'
(143)	*Yo va salí entero.*	'I'm going to be ok.'
(144)	*Nojotro va í.*	'We're going to go.'
(145)	*Nojotro va hablá cualquier cosa.*	'We're going to talk about anything.'
(146)	*Yo va colgá nomás.*	'I'm going to hang [coins as a birthday gift].'
(147)	*Nojotro va volvé otro día.*	'We'll come back another day.'
(148)	*Yo va hacé así.*	'I'm going to do [it] like this.'

In functional terms, at least some instances of *va* may be analyzed as having a
future/irrealis function. As regards the speakers' own grammatical interpretation
of *va* + INFINITIVE, it is likely that in most instances *va* still functions as an auxil-

iary verb, since in this dialect it is possible to place object clitics between *va* and the following infinitive:

(149)	*Yo va ti disí.*	'I'm going to tell you.'
(150)	*Yo va ti llevá jay.*	'I'll take you.'
(151)	*¿Quién va ti bañá?*	'Who is going to wash you?'
(152)	*Nojotro va ti visitá.*	'We're going to visit you.'

4.11. Summary: particles in Afro-Bolivian Spanish?

Empirical observation as well as direct questioning of speakers of the traditional Afro-Yungueño dialect reveals that most, if not all, instances of *ta, va,* and *ya* plus invariant verb continue to function as in modern Spanish: that is, they are progressive, future periphrastic and sentential adverbs, respectively. It is possible that, in a few idiolects, these elements have attained particle status, and that, in previous generations when the traditional dialect was spoken monolingually by all Afro-Yungueños, these elements behaved as particles rather than auxiliaries. While there is evidence for (past) "decreolization" of Afro-Yungueño Spanish in other respects, including (a) greater subject-verb and noun-adjective agreement, and (b) more extensive use of plural nominal and adjectival inflection, there is no evidence that *ta, va,* and *ya* once had particle status. Since there are no written attestations of earlier varieties of Afro-Yungueño speech (nor of contemporary varieties), and since the communal memories of the speech of earlier generations have all but disappeared, the evolutionary path of *ta, va,* and *ya* cannot be reconstructed with certainty.

Unlike *bozal* Spanish varieties in Cuba and Puerto Rico, Afro-Bolivian Spanish was never in contact with other creole languages, nor with languages of relatively recent immigration, such as Cantonese. Long-standing contact with Aymara is not responsible for the restructuring of Afro-Yungueño speech; at best, a few lexical items bear the imprint of Amerindian contact. By the end of the 16th century, Afro-Bolivians were for all intents and purposes cut off from evolving Latin American Spanish dialects (except for surrounding highland Bolivian varieties); the retention of archaic Spanish elements not found in other contemporary Bolivian dialects reflects this sociolinguistic isolation.

4.12. Copulative constructions

Within monolingual Spanish and Portuguese dialects there is little variation in the use of copular verbs. Copulative constructions vary widely among Spanish-

and Portuguese-derived pidgins and creoles (Lipski 1999c, 2000c). Spanish and Portuguese have two copular verbs: (1) *ser* (< Latin *esse* 'to be') expresses stable or permanent conditions, and can be used with predicate nominatives. And (2) *estar* (< Latin *stare* 'to stand') expresses temporary conditions or the results of a change of state; *estar* can only be used with adjectives, never with nouns. In general, Afro-Yungueño Spanish maintains the Spanish *ser* vs. *estar* distinction, albeit in the form of person/number-invariant verbs: *es/eh* and *ta* in the present, *era* and *taba* in the imperfect, and *fue* (the 3 s. preterite of Spanish *ser*) in the preterite. The Spanish preterite of *estar*, whose 3 s. form is *estuvo,* has not been retained in Afro-Yungueño Spanish. Examples of Afro-Yungueño copular constructions are:

(153)	*Nube **ta** bien rojo.*	'The clouds are really red.'
(154)	*Yo **ta** medio mal.*	'I'm not doing so well.'
(155)	*Eje qui **ta** allá no han di copiá.*	'That over there you shouldn't copy.'
(156)	*Eje lu mujé **ta** jay la cocina.*	'Those women are in the kitchen.'
(157)	*Ele **taba** atrá.*	'He was behind.'
(158)	*Mi lu huahua creo qui **taba** chiquitito.*	'My children, I think they were small.'
(159)	*si **es** un gaína o un conejo*	'whether it is a hen or a rabbit'
(160)	*Mi tata con mi mamá **es** nacío Mururata.*	'My father and my mother were born in Mururata.'
(161)	*Si nojotro lu negro tiene carro no **eh** di carro.*	'If we black people have a car, [we] are not for [having] cars.'
(162)	*Yo **eh** tu compadre.*	'I am your *compadre*.'
(163)	*No **era** pa luh persona mayó.*	'It wasn't for the elderly.'
(164)	*Asimihmo la gente **era** vivo.*	'People were astute like that.'
(165)	*Nojotro **era** pobrecito.*	'We were really poor.'

In general, Afro-Yungueño Spanish has no null copulas or adjectival verbs. Very occasionally, copulas are missing in conjunction with *asustao* 'frightened,' *miedo* 'fear, used in the sense of frightened,' and similar adjectives:

(166)	*Nojotro **asustao**.*	'We [were] afraid.'
(167)	*Nojotro **miedo** í.*	'We [were] afraid to go.'
(168)	*Ele **desconfiau** pueh.*	'She [was] suspicious, then.'

4.13. Existence and possession

In affirmative constructions, Afro-Yungueño Spanish generally maintains the distinction between Spanish *tener* 'to have' and non-auxiliary *haber* 'to exist':

(169) *¿Cuánto hijo pue oté **tiene**?*   'How many children do you have?'
(170) *¿Oté **tiene** coca?*   'Do you have any coca?'
(171) *Nojotro **tiene** vergüenza un poco.*   'We are a little ashamed.'
(172) *Lu qui **tenía** sus tata compró sus*   'Those who had fathers bought their
       zapato.   shoes.'
(173) *La río **tenía** lu planta como*   'The river [bank] had plants like snap
       vainilla.   beans.'
(174) ***Hay** unuh vena qui crece.*   'There are some veins that swell.'
(175) *Donde **hay** negro disi jay*   'Wherever there are black people they
       *siempre **hay** buya.*   say there is noise.'
(176) *Ni mucho papa **había** para*   'There weren't even many potatoes to
       comé.   eat.'
(177) *Negro pues **había** aquí.*   'There were black people here.'

To express lack of possession, the most traditional form of the Afro-Yungueño dialect is *nu hay* (< *no hay* 'there is not'). Examples (178) to (181) illustrate present tense usage; examples (182)-(184) show *nu había* (< Sp. *no había* 'there was not'), which is used for past reference:

(178) *Yo **nu hay** cajué.*   'I don't have coffee.'
(179) *Yo **nu hay** jay minga.*   'I don't have a replacement worker [in
                                                  the *coca*].'
(180) *¿Oté tiene coca? **Nu hay**.*   'Do you have any coca? I don't [have
                                                  any].'
(181) *Ele **nu hay** ningún marido nada.*   'She doesn't have any husband at all.'
(182) *Yo **nu había** ni tata casi ni*   'I didn't have a father and almost no
       mama.   mother.'
(183) *Yo **nu había** zapato pueh pa vistí*   'I didn't have shoes to wear.'
       pueh.
(184) *Yo **nu había** quen mi compra ni*   'I didn't have anyone to buy me shoes
       zapato ni bandera.   or flags.'

Occasionally, *tiene* 'has' and *tenía* 'had' are used with existential force, although this usage is not as systematic as the use of *nuay/nu abía* to express lack of possession:

(185) *Tantu plaga qui **tiene** ahora.*   'So many infestations that there are
                                                  nowadays.'
(186) *En eje cuarto **tiene** jay*   'In that room there is an echo-spirit.'
       anchancho.
(187) *Arapata ya **tiene** su lu carro.*   '[In] Arapata there are cars.'
(188) ***Tiene** un negrita qui taba aquí.*   'There was a black woman here.'

(189) **Tiene** *un señor aquí, acorda*   'There is a man here who remembers
      pueh de luh baile de lu negritu.   the dances of the black people.'

(190) *¿Qui lau* **tiene** *pueh mula?*   'Where are there mules?'

(191) **Tenía** *un señora, un negra.*   'There was a woman, a black woman.'

CHAPTER 5

PHRASE-LEVEL GRAMMATICAL CONSTRUCTIONS

5.1. Phrase-level grammatical constructions

Although in essence grounded in the grammar of the Spanish language as spoken worldwide, the traditional Afro-Bolivian dialect contains a number of significant departures from these patterns. The totality of these departures from contemporary Spanish, when added to the behavior of noun phrases, the verb phrases, and the highly altered phonological system, together yield a vernacular that stands in striking contrast to that of the other dialects and languages of Latin America.

5.2. Prepositions

In general, Afro-Yungueño speech uses Spanish prepositions in a fashion identical to other Spanish dialects. The major grammatical phenomenon that separates Afro-Bolivian Spanish from other varieties is the frequent omission of monosyllabic prepositions such as *a, de, en*, even in slow speech. In examples (1) to (15), the bracketed prepositions were omitted in the actual examples (in other dialects of Spanish, these prepositions are obligatory):

(1)	*Nació [en] Mururata.*	'[I] was born in Mururata.'
(2)	*Tengo un hermano allá [en] Coroico.*	'I have a brother there in Coroico.'
(3)	*Aprendió [a] tomá.*	'[She] started drinking.'
(4)	*En este tiempo di cosecha siempre nojotro va [al] trabajo.*	'In this harvest time we always go to work.'
(5)	*He ido [a] Caranavi seis año.*	'I went to Caranavi six years [ago].'
(6)	*Cuando gallo canta [a las] seis de la tarde.*	'When the rooster crows at six in the afternoon.'
(7)	*Los patrón vivían [en] La Paz.*	'The landowners lived in La Paz.'
(8)	*Patrón vivía [en] La Paz.*	'The owner lived in La Paz.'
(9)	*Awicha María ta [en] Brasil.*	'Old Maria is in Brazil.'[1]

---

[1] *Awicha*, the Aymara word for 'grandmother', is used by Afro-Bolivians as a respectful reference to elderly women. When used in the third person, an approximate English transla-

(10) *Trabajó hacienda [en] Tocaña.*   '[I] also worked on the hacienda in
                                                   Tocaña.'

(11) *Di ahí mi tata ha veniu buhcá*   'From there my father came to look for
     casa [en] Santa Ana, de ahí yo   a house in Santa Ana, and for that
     soy pues naciu [en] Santa Ana.   reason I was born in Santa Ana.'

(12) *Eyu salía [para] mi avisá aquí.*   'They came to tell me here.'

(13) *Yo lleva[de] Coroico també.*   'I also bring from Coroico.'

(14) *Nojotro iba lavá ropa [en] la río.*   'We went to wash clothes in the river.'

(15) *Ahí lu gente volvendo [del] la*   'Thus people returning from the
     cementerio tiene que cená.   cemetery had to then eat dinner.'

There are a few deviations from regional and international Spanish usage of
prepositions, in particular with the preposition *cun* (< Sp. *con* 'with'). *Cun* is
used to express age or temporary condition, where other Spanish dialects would
use *tener*:

(16) *Yo ta **cun** cabeza blanco.*   'My hair has turned white.'

(17) *Ele ta **cun** treintitreh año.*   'She is 33 years old.'

(18) *Yo estoy **cun** setenta y siete.*   'I am 77 years old.'

(19) *Ta **cun** la cabeza bien bañadito.*   'Her head [hair] is well washed.'

Cun may occasionally act as accusative marker:

(20) *Así han abusado **cun** nosotro.*   'That's how they abused us.'

(21) *¿Qué pue ta hací **cun** nojotro?*   'What are you doing to us?'

(22) *Mi mama va matá **cun** mi tata.*   'My mother is going to kill my father.'

It is also possible for *cun* 'with' to replace *y* 'and', but not to the extent found in
many Atlantic creole languages (Holm 1988: 206-207):

(23) *naranja **cun** cajué.*   'oranges and coffee.'

(24) *Mi tata **cun** mi mamá es nació*   'My father and my mother were born in
     Mururata.   Mururata.'

(25) *Mururuta **cun** Chijchipa, nojotro*   'Mururata and Chijchipa, we were
     siempre fue ... nojotro fue siempre   always, we were always together (=
     uno nomá.   were always sister communities).'

(26) *Algunos también tenía qui trabajá*   'Some only had to work two days, [that
     *doh día no mah, luneh **cun***   is, on] Mondays and Tuesdays.'
     marteh.

---

tion is 'old ...' When used in direct address, *awicha* corresponds approximately to English
ma'am, and is so glossed in the examples.

As in many other rural dialects of Spanish, *andi* 'where' (< Spanish *donde*) is used to denote 'at the house/home of':

(27) *Yo llegó **andi** mi hermana Juana*   'I arrived at the house of my sister
     ahí abajo.   Juana down there.'

(28) *Tiene que llegá **andi** tata (d)i*   '[The bridegroom] has to arrive at the
     novia.   house of the bride's father.'

(29) *Awicho Celia vivía **andi** tio*   'Old Celia lived in uncle Eusebio Sainz'
     Eusebio Sain.   house.'

Also found occasionally in Afro-Yungueño speech are Aymara-influenced possessives, based on *de ... su* 'of ... POSSESSIVE', but almost always in the order *su ... de* rather than the more Aymara-dominant *de ... su*. Thus one sporadically hears among Afro-Bolivians in the Yungas expressions such as *su casa di Juan* 'Juan's house', but almost never *de Juan su casa* 'Juan's house'.

(30) ***Su** mamá **di** mi papá ni siquiera*   'My father's mother was not a Larea.'
     era Larea.

(31) *Ese fue **su** mamá **di** Juan*   'That was Juan Vázquez' mother.'
     Vázqueh.

(32) *Cipriana era pues **su** mamá **di***   'Cipriana was old Gregorio's mother.'
     abuelo Gregorio.

(33) *Conoce ese awicho a **su** mujé **di***   'That old man knows Bonifacio's wife.'
     Bonifacio.

5.3. Questions and interrogative forms

Afro-Yungueño speech uses the Spanish interrogative words *¿qué/qui?* 'what', *quién* 'who?', *¿cuándo/cuándu?* 'when?', *¿cuánto/¿cuántu?* 'how much?' *¿cómo* 'how?', but more frequent is the two-word interrogative form *¿qui laya?* < Old Sp. *qué laya* 'what kind', in turn borrowed from Portuguese (Penny 1991: 234). This analytic form also found in other Ibero-Romance derived creoles, including Philippine Creole Spanish. Another typically creole two-word interrogative form is *¿quí lao?* < *¿qué lado?* 'where?' (lit. 'what side?'), typically used to express location. The directional locative interrogative, is *¿ándi?* 'where?', an archaic variant derived from Spanish *¿dónde?*. *Ande* is also found in other rustic Spanish dialects, including in the Canary Islands and New Mexico, as well as in archaic rural Bolivian Spanish of other regions. Although not common in other contemporary Bolivian Spanish dialects, *¿ándi?* has always been part of the rustic vernacular (e.g., Sanabria Fernández 1988: 32), as demon-

strated in numerous literary imitations of rural speech and in regionalist literature (34):

(34)   a.   *Después de cumplir su encargo, antes de irme a dormir, me pasé por*
              ande *tengo la imagen de la Mamita de la Bella y le prendí unas velas.*
              (Padilla Osinaga 1997: 318)
              'After running the errand, and before going to sleep, I passed by where I
              have the image of Mamita de la Bella and I lit some candles.'

        b.   *¿De* **ande** *querís que te recoja?* (Leyton 1967: 83)
              'Where do you want me to pick you up from?'

        c.   *Estábamos en la entrada del pueblo, metidos no sé cómo en la quinta de*
              don Melecio, **ande** *nos habíamos entrado de puro desorientados.* (Botel-
              ho Gonsálvez 1957: 42)
              'We were on the outskirts of town, I don't know how, but on Don Mele-
              cio's farm, where we had ended up because we were disoriented.'

Afro-Yungueño speech exhibits a few *in situ* questions (i.e., questions in which
the interrogative element has not been fronted):

(35) *¿Ote huahuay* **quién** *pues?*   'Whose *huahua* [child] are you?'
(36) *¿Bo tiene juamía* **de quién?**   'What family do you belong to?'
(37) *¿Aquí producía* **qué?**   'What was grown here?'

In situ questions are not found in other Bolivian Spanish dialects, but are fre-
quent in vernacular Brazilian Portuguese and in Angolan *musseque* Portuguese
(Lipski 1995c), in the latter case reflecting Kikongo and Kimbundu syntax.
Some Angolan literary examples are given in (38):

(38)   a.   *Está a chatiar mais velho* **porquê?** (Uanhenga Xitu 1977: 17)
              'Why are you bothering the old folks?'

        b.   *O quê você pensa a sua idade serve* **para quê?** {Vieira, (1985: 32)}
              'What do you think your age is good for?'

        c.   *Escola siô Bio duro* **quê?** (Castro Soromenho 1979: 156)
              'How long did Sr. Bio's school last?'

        d.   *Mas si entrar eu só do carnaval, faz* **quê?** (Uanhenga Xitu 1979: 71)
              'If I go to the carnival alone, what will I do?'

e. *Patrício era quê? [...] Socialismo é quê entao?* (Boaventura Cardoso 1977: 77)
    'What was Patricio [...] what is socialism?'

f. *Mas então saiu pra onde? [...] Lhe levaram porquê entao?* (Vieira 1980: 14)
    'But where did he go then? [...] Why did they take him?'

g. *Comi o quê entao? [...] Vavó, vamos comer é o quê? [...] Está onde, entao? [...] Tem é o quê?* (Vieira 1982: 8)
    'What did I eat? [...] Grampa, what are we going to eat? Where is he, then? What's happening?'

Non-inverted questions (i.e., INTERROGATIVE WORD + SUBJECT + VERB) are quite frequent in the traditional Afro-Bolivian dialect. The same configuration is also frequent in Caribbean Spanish, and in all Afro-Romance creole languages, but absent from all Andean dialects, all other Bolivian dialects included. Examples from spontaneous Afro-Yungueño speech include:

(39) *¿Ande oté ta?*   'Where are you?'
(40) *¿Qué oté ta tomá?*   'What are you drinking?'
(41) *¿Ande pue oté ta i?*   'Where are you going?'
(42) *¿Qui lado oté cayó?*   'Which side did you fall [on]?'
(43) *¿Qué pue oté hace?*   'What are you doing?'
(44) *¿Andi pue oté viví?*   'Where do you live?'
(45) *¿Andi pue oté ta trabajá?*   'Where are you working?'
(46) *¿Qué poh oté quiere?*   'What do you want?'
(47) *¿Qué oté ta hacé?*   'What are you doing?'
(48) *¿Qué poh oté comió?*   'What did you eat?'
(49) *¿Andi pue tía ta i?*   'Where are you going, ma'am?'
(50) *¿Para qué otene truju?*   'Why did you (pl.) bring [it]?'

Non-inverted questions in Afro-Bolivian Spanish are congruent with non-inverted questions in all Afro-Romance creole languages; this fact, combined with the absence of non-inverted questions in other Bolivian Spanish dialects, circumstantially hints at an Afro-creole connection. Other examples of Afro-Bolivian interrogatives are:

(51) *¿Qui laya eyu pesaba coca a huarco?*   'How did they measure, coca, by the huarco [an archaic measure]?'
(52) *Hacienda, ¿qui lao pueh fue?*   'Where was the hacienda?'

(53) *¿Qui lao oté trabaja anteh?*   'Where did you work before?'

(54) *Pero ¿qui lao va caí?*   'But where are [the seeds] going to

(55) *¿Cuánto huarco oté pesó?*   fall?'

(56) *¿Awicha ta con cuánto*   'How many *huarcos* did you weigh
     cumpleaño?   out?'

                          'How many birthdays have you had,
                          ma'am?'

5.4. Negative particles and negative constructions

The Afro-Yungueño dialect uses all patrimonial Spanish negative words, generally with the same meaning as in modern Spanish. In the traditional variety, Sp.
nadie 'nobody' is usually replaced by *ninguno* 'none': *ninguno ha yegau*
'nobody came'. In modernized speech, the popular Bolivian *nadies* 'nobody' is
frequently used.

The verb *tener* 'to have' remains invariant in most combinations (cp. *yo tiene
jay yuca* 'I have yucca', *nojotro tiene cajué* 'we have coffee'). To express lack of
possession, Afro- Yungueños (especially in Mururata and Chijchipa) use *nu hay*
(< *no hay* 'there is not'), as shown in Chapter 4 (p. 129), where "past" forms are
also given (cp. *nu había* (< Sp. *no había* 'there was not').

(57) *Yo nu hay cajué.*   'I don't have coffee.'

(58) *Yo nu hay jay minga.*   'I don't have a replacement worker [in
                          the *cocal*].'

(59) *¿Oté tiene coca? Nu hay.*   'Do you have any coca? I don't [have
                          any].'

(60) *Ele nu hay ningún marido nada.*   'She doesn't have any husband at all.'

(61) *Yo nu había ni tata casi ni mama.*   'I didn't have a father and almost no
                          mother.'

(62) *Yo nu había zapato pueh pa vistí
     pueh.*   'I didn't have shoes to wear.'

(63) *Yo nu había quen mi compra ni
     zapato ni bandera.*   'I didn't have anyone to buy me shoes
                          or flags.'

This usage is not present in other Ibero-Romance derived creole languages,
but it is found in the Zamboangueño dialect of Philippine Creole Spanish
(Chabacano), as demonstrated in the following examples of spontaneous speech
I recorded in Zamboanga (Lipski and Santoro 2007: 384-385).

(65) *Pwéde tu manehá máskin nuay
     lisénsya?*   'Can you drive even though [you] don't
                          have a license?'

(66) **Nuay** *ele compañero.*   'He doesn't have a companion.'
(67) *Tiene tiene trabajo, tiene* **nuay,**   'There are those who have work, and
    para **nuay,** *dipisil.*   those who don't; for [those who]
                                  don't, [it is] difficult.'

In Zamboangueño, *nuay* (= *nu hay*) is also used to negate verbs in the past/perfective tense:

(68) **Nuay** *yo andá porque yan [ya*   'I didn't go, because it was raining.'
    man] ulan.
(69) **Nuay** *pa uí kame.*   'We (excl.) didn't hear yet.'
(70) **Nuay** *kita puedé llamá.*   'We (incl.) couldn't call.'

Double negation of the sort *no tengo no* in which the second *no* is produced without pause or inflectional highlighting is found in several Afro-Iberian languages (Lipski 2000a, Schwegler 1996b). This construction is common in the vernacular speech of the predominantly Afro-Hispanic regions of the Dominican Republic and the Chocó in Colombia. It also appears in several 19th-century Afro-Cuban literary imitations, and finds a striking confirmation from an unexpected source: unpublished correspondence between the Cuban scholar José de la Luz Caballero and the American encyclopedist Francis Lieber. Lieber queried whether Afro-Cubans spoke a creole language. Luz Caballero's response confirms other observations, that *bozales* spoke imperfect Spanish but without the consistent restructuring and transmission to successive generations found in creole languages. He also gives clear evidence of double negation based on the *no ... no* pattern[2]:

> [...] como ya dije en mi respuesta, hay algunos modos de corromper el idioma empleado generalmente por todos los bozales, pero estos se refieren mas bien á las construcciones que no á la pronunciación; y esos módismos son precisamente los que se usan en el presente libro: he aqui los mas principales [...] 10° Repiten los negros casi siempre la negativa asi dicen vg. "no va á juntar no" "no va á salir no"

> [as I already said in my reply, the *bozales* have some general means of corrupting the language, but this refers more to constructions than to pronunciation, and these expressions are precisely those used in this book: here are some of the principal ones [...] the blacks almost always repeat the negative element, e.g., they say "no va a juntar no" {lit "I'm not going to get together not"}, "no va a salir no" {"I'm not going to leave not"}]

---

[2] I am grateful to Clancy Clements for providing me with a transcription of this fascinating document.

The same double negation pattern occurs in vernacular Brazilian Portuguese (Schwegler 1991b), and in the vernacular Portuguese of Angola, Mozambique, and São Tomé (Lipski 2000a). Similar double negation is found in the Portuguese-derived creoles of São Tomé and Principe; the related creole of Annobon uses only postposed negation, most probably derived from an original double paradigm.

The traditional Afro-Bolivian dialect almost never exhibits double negation based on the *no ... no* pattern; I have heard only a few cases of expressions such as *NO me ayuda NO* 'he doesn't help me at all', and even these may in reality be *no me ayuda, no* (with a "no" that serves as "afterthought", outside the main clause). However, the related *no ... nada* pattern, used with intransitive verbs in which *nada* cannot be acting as a direct object, occurs frequently enough as to be considered an alternative form of double negation. Some recorded examples are:

(71)	*ningún misa **nada***	'no mass at all'
(72)	*Yo no va i **nada**.*	'I'm not going at all.'
(73)	*No hacía valé **nada**.*	'He didn't give a good showing at all.'
(74)	*Nojotro no sabe ningún aymara **nada**.*	'We don't know any Aymara at all.'
(75)	*Oté no fue escuela **nada**.*	'You didn't go to school at all.'
(76)	*No va buscá ningún agua **nada** porque disi tiene arma.*	'[We] aren't going to get any water because they say there is a spirit.'
(77)	*Disi qui volaba pero ele no volaba **nada**.*	'They said that [she] flew but she didn't fly at all.'

The same construction appears frequently in vernacular Caribbean Spanish of several countries, although rarely attested in literature and never commented on by observers of language. Even though *nada* is ostensibly a pronominal form, in Caribbean Spanish, the construction *can* occur with intransitive verbs (unaccusative and unergative) as well as with expressed predicate nominals and adjectives. It usually occurs with no pause or change in intonation. Some overheard examples include:

(78)	*No es difícil **ná**.*	'It's not difficult.' {Puerto Rico}
(79)	*No llegó **nada**.*	'He didn't arrive at all.' {Venezuela}

Double negation with *no ... na(da)* appears occasionally in Dominican literature:

(80)   a.   *Dicen que Solito es malo; Solito no es malo **ná**.*
'They say that Solito is bad; 'Solito isn't bad at all'

(Caamaño de Fernández 1976: 29;
Henríquez Ureña 1966: 299) {19th-century popular song}

        b.   *Timoteo dizque era muerto; Timoteo no es muerto **ná**.*
'Timoteo was supposed to be dead; Timoteo isn't dead at all.'

(Prestol Castillo 1986: 47)

Cuban literature offers occasional instances of double negation with *no ... nada*:

(81)   a.   *Era un hecho inaudito y el sujeto aquel no debia ser tan bueno **nada**.*
(Herrera 1964: 45)
'It was an unheard of fact and that guy couldn't have been that good at all.'

        b.   *Un poco de polvo [...] no me baño **nada**.* (Soler Puig 1975: 77)
'A bit of powder [...] I don't bathe at all.'

        c.   *Espérese. No espero **nada**, este tipo es peligroso.* (J. Díaz 1966: 25)
'Wait. I won't wait at all; that guy is dangerous.'

        d.   *A usté no le intereso **ná**.* (Iznaga 1970: 21)
'You don't care about me at all.'

        e.   *No llueve, Ermidio; no me llueve **ná**.*(Iznaga 1970: 51)
'It's not raining Ermidio; it's not raining at all.'

In Venezuela, a song transcribed in the Afro-Venezuelan village of Caraballeda also exhibits a double negative:

(82)   *Dicen que mi Changó es mono*   'They say that mi Changó is cute'
        *Ma Changó **no** es mono **ná***   'but Changó isn't cute at all'
        Ma Changó lo que tiene   'but what Changó has'
        Que no lo saben bailá   'that they can't dance'

(Sojo 1986: 106)

A similar use of *na(da)* as double negator is found in a song transcribed in the Afro-Venezuelan community of Chichiriviche:

(83)   *Yo soy el Pájaro Negro*   'I am the black bird'
        cuando la gana me dá;   'whenever I feel like it'

> cuando no me da la gana   'when I don't feel like it'
> no soy pájaro **ná**!   'I'm not a bird at all.'
>
> (Sojo 1986: 258)

From vernacular São Tomé Portuguese comes (César 1969a: 334-336):

(84) *Não morre **nada**.*   'He's not dying at all.'

The same pattern is also attested in Mozambican Portuguese (Mendes 1981: 110):

(85) *Não vai embora **nada**!*   'He's not leaving at all.'

Examples from Angolan Portuguese include:

(86) *Tens dinheiro? Não tem **nada**.*   'Do you have money? I don't have any
                                            at all.' (Schuchardt 1888: 252)
                                            [1979: 70-71]
(87) *É verdade que eu robei! Mas*   'It's true that I robbed. But I didn't see
      *carta viu **nada**.*   any letter at all.' (Maria Archer, "A
                                            carta"; César 1969b: 704)

Such examples are probably not of recent origin. A very suggestive sentence from the Gold Coast, apparently used in 1621 by a woman as a reason for decapitating a slave (Jones 1995: 106) is:

(88) *siempre Comeer y non trabalhar,*   'always eating and not working, not at
      nada nada   all'

The sentence contains possibly Spanish elements (*siempre* 'always', *non* 'no'), and the sentence-final *nada* may be an emphatic afterthought; however, the correspondence with later Angolan and Mozambican Portuguese and vernacular Caribbean Spanish is striking.

Double negation with *no ... nada* is difficult to study for at least two reasons: first, it is transient in nature; and second, it passes unnoticed even by speakers who use this construction with some frequency. Informal questioning by the author in several Caribbean Spanish speech communities has revealed an almost total unawareness of this construction; when presented explicitly with examples actually produced by other speakers, most individuals consulted did acknowledge that double negatives of this sort were possible, although few admitted to ever using them.

5.5. Coordinate conjunctions and conjoined clauses

The Spanish coordinating conjunctions *y* 'and*'*, *o* 'or*'*, and *pero* 'but' are used in unaltered fashion in the traditional Afro-Bolivian dialect. This is true both within phrases and when conjoining entire clauses, as shown by (89)-(93):

(89)	*Yo **y** mi mamá iba.*	'My mother and I went.'
(90)	*hombres **y** mujé*	'men and women'
(91)	*Si es un gaína **o** un conejo.*	'If it is a chicken or a rabbit.'
(92)	*Lu guagua va, **pero** poco.*	'The kids go, but not much.'
(93)	***Pero** dici que ele subí.*	'But they say that he went up.'

Most Afro-Bolivians also use the Aymara-influenced Andean construction with phrase-final *pero,* where *pero* expresses politeness, doubt, or regret: *no está pero* 'he isn't home'. In these sentences, *pero* functions as a discourse marker rather than as a conjunction (Laprade 1976, 1981; Stratford 1989). This construction is more frequent in contemporary Spanish than in the traditional Afro-Yungueño dialect.

As mentioned previously, in Afro-Bolivian Spanish, *con* occasionally acts as a coordinating conjunction:

(94)	*Mi tata **con** mi mamá es nacio Mururata.*	'My father and my mother were born in Mururata.'

5.6. Complex sentence structure

Like contemporary Spanish, the traditional Afro-Bolivian dialect employs complex sentences (subordinate clauses are typically introduced by the complementizer *que,* and subordinating conjunctions by *porque*). In the traditional dialect, all verbs in subordinate clauses are derived from the Spanish indicative, even where contemporary Spanish would require a subjunctive form (examples 100, 103, 105-107).

(95)	*Esus palo no sirvi **porque** se va yená jai di poliya.*	'Those trees are no good because they will be full of termites.'
(96)	*Abuelo Calixto jai disi **que** murió.*	'They say that old Calixto died.'
(97)	*Los patrón y loh mayorodomo no dejaba **que** venía polecía.*	'The landowners and the overseers would not let the police come.'
(98)	*Pero dici **que** ele subí.*	'But they say that he went up.'

(99)   *Eje qui ta allá no han di copiá*   'Don't copy what's there [on the
       porque *no sirvi.*   blackboard], because it's wrong.'

(100) *Yo quiere* ***que*** *oté mi ehplica.*   'I want you to explain to me.'

(101) *Oté tiene que tomá todo* ***que***   'You need to take everything that the
       dostor ta ti dando.   doctor is giving you.'

(102) *Ele ya mira* ***que*** *ya senta.*   'He saw that [you] were sitting down.'

(103) *Tiene que gritá ...* ***pa que***   '[They] had to yell ... so Tocaña could
       escucha Tocaña.   hear.'

(104) *un mujé* ***que*** *está como tentación*   'a woman who is a temptation'

(105) *Yo quiere* ***qui*** *mi compra un*   'I want you to buy me a loaf of bread.'
       pancito.

(106) *Yo lu puntiaba cun barro cun*   'I spattered [my pants] with mud on that
       tierra ese lao pa qui ***disi*** *yo cayó*   side it could be said I fell so that
       pa que no ***nota*** *qui mi pantalón*   they wouldn't notice that my pants
       ta mojao di meau.   were wet with urine.'

(107) *Yo nuabía quen mi* ***compra*** *ni*   'I didn't have anyone to buy me shoes
       zapato ni bandera.   or flags.'

Since Afro-Yungueño Spanish is exclusively an oral language reserved for casual speech, the frequency of complex sentences is lower than would be found, for example, in formal discourse or written language. Nonetheless, with the exception of the absence of distinct subjunctive forms in subordinate clauses, Afro-Yungueño complex sentences are not notably different from those found in other varieties of Spanish.

5.7. Reduplication as intensification

Used as intensifying or augmentative construction, reduplication of nouns, verbs, adjectives, and adverbs is a common strategy in many creole (and non-creole) languages. Reduplication does occur in the traditional Afro-Bolivian dialect, but not to the extent found in many other creole languages. Examples include:

(108) *Bus taba **lleno-lleno**.*   'The bus was (really) full.'

(109) *Ta **suksa-suksa**.*[3]   'Dusk is falling.'

---

[3] *Suksa-suksa,* from Aymara *suksa* 'twilight', is used in the Nor Yungas Afro-Bolivian communities. In Chicaloma (Sud Yungas), the derived diminutive *suksita* is used.

5.8. Word order of major constituents in traditional Afro-Bolivian Spanish

Highland Bolivian Spanish, especially as spoken by Aymara- and Quechua-speaking bilinguals, strongly favors Object-Verb constructions, rather than the usual Verb-Object order found in most monolingual Spanish varieties. This is because Aymara and Quechua are O-V languages, and crossover into Spanish frequently produces combinations such as *limón cómprame* 'buy lemons from me', *casa tengo* 'I have a house'. These manifestly interlanguage combinations are stigmatized and avoided by educated speakers, but they are quite frequent in the Aymara-dominant communities that surround the Afro-Bolivian population in the Yungas. Despite the presence of O-V word order among their Aymara-speaking neighbors, Afro-Bolivians resort to this pattern rather infrequently. Representative examples of O-V order are:

(110)	*Yuca puro era.*	'There was only yucca.'
(111)	*Ni mucho papa había para comé.*	'There weren't even many potatoes to eat.'
(112)	*Puro mula se manejaba pue.*	'Only mules were used.'

Topicalized or left-dislocated sentences of the sort *Juan, lo que quiere es comer* 'what John wants is to eat' are almost never heard in Afro-Bolivian Spanish. "Predicate cleft" constructions found in Afro-Atlantic creoles such as Papiamentu (e.g., *(ta) pensa bo ta pensa* 'you're thinking' [Maurer 1988: 144]) are altogether absent from Afro-Bolivian speech.

CHAPTER 6

THE AFRO-BOLIVIAN LEXICON

6.1. Introduction

The lexicon of the traditional Afro-Bolivian dialects is predominantly drawn from rural Bolivian Spanish, with the phonetic modifications described in Chapter 2. A number of Aymara words are used in both the traditional dialect and contemporary Spanish, as detailed in Chapter 7.

Only a handful of words are exclusive to the Afro-Yungueño dialect cluster. This chapter includes these words as well as other lexical items that typify Afro-Bolivian speech, particularly those referring to coca cultivation. The Afro-Bolivian lexicon can be logically divided into three parts, in addition to Spanish words shared with the rest of Bolivia. First, there are several items derived from Spanish (including general Latin Americanisms originally borrowed from other indigenous languages) or Spanish words with altered meaning. Second, there are numerous words of Aymara origin, some assimilated to Spanish morphology and others modified only to conform to Spanish phonotactics. Finally, there is a handful of words of unknown origin, for which some researchers have suggested African sources.

6.2. Lexical items derived from Spanish[1]

agradé   'to give thanks'.
             < Sp. *agradecer*

andi   'where'
             < Sp. *donde,* archaic *onde* (in turn from Latin *de unde*)

apagavela   'small moths attracted to lights and flames'
             < Sp. *apaga* 'put out' + *vela* 'candle'

---

[1] Aymara-derived vocabulary that in some dictionaries and orthographic systems would be written with *k* and *w* are represented orthographically as Spanish words, with *c/qu* and *hu*, respectively. An exception is *awicha* 'grandmother,' widely written in Aymara orthography by Bolivian speakers of Spanish.

arroba (de huascazos)   '25 lashes with a *huasca* whip, a common punishment during the hacienda period'
    < Sp. *arroba* 'measure of 25 lbs.' and (probably) Quechua *huasca* 'whip'

atabul   'coffin'
    < Sp. *ataúd*

ayere   'yesterday'
    < Sp. *ayer*, with paragogic vowel

cesto   'Measure of 32 lbs., used in buying and selling coca leaves'
    < Sp. *cesto* 'large basket'

chapaleá   'to become covered with mud from walking through a muddy spot'
    < Sp. *chapalear* 'to splash by striking or stomping on the surface of water'

cinisia   'ashes'
    < Sp.*ceniza*

cocala   'field of coca plants'
    < Sp. *cocal*

comadre/compadre   In additional to the usual Spanish meanings of adults who share god-parent relationships with one another's children, these terms are frequently used as respectful forms of address, and are thus parallel to hypocoristic *tío/tía*.

coreá   'to clear the weeds from an orchard'
    < Sp. *corear* 'to hoe, chop weeds'

cotencia   'woven cloth about the size of a small table cloth,' used by women in the Yungas to carry small parcels, bundled and wrapped around the neck while walking.
    < Sp. *cotensia* 'sack cloth'

cu   'to sit down'
                                < Sp. *culo* or Port. *cu* 'arse'

corte   'a series of *huachos* or strips of land, an archaic meas-
                            ure used to describe the amount of land (to be) cleared
                            in a coca plantation'
                                < Sp. *corte* 'section [e.g., of land]'

da dioselupai   'to give thanks'
                                < Sp. *dar* 'to give' + *Dios se lo pague'* 'may God repay
                                you.' Cp. *diojelupai* below.

diojelupai/diosolupai   'thanks, thank you'
                                < Sp. *Dios se lo pague* 'may God repay you.' This is
                                the traditional way of expressing thanks. It is pro-
                                nounced as a single word and among the few Afro-
                                Bolivians who attempt to write the traditional dialect,
                                it is also written this way (as exemplified in the
                                Appendix). Guevara (1968: 81) mentions the similar
                                fused forms *diosolopay* and *diosolopague* in popular
                                Ecuadoran speech.

ele   'he/she/it'; genderless third person singular subject
                            pronoun, used for both masculine 'he' and feminine
                            'she'
                                < Sp. *él* 'he' with paragogic vowel

estera   'rustic mat or sleeping pallet, usually made from dried
                            banana fibers'
                                < Sp. *estera* 'wickerwork'

eyu   'third person plural pronoun, used for both masculine
                            and feminine'
                                < Sp. *ellos* 'they (masc.)'

guaracha   'rustic wooden bench'
                                < Sp. *guaracha* 'awning, barbecue pit'

hojeá   'to remove dry and wilted leaves from banana plants'
                                < Sp. *hojear* 'to shake leaves' < *hoja* 'leaf'

huacho   'an archaic measure of land, used to describe the width of strips
                      of land'
                        < Sp. *guacho* 'furrow'

huasca   'rustic whip, used to punish *peones* during the hacienda period'
                        < *huasca* 'whip,' a general South Americanism originally of
                          Quechua origin (the word is also *huasca* in Quechua, with the
                          meaning of `whip').

¿insé?   'really, no kidding?'
                        Pronounced with steeply rising interrogative intonation to express
                        disbelief or surprise. It may be a shortening of Sp. *¿en serio?*
                        'really?' Montaño Aragón (1992: 272) glosses this word as
                        "*¿qué dice?*" 'what are you saying?', but the true meaning is
                        not to request a repetition but rather as an interjection requiring
                        no response.

jondía   'to hurl or throw'
                        < archaic Sp. *jonda* (modern Sp. *honda*) 'slingshot'

mama   'mother'
                        < Sp. *mamá* 'Mom, mother,' with stress shift to the first syllable

manta   used with female names, roughly meaning 'sister' (e.g., *manta
                      Juana*)
                        < Sp. *hermanita* 'sister (dim.)'

ojala   'I wish, if only'
                        < Sp. *ojalá* 'if only, may God wish' with stress shift from the last
                          to the penultimate syllable ([o-'ha-la]

oté   'you'; second person singular pronoun, used in both familiar
                      and formal contexts
                        < Sp. *usted* 'you (formal, sing.)'

otene   'you (pl.)'; second person plural subject pronoun
                        < Sp. *ustedes* 'you (formal, pl.)'

palanganiá   'to gossip or spread rumors'
                        < Sp. *palanganear* 'to boast,' < *palangana* 'chatterbox, boastful
                          person'

picarado

'to remove dirt from around a recently transplanted coca plant after a heavy rain'
> < Sp. *picar* 'to dig, chop with a pick'

platano

'plantain'
> < Sp. *plátano* ['platano], with stress shift ([pla'tano])

polilla

'termite'
> < Sp. *polilla* 'moth'

pongo

'domestic labor required of male *peones* during the hacienda period in the Yungas
> < *pongo* 'indigenous male servant,' a general South Americanism originally of Quechua origin. Cp. Quechua *pongo* 'laborer'.

sanjuaneá

'to plant seeds by scattering'
> < Sp. *San Juan* 'Saint John'

també

'also'
> < Sp. *también*. *Tambe* is also used in Papiamentu. Portuguese *tamb*é*m* may also be implicated here.

tata

'father.' Also used with male names to mean 'grandfather' (e.g., *tata Sai [Salles]*)
> < colloq. Am. Sp. *tata* 'daddy'

tatito

a term used by Afro-Bolivians to refer to indigenous persons
> < the diminutive of Sp. *tata* 'daddy'

tiestu

'earthenware vessel for roasting coffee'
> possibly < Sp. *tostar* 'to roast,' *tuesto* 'I roast'

tío (male)/**tía** (female)

Term used in the traditional Afro-Bolivian dialect as respectful address form for adults, both by children and by adults. The same term is also frequently used as subject pronoun indicating greater respect than the neutral *oté,* which assumes the functions of Spanish familiar *tú* and formal *usted*.
> < Sp. *tío* 'uncle,' *tía* 'aunt'

John Lipski

viudita a variation of the mysterious female figure that appears at night to frighten passersby
  < the diminutive of Sp. *viuda* 'widow'

zanjeo/zanjío 'process of digging furrows on the hillside for new coca plantings'
  < Sp. *zanja* '[drainage] ditch'

6.3. Lexical items derived from Aymara

Aymara nouns and adjectives are usually adopted into Afro-Bolivian Spanish with only phonotactic modifications: aspirate and glottalized consonants are replaced by simple occlusives, and the Aymara uvular stop /q/ is replaced by the Spanish velar stop /k/. Aymara verbs are typically stripped of the infinitive ending *-aña,* and fitted with the Spanish first-conjugation suffix *-á (-ar)* or *-iá (-ear).*

The following list is a selection of commonly-used Aymara borrowings into Afro-Bolivian Spanish. Aymara etymologies have been checked with dictionaries[2] as well as with several Aymara speakers, from the highlands and from the Yungas.[3] Putative Aymara etymologies that were given by informants but could not be verified in dictionaries are marked with an asterisk. Aymara has been written with several different orthographic systems, and the entries below reflect the prevailing trends in the reference works consulted.

ahuaytañá 'to cover with leaves or cloth'
  < Aymara *ahuayt'asiña* 'to cover one's daily outfit with a blanket'

aicatá 'to revive a cooking fire'
  < Aymara *aycataña* 'to prop up, to revive a fire'

anchancho 'an evil spirit manifested by an echo in abandoned houses or

[2] For instance: Ayala Loayza (1988), Bertonio (1879), Büttner, Condori Cruz, and Llanque (1984), Carvajal Carvajal, Huanca Tórrez and Vásquez (1978), Cotari, Mejía, and Carrasco (1978), Deza Galindo (1989), Ebbing (1965), Gómez Bacarreza (1999), Layme Pairumani (2004), Layme et al. (1992), Lucca (1983), Miranda S. (1970), M. Paredes (1971), Ross (1958), Tarifa Ascarrunz (1990), Van den Berg (1985), Yapita (1979).
[3] Special thanks are due to Juan de Dios Yapita for La Paz Aymara and Luis Mamani (from Dorado Grande) for Aymara data from the Yungas.

other frightening places, also a mythological creature that frightens travelers'

> < Aymara *anchanchu* 'malignant spirit said to inhabit abandoned mines,' also an eco, especially in abandoned houses and dark hollows' (Deza Galindo 1989: 33; Miranda S. 1970: 111; Van den Berg 1985: 24). Since some Afro-Bolivians believe the *anchancho* to take an animal form, there may be some crossover with prenasalized Sp. *chancho* 'pig' > **nchancho* > *anchancho*.

ancu   'hard'

> < Aymara *anku* 'hard, tough [said of meat]'

awicha   'a term of respect / used to address or refer to elderly women'

> < Aymara *awicha* 'grandmother, elderly woman'

awicho   'occasionally used to refer to elderly men'

> analogously formed from Aymara *awicha* 'grandmother, elderly woman'

cahuirá*   'to toast leaves in the sun or over a fire'

> < Aymara *khahuiraña* 'to soften (in the sun)'

cainá   'to work in one agricultural spot all day'

> < Aymara *jaymaña* 'to work on communal lands.' Some Aymara speakers from the Yungas suggest the origin in Aymara *khamasiña* 'to rest.'

caracayo   'barefoot'

> < Aymara *q'aracayu* 'barefoot'

cayana*   'pot shards'

> < Aymara *kallamo* 'pieces'

chacuru   'implement made of sticks for hanging things to dry'

> < Aymara *ch'akuru* 'metal stake'

chacantá   'to become stuck in the mud (said of vehicles,' usually in the participle form *chacantao*)

> < Aymara *chacantaña* 'to obstruct' and *chacantayaña* 'to block a roadway'

chajchuquipá   'to sprinkle water'
                     < Aymara *ch'ajhchuña* 'to sprinkle'

chajchurá   'to sprinkle water on a dirt floor to keep down the dust'
                     < Aymara *ch'ajhchuña* 'to sprinkle'

chajeá   'to pound or mash'
                     < Aymara *ch'ajheña* 'to pound, mash'

chalalí*   'to shout'
                     < Aymara *chalaliña* 'to shout loudly'

chamisa*   'small sticks, kindling'
                     < Aymara *ch'umisa* 'small sticks'

chaypu   'dawn or early dusk'
                     < Aymara *cchayphu* "crepúsculo; claridad que se presenta desde
                     que se pone el sol hasta que anochece" [dusk; twilight that
                     stretches from sunset until darkness] (Carvajal Carvajal, Huan-
                     ca Tórrez and Vásquez 1978: 14); also *cchapu* with the same
                     meaning (Miranda S. 1970: 136)

chilcatá*   'to prop up, an object, a baby'
                     < Aymara *chilcatam* 'prop, support'

chilpañá*   'to prop up or block off'
                     < Aymara *chilpañam* 'support'

chiuli   'baby chick'
                     < Aymara *chiuli* 'chick, duckling'

cho   'a vocative, approximately "hey" usually accompanied by the
                     name of the person being addressed'
                     < Aymara *cchuy* 'hey! look!'

chojtá   'when rain dampens cut coca leaves before they can thorough-
                     ly dry'
                     < Aymara *cchojhtáña* 'to purposely urinate on someone or some-
                     thing'; also Aymara *llujtaña* 'to moisten'

churahui 'cloudy, with the possibility of rain'
< Aymara *ch'urahui* 'cloudy'

cojoro 'dried bark from banana trees, used to make rustic mats'
< Aymara *kojoro* 'banana leaves used to carry coca leaves' (Miranda S. 1970: 129)

cuyá, cuyuntá 'to take care of a cooking fire, covering the coals with ashes overnight'
< Aymara *aqayaña* 'to feed a fire'

huaquichá 'to prepare food'
< Aymara *huaquichaña* 'to prepare'

huarco 'an archaic measure of weight, used when buying and selling coca'
< Aymara *huarcu* 'a measure of weight originally worth 80 *centavos* (1/100 of a peso)

janquí 'to bite'
< Aymara *jankhina* 'to gnaw'

jaturá 'to chew'
< Aymra *jaturaña* 'to nibble, scrape with the teeth'

jawintau/jawirau 'to become muddy'
< Aymara *jahuiña* 'to paint, smear'

jay an element frequently used to punctuate Afro-Bolivian discourse. Illustrated more fully in Chapter 7, *jay* conveys no specific meaning to a sentence but rather adds an aspect of familiarity.
< Aymara *jay,* an interjection meaning approximately 'what?' or 'listen!'

jilacata 'work-team leader of field labor gangs during the *hacienda* period of the Yungas, prior to the reforms of 1952'
< Aymara *jilaqata* 'local indigenous authority,' < Aymara *jila* 'older brother'

jinchucha 'the first harvest of a new *cocal*'
< Aymara *jinchuchaña* 'harvest coca leaves'; also 'place handles on a ceramic receptacle'

jurcurá 'to hoe or dig in the dirt'
< Aymara *joryqhoña* 'to scratch, gouge'

larpa 'rickety, weakling (said of a child born prematurely)'
< Aymara *larpha* 'rickety, prematurely born'

masí 'to chop weeds from around mature coca plants.' The nominal form is *el masi*.
< Aymara *masiña* 'to remove weeds from a coca field' (Miranda S. 1970: 202). Some Aymara speakers claim that it is not of Aymara origin, although all Aymaras in the Yungas know and use this word.

matachá* 'to sprinkle coca leaves with water to soften them so they do not crumble when placed into sacks for the market'
< Aymara *matachiña* 'to soften'

minga 'substitute laborer, temporarily replacing a *peón* who was ill or otherwise indisposed during the hacienda period in the Yungas'
< Aymara *mink'a* or *minq'a* 'laborer, substitute'

mitani 'domestic labor required of female *peones* during the hacienda period in the Yungas
< Aymara *mit'ani* 'unpaid female labor in the house of a colonist'

nina-nina 'lightning bug or firefly'
< Aymara *nininina* 'firefly'

pincará 'to remove weeds from around recently sprouted coca plants'
< Aymara *phincataã* 'to mound up agricultural products'

pitará 'to remove weeds from around young coca plants'
< Aymara *p'itaraña* 'to crochet, to cut slivers with a sharp object'

pocaquí 'full, crowded'
< Aymara *phoqa* 'full'

quepechá 'to wrap up'
< Aymara *q'epichaña* 'to wrap up'

quichí 'to harvest coca by picking the leaves'
< Aymara *k'ichiña* 'to pinch,' to pick coca leaves in the Yungas' (Miranda S. 1970: 181)

quiquiriá 'to struggle with a heavy object'
< Aymara *k'ik'i* 'full, dense'

quisima 'soot from a cooking fire that adheres to the inside of a dwelling'
< Aymara *qhesima* 'soot'

quisturá 'to puncture'
< Aymara *khistuña* 'to chew, tear apart with the teeth'

rejuiciliu 'lightning flash'
< Aymara *llijulliju* 'lightning flash'

sangararau 'tangled up'
< Aymara *sankhu* 'thick, dense'

suxa-suxa 'dusk' (see also *suxita* below)
< Aymara *sujsa* 'last evening light or first morning light'

suxita 'dusk' (in Chicaloma, Mururata, and Chijchipa)
< Aymara *sujsa* 'last evening light or first morning light', with Spanish-derived diminutive suffix –*ita*.

timpi 'a *contencia* or cloth full of harvested coca leaves'
< Aymara *t'imphiña* 'to carry objects in a corner of one's dress or apron'

tiquili 'a stick or pole serving as support'
< Aymara *tikilja* 'support, wooden support pole'

6.4. Lexical items of uncertain origin

candambira 'a word forming part of the *mauchi* funeral song.' One of the repeated verses of the *mauchi* is *candambira mauchi, candambira*.

Rey Gutiérrez (1998: 188) offers a Kikongo etymology for *candambira*: "es la deformación de KANDA que significa familia y MBIRA que es llamada. En la concepción religiosa de la negritud, la persona muere cuando su familia que está en el más allá lo ha llamado" [it is the deformation of KANDA, which means family, and MBIRA which is a call. In the black concept of religion a person dies when the person's family which is already in the beyond calls for the person]

chahuirá   'to handle or grope a person or food'

possibly < Aymara *q'allphiña* 'to grope or stroke.'

cocotao   'stripped, bare, said of land'

jajará/jajareá 'to chop or pull out weeds in heavy earth, struggling'

possibly from Spanish *jalar* 'to pull, tug'

mauchi   'the traditional Afro-Bolivian funeral chant, performed upon return from the cemetery after an adult has been buried'

Rey Gutiérrez (1998: 188) suggests a Kikongo origin for the word *mauchi*: "MA: prefijo Kikongo que indica la pertenencia. UCNI: es la deformación de UNSI que significa dentro de la tierra, U: dentro, NSI: tierra. Mauchi se refiere a la tierra" [MA, Kikongo prefix that indicates belonging; UCNI is the deformation of UNSI that means within the earth; U within, NSI earch. *Mauchi* refers to the earth]

miti   'a measure of coca leaves, that fits into a *cotencia*, approximately 2 lbs.'

ñanga   'a timid person, a crybaby'

possibly < Aymara *ñanqha* 'cruel, scornful, evil'; the derived word in Afro-Yungueño Spanish is *ñanguerío* 'timidity'

ñanguingui 'boasting, idle chatter'

possibly derived from Aymara *ñanqha*; see *ñanga* above.

saya   'traditional Afro-Bolivian dance, accompanied by drums.

Rey Gutiérrez (1998: 102) derives *saya* from Kikongo *nsaya* meaning communal labor.

zemba   'a traditional Afro-Bolivian dance similar to the Rio Plata *candombe*, now rarely performed'

Rey Gutiérrez (1998: 216) suggests a Kimbundu word meaning 'navel' or 'striking the navel' as a possible source: "de ahí que

una de las figuras de este baile sea, precisamente, la "ombligada". Fue traída por los esclavos provenientes del área cultural
Angola-Kongoleña. Semba lo mismo que Samba. En la semba
los bailarines se chocan o empujan con el vientre. También se la
denomina "golpe de frente" o "golpe pélvico" [one of the dance
steps is precisely the *ombligada* {belly thrust}. It was brought
by slaves from the Angola-Kongo region. *Semba* is the same as
samba. In the *semba* the dancers bump each other and thrust with
the belly. The dance step is also called "frontal bump" and
"pelvic bump"].

CHAPTER 7

AYMARA INFLUENCE IN AFRO-BOLIVIAN SPANISH

7.1. Aymara and Aymara-influenced Spanish in contact with Afro-Yungueño Spanish

Throughout their residence in the Yungas –a residence that spans at least the past two centuries, and probably also the early colonial period, when black slaves lived in the highlands– Afro-Bolivians have been outnumbered by surrounding Aymara-speaking population. Until relatively recently, i.e., well into the 20th century, many of the Aymara communities in the Yungas were essentially mono-lingual, a fact that has been proposed as contributing to the maintenance of the traditional Afro-Bolivian dialect for so long in unmodernized form, even as Afro-Bolivians acquired and used Aymara.

With the spread of competence in *castellano* among neighboring Aymaras, the immediately recognizable Aymara-influenced interlanguage heard through-out highland Bolivia came into contact with the Afro-Yungueño dialect. This nat-urally raises the question as to how much of the non-patrimonial Spanish compo-nent of Afro-Bolivian Spanish might in fact reflect not just the heritage of former L$_2$ *bozal* learners of Spanish, but also (maybe even only) the imprint of Aymara-influenced Spanish. Given the considerable cultural syncretism observed among Afro-Yungueños, immediately noticeable in female attire but going much deep-er, this question deserves special attention. While it is true that research conduct-ed for the present project has uncovered no plausible Aymara sources for the most striking grammatical restructuring of Afro-Aymara Spanish, it is also the case that Afro-Bolivians use numerous Aymara lexical items and phrases in such an integrated fashion as to indicate coexistence for considerable time. Some of these lexical items are examined in the next section.

7.2. Aymara and Aymara-influenced lexical elements in Afro-Yungueño Spanish

7.2.1. THE FILLER ELEMENT *JAY*

The most striking and most frequent non-Spanish lexical item in Afro-Yungueño Spanish is *jay,* used to punctuate utterances, and considered by both Afro-Bolivians and other observers as the quintessential feature of black Bolivian speech. When used in Afro-Yungueño speech, *jay* has no independent semantic content; that is, the omission of *jay* would never change the meaning of an utterance. At the same time, elicitation of many sentences from Afro-Bolivian speakers always produces *jay* as an integral component; when queried, speakers reply that the sentence sounds "right" with *jay*, and a bit "empty" without it. One Afro-Bolivian speaker felt that *jay* is most frequently used with past-tense reference, but my observations do not bear this out.

Typical examples of the use of *jay* in Afro-Yungueño speech are:

(1)	*Yo no fue jay.*	'I didn't go.'
(2)	*Ahora días jay corto, hay que avanzar trabajo di madrugada.*	'Now that the days are shorter we have to start working earlier in the morning.'
(3)	*Ya murí jay hace tiempo.*	'[She] died a long time ago.'
(4)	*Francisco jay ya mauchió.*[1]	'Francisco died.'
(5)	*Así jay era.*	'That's the way it was.'
(6)	*Yo no sabe jay.*	'I don't know.'
(7)	*Yo nuay jay minga.*	'I don't have a replacement worker.'
(8)	*Yo ta i jay.*	'I'm going.'
(9)	*Yo ta vení jay del pueblo.*	'I'm coming from town.'
(10)	*Lu profesor taba jay marchandu.*	'The teachers were marching.'
(11)	*No hay jay pa velá.*	'There is nothing for the wake.'
(12)	*Así jay mi ha dició.*	'That's what [he] told me.'
(13)	*Ya miró jay.*	'I saw [it].'
(14)	*Hay que civilizá jay.*	'It's necessary to get civilized.'
(15)	*Eje lu mujé ta jay la cocina.*	'Those women are in the kitchen.'
(16)	*Yo tiene jay yuca.*	'I have yucca.'
(17)	*Nojotro vino jay Coroico.*	'We came from Coroico.'
(18)	*Ayere yo fue jay.*	'I went yesterday.'
(19)	*Yo sigui jay cuyuntando.*	'I'm still banking the fire.'
(20)	*Yo disió jay.*	'I said [it].'
(21)	*Yo va ti llevá jay.*	'I'm going to take you.'
(22)	*¿Quién jay lo ha dició?*	'Who said it?'
(23)	*Ele anda jay.*	'He/she is going.'
(24)	*Yo ta comeno jay.*	'I'm eating.'
(25)	*Ele jay ta vení.*	'He/she is coming.'

---

[1] The word *mauchi*, of uncertain etymology (see Chapter 6), refers to the traditional Afro-Bolivian funeral ceremony. A few speakers have created the analogical verb *mauchí* 'to die'.

(26) *Mujé no trabaja jay en eje pueblo.*   'Women don't work in that village.'
(27) *Esus palo no sirvi porque se va*   'Those trees are worthless because they
     yená jay di poliya.   will be filled with termites.'
(28) *Abuelo Calixto jay disi que murió.*   'They say that Calixto died.'
(29) *Asti recordá jay.*   'You must remember.'
(30) *Eje cholo jay llegó.*   'That Indian arrived.'
(31) *Yo ta jay bien.*   'I'm doing well.'
(32) *Nojotro lu genti antiguo sabemo*   'We older people know what things are
     jai qué cosa es bueno.   good.'

Jay also occurs in partially modernized Afro-Yungueño speech, in which full subject-verb and some noun-adjective agreement are found. *Jay* is sometimes used by non Afro-Bolivians when speaking to black Yungueños. Some examples of *jay* in partially modernized speech are:

(33) *Aquí levantamo jay temprano.*   'We get up early here.'
(34) *Cuando mis hermana vivía,*   'When my sisters were alive, they did
     hacían jay semana.   chores.'
(35) *Ustedes deben tener jay algo que*   'You must have something to
     recordar.   remember.'
(36) *No sé ustede cómo jay hacían en*   'I don't know how you did at home.'
     casa.
(37) *Ayere jay ha hecho un sol.*   'Yesterday the sun was very strong.'
(38) *He ido jay a la [sic] pueblo.*   'I've gone to town.'
(39) *Sería bueno jay que pensemos en*   'It would be well for us to consider
     eso.   this.'

Of Aymara origin, *jay* is used both in contemporary Aymara and to a much lesser extent in Aymara-influenced Spanish. Aymara *jay* means roughly 'what?' or 'hey!'[2], and is employed when responding to someone calling out. Typically employed by itself, Aymara, *jay* can also function as a tag question, meaning 'right?'. However, in vernacular urban and rural Aymara, it also appears at the end of the sentence or sentence-medially, as a tag phrase, roughly equivalent to the use of *yo* [joɥ] in contemporary vernacular African American English in the United States. Traditional Aymara speakers do not transfer this item into their Spanish, but

---

[2] http://www.lenguandina.org/ gives the following definition: '*jay* interjección de uno que da señal de que oye, siendo llamado' [an interjection from one who has been called, indicating that he is listening]. Carvajal Carvajal et al. give the following definition: "*jay*: intj. ¿qué?; expresión generalmente usada en las respuestas, equivale a 'qué cosa'" [interjection 'what'; an expression generally used in replying, meaning 'what?'] (1978: 32). Deza Galindo has this entry: '*jay*: interj. ¡qué! ¡oye!' [interjection, 'hey!', 'listen!'] (1989: 97).

bilinguals sporadically use *jay* (with variant *ja*) in their Spanish discourse. Bolivian popular literature occasionally represents this usage. For example, in the novel *Zambo Salvito* (Paredes Candia 1988: 21), an indigenous woman addresses two black protagonists as follows: "Ustedes **jay** son dos bocas, si quieres quedate por la comida" [you have two mouths to feed; if you like, stay for dinner]. Botelho Gonsálvez' (1941) *Coca,* a novel set in the Yungas, has the following examples:

(40) *Asina **jay** jué, compañeros.*   'That's how it was, comrades.' (p. 17)

  *¡Choy! ¡**Jay**! ¡La güena mula!*   'Hey, the good mule.'(p. 18)

  Ay, choy, es muy poco; seraps tres   'Ah, it's too little; it's only three pounds
  libras de coca y una botella de   of coca and a bottle of liquor,
  *trago, ¿**jay**?*   right?'(p. 55)

  Güeno, pos habrá usté notado un   'OK. you must have noticed a sudden
  cambio repentino en Marucha,   change in Marucha, right?' (p. 119)
  *¿**jay**?*

  *Bueno, dime una cosa ... ¿**Jay**?*   'Well, tell me something … what? he
  consintió, moviendo la cabeza.   answered, nodding his head.' (p. 123)

Other literary examples include those in (41):

(41) *No doña Petrona, tempranito **ja**,*   'No, Doña Petrona, I went to my plot of
  mey ido al tambo, para   land early to get fresh fruit.'
  agarrarme fruta fresca.
  (Barrera Gutiérrez 2000a: 21)

  Bueno, mi nombre es Eulogia,   'Well, my name is Eulogia, I'm single
  *soltera **jay** son no tengo*   and not engaged.'
  compromiso. (Barrera
  Gutiérrez 2001: 64)

  Nara sempre mama, nara, sultera   'Nothing, mother, I'm single.'
  jay suy. (Barrera Gutiérrez
  2000b: 98)

  *No es para tanto ... joven es **jay**.*   'It's no big deal … he's young.'
  (Barrera Gutiérrez 1996: 113)

  *El también, **jay**, se ha desviado*   'He's really gone out of his way
  trabajando para la chica.   working for the girl.'
  (Díaz Villamil 1946: 30)

  *Pero Mamita. todos **jay** están*   'But Mom, everybody's dancing that
  bailando lo mismo. (Díaz   way.'
  Villamil 1946: 116)

  *Estos bailes **jay** hacen conservar*   'Those dances keep one in shape, they
  la línea, como dicen. (Díaz   say.'
  Villamil 1946: 117)

De mis ekhekhos, jay le estoy diciendo, joven. (Díaz Villamil (1987: 7))
'I'm talking about my *ekhekhos* {statues of a mythological figure}, young man.'

¡Hua, cómo nomás! Si el domingo nomás jay he estado con ustedes. (Díaz Villamil 1986: 37)
'What do you mean? I was with you just last Sunday.'

Por eso también jay yo les he de cuidar del trago. (Díaz Villamil 1986: 31)
'For that reason also I have to keep them away from liquor.'

Choy Molina, tu oficio no te da para nada, y yo tengo que hacer con nuestras hijas de panadera, lavandera y cocinera, porque sinós nos muriéramos, jay, de hambre. (Mendoza López 1970: 65)
'Hey Molina, your job doesn't pay anything, and I have to be a baker, a washerwoman and a cook with our daughters because otherwise we'd starve.'

Por que'ps siempre ha de estar apenada mi pogre chica, ja? Salmón (1988: 37)
'Why are you always so unhappy, poor girl, eh?'

Servicial, jay, es. (Salmón 1988: 46)
'She's really helpful.'

¡Es aprendiz, jay! (Salmón 1989: 36)
'He's just an apprentice.'

The use of *jay* to curry favor is a typical strategy used by Aymara market vendors (the majority of which are women), as demonstrated for example in Wilder Cervantes' *La sanguchera de la esquina* (2001):

(42) *Sanguches, niñitos. Con aceite, jay son!*
'Sandwiches, kids, with oil.' (p. 54)

De carne y huevo jay son.
'They have meat and eggs.' (p. 123)

De carne importada de Viacha, ¡jay! son.
'They have meat imported from Viacha.' (p. 141)

These literary imitations demonstrate both similarities and differences with respect to Afro-Bolivian Spanish. In the latter dialect, for example, *jay* never appears in tag questions, and is more frequently employed sentence-internally than sentence-finally. The most noteworthy difference is overall frequency: while used constantly in Afro-Bolivian Spanish, *jay* is quite rare in observed vernacular Spanish as spoken by Aymara-dominant Bolivians. The ultimate source of Afro-Bolivian *jay* is clearly Aymara, but Afro-Bolivians have created innovative combinations of their own.

7.2.2. *Tío* AND *TÍA*

In the Afro-Yungueño dialect, adults not related to the speaker are referred to as *tío* (male) and *tía* (female). This is true not only when children speak, but even among adults who greet one another. *Tío/tía* is often used in direct address to adults, instead of the pronoun *oté*; this may be because, in the traditional Afro-Bolivian dialect, there is no pronominal distinction between familiar and formal second-person address, as in modern Spanish *tú/vos* vs. *usted*. This is similar to Brazilian Portuguese, in which the familiar pronoun *tú* is absent from most dialects (in formal direct address, *o senhor* 'the gentleman' and *a senhora* 'the lady' are employed instead). The same also holds for Sephardic (Judeo) Spanish –which split off from Peninsular Spanish before *usted/ustedes* emerged as pronouns of respect– where *él/ella* serve as formal direct address pronouns. Afro-Bolivian *tía* as direct address pronoun is exemplified in:

(43) *¿Tía ta bien nomah?*   'Are you well, ma'am?'
(44) *¿Andi pue tía ta í?*   'Where are you going, ma'am?'

Aymara speakers in Bolivia use the same greeting (using Spanish *tío* and *tía* rather than the Aymara equivalents) with the same pragmatic matrix. Given that this usage is not found elsewhere in Bolivia, and given the historical demographic balance in which small groups of Afro-Bolivians were surrounded by large established Aymara communities, it is possible that the greetings *tío* and *tía* among Afro-Yungueños reflect prevailing Aymara usage.[3]

7.2.3. *AWICHA*

Elderly Afro-Bolivian women are referred to by the Aymara word *awicha* 'grandmother', just as Aymara speakers do in their own speech communities. Elderly men receive the title *abuelo* rather than the Aymara equivalent. Aymara speakers frequently make the same dichotomy, using *awicha* and *abuelo*. Aymara speakers rarely use *awicha* in their Spanish, but the same word is routinely employed in Afro-Bolivian Spanish. The analogical form *awicho* is sometimes used among Afro-Bolivians.

---

[3] Armin Schwegler (personal communication) reminds me that *tío* > *cho* and *tía* > *cha* are common vocatives in Palenquero and in Chocó, Colombia. In *Chimaⁿkongo: lengua y rito ancestrales en El Palenque de San Basilio* (1996, vol. 2: 256), Schwegler suggests that the Afro-Portuguese-derived hypocorisms *cho* and *cha* were probably already part of the linguistic repertoire of many Kongo/Angolan slaves that were shipped to Latin America.

7.2.4. CHO

Characteristic of Afro-Yungueño speech, and part of stereotypes used by neighboring speech communities when imitating their language, is the salutation *cho*. *Cho* is used as a greeting, similar to the use of *che* in the Guaraní-speaking area and in the Rio de la Plata, but actually represents a modification of Aymara *chhuy* (more often pronounced as *chuy* or *choy*). Examples include:

(45) **Cho**, *¿andi pueh tah yendo?*   'Hey, where are you going?'

(46) **Cho**, *hasti tendé huajaya in eje*   'Hey, spread some coca leaves on that
     cotencia.   drop-cloth.' (from Angola Maconde
                                            2000: 13)

Aymara speakers often introduce *choy/chuy* when speaking Spanish, the same as Afro-Bolivians. Some literary examples are given in (47):

(47) **Choy** *no seas zonzo.* (Díaz   'Hey, don't be a fool.'
     Villamil 1986: 49)

Choy, *apurate. ¡No mauleyes!*   'Hurry up, don't malinger.'
(Salmón 1998: 16)

Choy, *Riguchito.* (Salmón 1988: 45)   'Hey, Riguchito.'

*¡***Choy**, **choy**, **choy***! *¿Creyo que*   'Hey, are you calling me an old
me estás llamando vieja?   woman?'
(Wilder Cervantes 2001: 14)

Choy *llocalla, retírate ampe, tey*   'Hey girl, go away, I'm telling you.'
dicho. (Barrera Gutiérrez
2000a: 15)

Choy, *llevame pues, yo más*   'Hey, take me along, I want to go.'
quiero ir. (Barrera Gutiérrez
2001: 19)

Choy, *Francisco, no te duermas.*   'Hey Francisco, don't fall asleep.'
(Botelho Gonsálvez 1945: 55)

Choy, *¿que's eso?* (Botelho   'Hey, what's this?'
Gonsálvez 1941: 14)

Ay, **choy**, *es muy poco.* (Botelho   'It's too little.'
Gonsálvez 1941: 55)

Choy, *¿acaso he nacido con*   'Hey, do you think I was born wearing
ropas? (Botelho Gonsálvez   clothes?'
1941: 124)

Choy *Juancho ... levantate, ya*   'Hey Johnny, get up, it's 7:00 already
son las siete y el colectivo   and the bus is coming soon.'
dentro de un rato va pasar.
(Paredes Candia 1989: 15)

7.2.5. *ASTI*

Asti < Sp. *has de* 'you must', reflects the Aymara 3-vowel system (with its high front vowel [i]) and realization of Spanish intervocalic /d/ as [t]. *Asti* is used in the traditional Afro-Bolivian grammar as an invariant form, even with the singular pronoun *oté* 'you' and with plural *otene* 'you (pl)'. In the Afro-Yungueño dialect, as in Aymara-influenced Spanish, *asti* can have future imperative reference when in the affirmative (ex. 48), and often carries a warning note or admonition in the negative (ex. 48-50). In other contexts, *asti* can express simple probability (ex. 52).

(48)	*Cho,* **hasti** *tendé huajaya in eje cotencia, nu**asti** olvida di remira.*	'Please spread out the coca leaves on the drying cloth; be sure to keep an eye on the weather.' (Angola Maconde 2000: 13-14)
(49)	*¡No* **asti** *sembrá!*	'Don't plant!'
(50)	*¡No* **asti** *í!*	'Don't go!'
(51)	*¿Qué* **asti** *sembrá?*	'What will you (probably) plant?'
(52)	**Asti** *recordá jay.*	'You got to remember [it].'

In other varieties of Bolivian Spanish, *asti* only occurs with second-person singular reference, corresponding to the subject pronouns *tú/vos*; the full paradigm of other forms is also found, including *hemos de* 'we must', *han de* 'they must', *he de* 'I must'. Bolivian literature contains many examples of *asti* in vernacular speech. *Asti* is not always attributed explicitly to Aymara speakers, but is exclusively found in the most popular registers, which are heavily influenced by Aymara. Some literary examples are given in (53):

(53)	*Vas a estar sintonizando la radio y cuando hayga un gol me* **haste** *avisar.* (Salmón 1999a: 13)	'You'll be listening to the radio, so let me know when a goal is scored.'
	Si me quieres, me has dicho, me **haste** *esperar.* (Díaz Villamil 1986: 22)	'If you love me like you say, you'll wait for me.'
	Ahora **has de** *saber que soy valiente.* (Alarcón 1997: 25; written 1936)	'Now you'll see that I'm brave.'
	No **haste** *hacer en otra hija.* (Salmón 1988: 53)	'You won't do that to another daughter.'
	Por algops eres abogado, y lo **haste** *estar haciendo acortar.* (Salmón 1999b: 30)	You're a lawyer for a good reason, you should remember.'

7.2.6. OTHER AYMARA LEXICAL ITEMS

In the Afro-Yungueño dialect, many lexical items of Aymara origin are used in daily speech (Chapter 6), where they have the same meaning as in Aymara. Most frequent are *suksa-suksa* or *suksita* (Aymara *suksa*) 'early evening light'; *chaypu* 'dawn or dusk'; *churahui* 'overcast sky'. All Aymara words used in daily Afro-Bolivian discourse refer to meteorological phenomena or the agricultural cycle.

7.3. Aymara-Spanish phonetics vs. Afro-Bolivian phonetics

Impressionistically, Afro-Bolivian Spanish phonotactics differs radically from both monolingual highland Bolivian varieties and Aymara-influenced interlanguages. As described in Chapter 2, all highland varieties are characterized by strong pronunciation of word-final /s/ and trilled /r/, both of which disappear in the traditional Afro-Bolivian dialect. Bolivians of all dialect zones, including Aymara-influenced Spanish, distinguish /x/ and /φ/, giving the latter phoneme a clearly lateral articulation. The traditional Afro-Bolivian dialect merges /x/ and /φ/ in favor of a weakly articulated [φ].

Despite centuries of contact between Aymara and Afro-Bolivian Spanish, the only potential overlap lies in the behavior of unstressed vowels. In Afro-Bolivian Spanish, word-final unstressed /o/ usually becomes [u], and word-final unstressed /e/ becomes [i]. This trait has been documented for other Afro-Hispanic varieties, from the 16th to the 19th centuries (see the texts and analysis in Lipski 2005), particularly in neighboring Afro-Argentine and Afro-Uruguayan speech. These changes have become effectively lexicalized in most words, so that the underlying form of the third person plural pronoun (derived from Spanish *ellos* /'eʝos/) is now /'eʝu/ in the Afro-Bolivian dialects. Some word-internal unstressed mid vowels occasionally undergo the same raising, particularly in pretonic position, but this is not common, and has not been lexicalized. Unstressed clitics such as the preposition *di* < *de,* or the generic article *lu* < *los,* have also been lexicalized with high vowels. This carries over into partially modernized Spanish, as shown by the following examples:

(54)	*Ese tía es mamá **di** [de] fulano.*	'That women is so-and so's mother.'
(55)	*Yo mi **caiu** [me he caído].*	'I fell down.'
(56)	*Otene fue **caí** [caer].*	'You (pl.) fell down.'
(57)	*Han **yigao** [llegado] lu(s) trabajadó.*	'The workers have arrived.'
(58)	*Mañana **imos di** [hemos de] comé.*	'We'll eat tomorrow.'

The Aymara vowel system contains only the three phonemes: /i/, /a/, and /u/. Aymara speakers routinely neutralize Spanish /i/ and /e/, /o/ and /u/ in all positions, including those bearing full stress. Although Bolivian literature often portrays Aymara-interfered speech as freely confounding these pairs of vowels, [i] and [u] usually prevail. Bolivian regionalist literature frequently portrays this vocalic neutralization, which is a staple in the popular theatrical presentations of writers such as Raúl Salmón and Juan Barrera Gutiérrez (see the examples in Chapter 2, page 66). Although the raising of unstressed final vowels in Afro-Bolivian Spanish may have been reinforced by the gradually emerging Spanish interlanguage of their once monolingual Aymara neighbors, the behavior of Spanish vowels in the two systems is typologically different enough to suggest an independent origin in the Afro-Yungueño dialect. Most importantly, Spanish stressed /i/ and /e/ are never systematically altered in Afro-Bolivian Spanish, which further leads me to conclude that vowel raising (even in stressed syllables) in the Afro-Yungueño dialect has its roots in language contact.

7.4. Morphosyntax: Aymara-influenced Spanish as a possible locus of transmission

In light of the significant departures from Spanish morphosyntax found in Afro-Yungueño speech (Chaps. 4-5), it is necessary to consider patterns of Aymara-influenced Spanish. This will help us determine whether any of the Afro-Bolivian traits originated in contact-induced Aymara-Spanish interlanguage. There are few morphosyntactic similarities between traditional Afro-Bolivian Spanish and Aymara-influenced Spanish, except for the general gravitation toward Object-Verb word order in Afro-Bolivian Spanish, a trait found in most highland varieties even among monolingual Spanish speakers. Several specific cases of Aymara-influenced Spanish are discussed in detail below.

7.4.1. NOMINAL AND VERBAL MORPHOLOGY

Aymara speakers routinely experience difficulties with Spanish nominal and verbal morphology, in fashions similar to other L2 learners. Aymara-interfered Spanish is characterized by considerable vacillation in subject-verb agreement, including the frequent combination of the formal subject pronoun *usted* 'you' with verbs corresponding to the second person familiar pronoun *tú*. This is similar to patterns observed in Equatorial Guinea (Lipski 1985a), and may respond to the same colonial and post-colonial discourse structure: in both Equatorial

Guinea and the Andean dialects of Bolivia, the natively spoken Spanish dialects acquired as a second language by Africans and Native Americans, respectively, are characterized by prominently sibilant word-final /s/, which makes the 2nd person singular *tú* forms highly prominent. At the same time, native Spanish speakers imposed an asymmetrical address pattern on the subaltern groups, referring to the native populations with the familiar *tú* forms irrespective of age and status, but requiring the respectful *usted* patterns from the indigenous populations. Given that neither the native languages of Equatorial Guinea nor Aymara have two series of second-person pronouns (and also that languages of the Bantu family do not inflect verbs for person and number via suffixes), hybrid combinations of *usted* + verb form ending in the *–s* corresponding to *tú* have resulted. Some literary examples from Bolivia include the examples in (59), from Raúl Salmón's *El partido de la contrapartida* (1969):

(59) *Y si **usti ti pasas** de on minoto, 1.000- Bs.* (p. 442)
'And if you go over one minute, [it costs] 1000 Bolivianos.'

*Usté **tienes** que vérmelo usté.* (p. 443)
'You have to see him.'

*¿Acaso no **sabes usté**?* (p. 445)
'I suppose you didn't know.'

*Usté ya lo **vas** a conocer.*(p. 455)
'You're going to meet him.'

*Tu comadre de **usted** siempre dice.* (p. 456)
'Your *comadre* always says.'

*¿No **queres** quedarte **usted** un ratito?* (p. 457)
'Won't you stay for a while?'

*Ostí **nicisitas** salvación in la Jerceto di Salvación.* (p. 463)
'You need to be saved by the Salvation Army.'

Mendoza (1991: 145) offers the example *Señoras, ¿ustedes de que zona es?, nos decía.* 'Ladies, what area are you from?', which demonstrates another facet of Aymara-Spanish interlanguage, namely the use of a second-person plural pronoun with a third-person singular verb. The same pattern of formal pronoun plus verb corresponding to the familiar second person pronoun occurs in vernacular Angolan Portuguese, for the same reasons as in the Spanish of Equatorial Guinea, as shown in the Angolan literary examples in (60) and the Equatorial Guinea examples in (61):

(60) *Mas **você sabes** porque o **teu** pai não gosta do Mbenza.* (Uanhenga Xitu 1977: 153)
'But you know that your father doesn't like Mbenza.'

*Se **você queres** eu vou lá te ensinar ainda.* (Vieira 1985: 15)
'If you like, I'll take you there to show you.'

*Kangatu, **você vejas** lá! Cuidado!*
(Vieira 1985: 33)

'Kangatu, look there. Be careful!'

*Cala-**te** a boca, Xanxo. **Vocé** já
não **respeitas** mais-velho?*
(Vieira 1985: 34)

'Shut up, Xanzo. Don't you respect
your elders any more?'

*Oia lá, ó Joaquim ... **você** não
namoraste um laparica
chamado Joana?* (Ribas 1969:
23)

'Hey Joaquim, ... didn't you fall in love
with a girl named Joana?'

*Ó amico! **Você** como **passaste**? ...
Antão é **você**? Quando
chegaste? ... ó amico, **você**
não **tiraste** o chapéu?* (Ribas
1969: 24)

'Hey friend, how was it? ... And you?
When did you arrive? ... Hey
friend, didn't you take off your hat?'

***Você tens** a carta?* (Ribas 1969:
116)

'Do you have the letter?'

*Ó amico Sabastião, **você estás** aí?*
(Ribas 1969: 144)

'Hey friend Sebastian, are you there?'

*Não sei, quando cheguei na porta
só vi dar mão e **você ficaste**
calado.* (Xitu 1979: 44)

'I don't know, when I got to the door I
offered my hand and you remained
silent.'

*Ai, Titino, **você viste**, jura ainda?*
(Rocha 1977: 22)

'Hey, Titino, did you see it, do you
swear to it?'

*Olha inda velho Bernardo
camabuim, **você mastigas**
como é?* (Cardoso 1977: 74)

'Hey old Bernardo, can you still chew?'

*Melhor **você dizes** naquele homem
se mano Xico chega, a gente
está lhe esperar na muralha.*
(Vieira 1980: 14)

'Better you should tell that man if Xico
comes, we're waiting for him by the
wall.'

*Eu sei **você conheces** bem
Silvestre.* (Vieira 1980: 22)

'I know that you know Sylvester well.'

*Então, **você**, menino, não **tens** mas
é vergonha?* (Vieira 1982: 8)

'Hey kid, aren't you ashamed?'

***Você esqueceste** o sábado?* (Vieira
1982: 30)

'Did you forget about Saturday?'

(61) *Perdone mi jefe, pero como **usted**
no me **habías** dado la orden.*

'Excuse me boss, but since you hadn't
ordered me.' (Laurel 2000: 3)

Usted mandas.

'You're in charge.' (Bibang Oyee 2002:
29)

Usted dijiste.

'You said [so].' (Bibang Oyee 2002: 29)

Usted me dijo que venga contigo.   'You told me to come with you.' (Quilis
     and Casado-Fresnillo 1995: 188)
Usted me pedistes un favor.   'You asked me for a favor.' (Quilis and
     Casado-Fresnillo 1995: 188)

The inconsistent use of the formal second-person singular pronoun with a verb form corresponding to the familiar pronoun is altogether different from Afro-Yungueño speech, in which the verb form is invariant with respect to person and number. At the same time, the Afro-Bolivian dialect is nearly unique among all Romance-derived creole languages and other Afro-Hispanic dialects in having adopted the Spanish formal pronoun *oté* (< *usted*) as sole second-person singular pronoun.[4]

7.4.2. LACK OF NOUN-ADJECTIVE GENDER AGREEMENT

Aymara does not distinguish grammatical gender in nouns or adjectives, and Aymara-Spanish interlanguage frequently exhibits lapses of noun-adjective agreement, as well as incorrect gender assignment in nouns (Laime Ajacopa 2005: 46; Lucero Mamani 2003). There is frequent gravitation toward the masculine gender as the universally unmarked form (Laime Ajacopa 2005: 46), but not to the extent of complete replacement of all gender concord by the masculine, as in Afro-Bolivian speech. Some Aymara-Spanish interlanguage examples are:

(62) *nuestro merienda*   'our snack' (Laime Ajacopa 2005: 46)
(63) *nuestro realidad*   'our reality' (Laime Ajacopa 2005: 46)
(64) *un costumbre*   'a custom' (Laime Ajacopa 2005: 46)
(65) *otro de las tradiciones*   'another tradition' (Laime Ajacopa 2005: 46)
(66) *el granizada*   'the sleet' (Mendoza 1991: 189-191)
(67) *una lápiz roto*   'a broken pencil' (Mendoza 1991: 189-191)
(68) *Bien oscuro siempre era esa tela.*   'That cloth was very dark.' (Mendoza 1991: 189-191)
(69) *un sequía*   'a drought' (Mendoza 1991: 189-191)

---

[4] The ritualized Afro-Hispanic language of the *congos* of Panama employs the pronoun *utene* < *ustedes* 'you (pl.)' for all second-person references, singular and plural (Joly 1981, 1984; Lipski 1986h, 1986i, 1989a, 1997).

Given that Aymara speakers living in proximity to speakers of the traditional Afro-Bolivian dialect have acquired Spanish relatively recently, it is unlikely that the suspension of grammatical gender in Afro-Yungueño Spanish is due to imitation of the Aymara-Spanish interlanguage, although the latter could well have retarded the gravitation towards the modern Spanish patterns.

7.4.3. DOUBLE POSSESSIVES

Aymara-influenced Spanish makes frequent use of double possessives, of the sort *su mamá de Juan* 'lit. his/her mother of Juan = Juan's mother' and the even more basilectal *de Juan su mamá*. Lucero Mamani (2003) and Laime Ajacopa (2005: 46) point to examples such as *eso era mi visión de mí* 'it was my view'. Mendoza (1991: 190) offers *de la Juanita su mamá era* 'it was Juanita's mother', *a su papá de tu amiga* 'your friend's father', *su juguete de tu hermano* 'your brother's toy'. Similar constructions are used by Afro-Bolivians when speaking contemporary Spanish, although constructions with displaced object of the sort *de Juan su mamá* 'Juan's mother' are rather uncommon. A few double possessives are found in the traditional Afro-Yungueño dialect, with the most common configuration being *mi ... di mí*, as in *MI idea DI MÍ* 'my idea'. Such combinations are infrequent in Afro-Bolivian Spanish, which suggests recent intrusions from the surrounding Aymara-Spanish interlanguage.

7.4.4. OBJECT-VERB WORD ORDER

Aymara-Spanish and Quechua-Spanish interlanguage employ OBJECT-VERB and PREDICATE ADJECTIVE-VERB word order much more so than monolingual Spanish varieties, with the frequency of displaced O-V combinations inversely correlated with proficiency in Spanish. Mendoza (1991: 245-247) provides a transcription of an interview with an interlanguage speaker, in which examples like the following recur frequently (Objects and predicate adjectives are given in small caps):

(70) *MI PUEBLO frío es.*   'My town is cold.'
(71) *EL CHOÑO [chuño] dejamos.*   'We leave the *chuño* [dehydrated potato].'
(72) *CÁSCARAS pelamos.*   'We peel off the skin.'
(73) *VACA hay pero mayoría no come.*   'There are cows, but the majority doesn't eat [beef].'

(74) *DE OVEJA nomás tenemos harto.*   'We have a lot of sheep.'

(75) *CARNE DE OVEJA nosotros*   'We cook mutton.'
   cocinamos.

Object-Verb constructions are occasionally used when Afro-Bolivians speak contemporary Spanish, but non-topicalized O-V constructions almost never occur in the traditional Afro-Yungueño dialect, which demonstrates a resistance to one of the most robust syntactic features of Aymara-Spanish interlanguage.

7.4.5. ELISION OF DEFINITE ARTICLES

Elision of normally required definite articles, particularly in subject position, does occur in both Quechua-Spanish and Aymara-Spanish interlanguage, since neither of the two principal Andean languages employs definite articles. Mendoza (1991: 127-128) notes that in contemporary Bolivian Spanish, elision of the definite article occurs only in the most popular variants, by definition reflecting an indigenous substrate; this occurs most often with displaced subjects in O-V constructions: *[EL] CUADERNO no ha podido encontrar siempre* 'I couldn't find my notebook' (120), *[EL] PERRO nomás había sido* 'it was just a dog' (1991: 188). Elimination of the definite article in object constructions also occurs (1991: 188): *quiero ver [EL] CUARTO* 'I want to see the room'. Although Mendoza refers to the elided article as "una forma básica en el interlecto" [a basic form in the interlanguage] (1991: 188), his own transcriptions of interlanguage speakers provide almost no examples of elided articles. My own observations during several visits to Bolivia suggest that article deletion occurs frequently only in the first stages of acquisition of Spanish by adult speakers of Aymara, i.e., among highly Aymara-dominant semi-bilinguals, and drops off rapidly thereafter.

   The traditional Afro-Yungueño dialect is characterized by the frequent omission of definite articles; but when speaking contemporary Spanish, Afro-Bolivians rarely delete the definite article. By inference this suggests that the ultimate source of null definite articles in Afro-Yungueño Spanish is not Aymara-Spanish interlanguage, which came into contact with the traditional Afro-Bolivian dialect relatively recently. The typological similarities of null definite articles between Afro-Bolivian Spanish and vernacular Afro-Portuguese varieties (Brazil, Helvécia, Angola) provide a more plausible scenario, although later contact with Aymara-influenced Spanish may have reinforced Afro-Bolivian null articles.

7.5. Summary

Given the significant gaps in the oral and written history of Afro-Bolivians in the Yungas, the full extent of Aymara influence on the Afro-Yungueño dialect may never be determined with certainty. Currently, Afro-Yungueño Spanish and Aymara-influenced varieties from the same region are quite different; outside observers can easily distinguish the two ethnolinguistic varieties, and both Afro-Bolivians and Aymara Spanish speakers interviewed for the present study acknowledge these differences. It is conceivable that in past centuries Afro-Yungueño speech may have been more significantly altered by contact with the Aymara language or with the Spanish as spoken by Aymara-dominant bilinguals. The oldest living memories tapped for the present study, representing an individual born around 1890 and with recollections extending at least half a century before that, do not show evidence of a greater influence of Aymara. That Afro-Yungueño Spanish cannot be simply reduced to the residue of Aymara-induced contact phenomena can only be established inferentially, by demonstrating significant features of Afro-Yungueño speech that have never been documented for any other Andean variety formed in contact with indigenous languages, and which at the same time are also found in other Afro-Hispanic dialects, both contemporary and reconstructed from written imitations from centuries past. One can also point to prominent features of Aymara-influenced Spanish that fail to appear in Afro-Bolivian speech, although such cases are not convincing if taken in the absence of exclusively Afro-Yungueño traits. Table 7.1 summarizes the results of this comparison.

TABLE 7.1
A comparison of Afro-Yungueño and Aymara-Spanish varieties

Feature	Afro-Yungueño	Aymara-Spanish	Other Afro-Hispanic
O-V word order	rare	frequent	almost never
3 s. as invariant verb	always	one of many instances of unstable subject-verb agreement	all Afro-Iberian pidgins and creoles, Spanish of Equatorial Guinea
invariant plural article *lu(s)*	nearly always	never	some Afro-Río Platense
masculine gender only	always	some	all Afro-Iberian pidgins and creoles; some in Spanish of Equatorial Guinea and earlier Afro-Hispanic
bare plurals	frequent	never	vernacular Brazilian and Angolan Portuguese, earlier Afro-Hispanic; Chota Valley
invariant plurals	very frequent	almost never	Chota Valley
null definite articles	very frequent	some	vernacular Brazilian/Angolan Portuguese, some earlier Afro-Hispanic
/o/ > [u] /e/ > [i]	final atonic and clitic only	much neutralization in all tonic and atonic positions	some final atonic in Río Platense and earlier Afro-Hispanic speech

CHAPTER 8

THE STATUS OF AFRO-BOLIVIAN SPANISH

8.1. Introduction

The preceding chapters have described the traditional Afro-Yungueño Spanish dialect in sufficient detail as to demonstrate considerable restructuring vis-à-vis modern Spanish in other areas of the world. The grammatical differences between the Afro-Yungueño dialect and other contemporary varieties are as systematic and far-ranging as, for example, those that separate Spanish from its sibling Ibero-Romance languages, such as Galician, Asturian, Aragonese, and even Portuguese and Catalan. The Afro-Yungueño dialect is spoken natively (and until recently was spoken monolingually), exclusively by descendents of African slaves brought to Bolivia during the colonial period. The traditional dialect bears the imprint of earlier learners' varieties, e.g., in the simplification of verbal inflection and the suspension of gender concord in the noun phrase.

Although sharing some basic similarities with Aymara speakers' approximations to Spanish, Afro-Yungueño Spanish contains fundamental structures that cannot be attributed to contact with Aymara, or with Aymara-Spanish bilinguals. At the same time the emergence of innovative structures such as plural possessives and demonstratives, imperatives of the form *no qui* + INFINITIVE, and the use of *nuay* and *nuabía* for possession bespeaks of stabilization of an earlier L2 variety in the Afro-Bolivian speech communities. The precise status of Afro-Yungueño Spanish within the framework of contact-induced languages remains to be established.

8.2. Is Afro-Yungueño Spanish an Afro-Hispanic (post-*bozal*) survival?

The title of this section may seem to embody a rhetorical question, but in fact an answer to this question is not as simple as it first appears. The traditional Afro-Yungueño Spanish dialect contains no words of undisputed African origin,[1] nor are there morphosyntactic structures that point unmistakably to one or more spe-

---

[1] Except for Africanisms used widely throughout Latin America, such as *ñame* 'yam' and *mondongo* 'tripe stew.'

cific African languages. The lack of documentation on earlier stages of Afro-Yungueño Spanish (the first written attestations are less than two decades old, and the oldest recorded speakers of the traditional dialect were born in the 20th century) together with the sketchy historical data on the presence of Afro-Bolivians in the Yungas mean that the question of origin must be approached circumstantially. As in a court of law, means, motive, and opportunity must be demonstrated, together with comparable evidence from acknowledged Afro-Iberian languages past and present. In this respect, Afro-Yungueño Spanish is not substantially different from Papiamentu, a language widely acknowledged to be an Afro-Iberian creole, but for which specific African roots cannot be traced with certainty.

Afro-Yungueño Spanish is spoken only by descendents of African slaves in isolated Yungas communities. It is spoken as a monolingual native language, and has been at least as far back as collective community memories can be extrapolated –perhaps a century and a half. The traditional Afro-Yungueño dialect is qualitatively and quantitatively different from the L_2 Spanish of neighboring Aymara speakers (Chapter 5). At the same time we recall that Afro-Yungueño Spanish has absorbed many Aymara lexical items (Chapter 6).

As summarized below (section 8.3 and Table 8.1), Afro-Yungueño Spanish shares many similarities with contemporary Afro-Iberian creole and semicreole languages, and with descriptions of pidginized Spanish as spoken by Africans in earlier centuries. These morphosyntactic common denominators are not shared by any variety of Spanish that does not result from previous contact with African languages or with Africans' acquisition of Spanish in multilingual slave holdings. According to the historical sources reviewed in Chapter 1, Africans taken as slaves to colonial Bolivia had to acquire Spanish by ear, with no formal instruction, and often with limited access to native speakers of Spanish.[2] Once Afro-Bolivians arrived in the Yungas, Afro-Yungueño Spanish spent an undetermined but evidently considerable time away from native speakers of Spanish, all the while maintaining a cultural and linguistic distance from their Aymara-speaking neighbors. Although no collective awareness of Africa or African customs survives in the Afro-Bolivian communities, there has always been a strong sense of being *negros,* different culturally and linguistically from other Bolivians. This ethnic awareness has probably been instrumental in the retention of the traditional Afro-Yungueño dialect until the most recent generations.

---

[2] The archaic elements in Afro-Yungueño Spanish suggest that this dialect was formed several centuries ago: they include *truju* (modern Sp. *trajo*), which is the preterite of *traer* 'to bring'; *andi* (modern Sp. *donde*) 'where'; *jondiá* (modern Sp. *honda* 'slingshot') 'to shoot with a slingshot.'

The circumstantial evidence just reviewed points to the conclusion that Afro-Yungueño Spanish is an Afro-Hispanic variety that first arose when African-born *bozales* and their immediate descendents acquired Spanish as a second language during the colonial slave society. Contact with neighboring Aymara speakers resulted in lexical accretions, but evidently had little effect on Afro-Yungueño grammar. There is no competing hypothesis that accounts for the full range of data. Consequently, Afro-Yungueño Spanish will be evaluated within the framework of Afro-Iberian languages.

8.3. Is Afro-Yungueño Spanish a creole language?

Despite the considerable bibliography on creole languages and the fact that every creolist "knows" which languages are creoles, there is not a single universally accepted definition of creole. Definitions or working assumptions fall into three basic categories. Some accounts of creole language describe them entirely in terms of their cultural and social history. Other proposals concentrate on the stages of formation and transmission of pidgins into creoles. Finally, some definitions of creole languages include essential structural elements postulated as being part of most or all creole languages. In practice, both formal and working definitions of creole languages combine aspects of each of these categories. At one end of the scale, DeGraff limits himself to a sociohistorical/geographical definition:

> "Creole languages" refer to the speech varieties that were created in many of the newly-created communities –the "Creole" communities– in and around the colonial and slave-based plantations of the "New World" in the 17th-19th centuries. These Creole communities emerged relatively abruptly as the result of Europe's colonization of the Caribbean [...] creole languages thus developed among Europeans and Africans in the colonial Caribbean.

(DeGraff 2005: 541)

This echoes Mufwene: "Historically, a creole language variety is also one that was originally assumed to be spoken by a creole population typically in one of the European tropical and island colonies in the eighteenth and nineteenth centuries" (1997: 54). Mufwene feels that pidgin and creole are "names assigned to particular languages by a baptismal protocol which did not always check whether or not some ontological criteria were met" (1997: 55). He ultimately prefers to describe these contact varieties in terms of usage: "Creoles differ from pidgins in being vernaculars, serving as the primary means of communication for their users, while pidgins are used only for special, limited functions, such as trade with a foreign group" (1997: 52). Holm gives another definition: "a *creole* has a jargon or a pidgin in its ancestry; it is spoken natively by an entire speech community, often one whose ancestors were displaced geographically so that their ties with their original language and sociocultural identity were partially broken. Such social conditions were often the result of slavery" (2000: 6). This quasi-definition says nothing about the linguistic structure of creole languages, but instead addresses only their ancestry. Mühlhäusler (1997: 7-13) reviews many definitions, ultimately settling implicitly on the notion that a creole language is a nativized form of an earlier pidgin, although admitting of alternative scenarios. Romaine (1988: 38-41) also offers a variety of perspectives, centering on the notion of a creole as an expanded and nativized pidgin, a notion that has been established in creole studies at least since Hall (1966: xii). Thomason and Kaufman (1988: Chaps. 6-7) are among the many linguists who focus on the partial or total break in transmission of a native language to subsequent generations as the basis for creole language genesis.

A number of linguists have proposed structural features of creole languages. Such putative lists must be combined with sociohistorical information about the formation of the languages in question, since it is generally accepted that while there may be linguistic features common to most or all creole languages, the pedigree of a creole language cannot be determined by linguistic features alone (the same features also occur in languages that no one would consider creoles).

Much of the discussion about the nature and typology of creole languages was initiated by Bickerton (1981: Chap. 2), who viewed creoles as resulting from the intersection of traits specific to the lexifier and substratum languages and universal "bioprogram" features common to all human language. Although not all of Bickerton's proposals have withstood the test of time in subsequent creole studies, none is completely without merit, and all deserve mention here. Bickerton asserted that most creole languages have an article system with "a definite article for presupposed-specific NP; an indefinite article for asserted-specific NP; and zero for nonspecific NP" (1981: 56). This matches the article system of Afro-Yungueño Spanish –the Bolivian variety studied in this book–, and as such contrasts rather sharply with modern Spanish, whose article system, like that of other Romance languages, requires definite articles for non-specific subject NPs. In creole languages, WH-questions words are "directly preposed to the declarative form of the sentence" (Bickerton 1981: 70). This feature is similarly characteristic of Afro-Yungueño Spanish, in contrast to all other South American dialects of Spanish (those of Highland Bolivian included). Bickerton also notes the extreme scarcity of passive constructions in creole languages, most of which use simple juxtaposition and rules of interpretation, in which for transitive verbs, NVN is interpreted as actor-action-patient, and NV as patient-action. Afro-Boli-

vian Spanish conforms to this characterization; true Spanish passives based on
ser 'to be' are not used, and Spanish pseudo-passives *se* such as *se dice* 'it is
said' are usually replaced by simple verbs lacking this erstwhile reflexive clitic:
disi 'it is said'.

Creole languages typically use a single verb meaning 'to have' to express
both possession and existence. This does not usually occur in Afro-Yungueño
Spanish, which maintains the patrimonial Spanish distinction between existential *haber* 'to have, to exist' and *tener* 'to have, to possess, etc.' Very occasionally, *tiene* < *tener* 'to have' is used with existential meaning, as shown in Chapter
4, section 4.13, and repeated here (1-7):

(1)	*Tantu plaga qui **tiene** ahora.*	'So many infestations that there are nowadays.'
(2)	*En eje cuarto **tiene** jay anchancho.*	'In that room there is an echo-spirit.'
(3)	*Arapata ya **tiene** su lu carro.*	'[In] Arapata there are cars.'
(4)	***Tiene** un negrita qui taba aquí.*	'There was a black woman here.'
(5)	***Tiene** un señor aquí, acorda pueh de luh baile de lu negritu.*	'There is a man here who remembers the dances of the black people.'
(6)	*¿Qui lau **tiene** pueh mula?*	'Where are there mules?'
(7)	***Tenía** un señora, un negra.*	'There was a woman, a black woman.'

A more systematic exception is the use of *nu hay* 'don't have' (< Sp. *no hay*
'there is not') and *nu había* 'didn't have' (< Sp. *no había* 'there was not'), as
described in Chapter 4, section 4.13, and repeated here (8-14):

(8)	*Yo **nu hay** cajué.*	'I don't have coffee.'
(9)	*Yo **nu hay** jay minga.*	'I don't have a replacement worker [in the *cocal*].'
(10)	*¿Oté tiene coca? **Nu hay**.*	'Do you have any coca? I don't [have any].'
(11)	*Ele **nu hay** ningún marido nada.*	'She doesn't have any husband at all.'
(12)	*Yo **nu había** ni tata casi ni mama.*	'I didn't have a father and almost no mother.'
(13)	*Yo **nu había** zapato pueh pa vistí pueh.*	'I didn't have shoes to wear.'
(14)	*Yo **nu había** quen mi compra ni zapato ni bandera.*	'I didn't have anyone to buy me shoes or flags.'

The existence of this form suggests that in earlier stages of the language, there
was greater overlap between existential and possessive constructions.

Many creole languages, including some formed in contact with African languages, exhibit adjectival verbs. Also, these same languages tend not to have copulas in predicative adjective constructions. In Afro-Bolivian Spanish, the copulas behave as in Spanish, although *ta* < *estar* 'to be' (location, temporary state) sometimes assumes functions relegated to *ser* 'to be' (permanent nature) in modern Spanish. This is in line with Afro-Iberian creoles like Palenquero, Papiamentu, São Tomé, Príncipe, and Annobón, which use copulas with predicate adjectives.

Yet another feature attributed by Bickerton to most creole languages are movement rules that front focused or topicalized constituents. This is an option occasionally available in modern Spanish, and also present in the varieties spoken in the Yungas. Given the occasional penetration of Aymara-induced O-V word order in some manifestations of Afro-Yungueño Spanish (see Chapter 7, pp. 172-173), what appear to be fronted objects may in fact be an alternative choice of an interlanguage O-V word order.

Bickerton (1981) work on creoles devotes most of his efforts to demonstrating similarities among Tense-Mood-Aspect (TMA) systems, typically based on preverbal particles. As shown in Chapter 4, the Afro-Bolivian verb phrase cannot be accurately described as based on "TMA particles + AN INVARIANT STEM". At the same time, several factors combine to suggest a transitory TMA-based system for Afro-Bolivian Spanish. These include the invariant nature of the verb in the most traditional form of the dialect, the occasional appearance of *ta* plus a reduced form of the gerund that approximates the Afro-Yungueño infinitive, the ambiguous use of the adverb *ya* 'already' and periphrastic future constructions based on *va* 'go', This system coexists with a closer approximation to the modern Spanish verb phrase and is reminiscent of the grammars proposed for Afro-Cuban *bozal* Spanish by Ziegler (1976) and Castellanos (1990).

Koopman and Lefebvre (1981: 216) also seek to identify a number of key structural features of creole languages: (a) the vocabulary is defined in terms of major syntactic features such as noun, verb, adjective, adverb, and major morphosyntactic categories such as tense; (b) the structure of the lexicon is reflected in base rules containing positions defined in terms of major and minor features, which provides for auxiliaries, determiners, and topic positions. Koopman and Lefebvre's generic definition presumably fits all natively-spoken natural languages, and is useful in describing creole languages only with respect to the expansion of an original pidgin.

In addressing the question as to whether Afro-Bolivian Spanish is a creole language –perhaps in the final stages of decreolization– it is useful to compare its features with other acknowledged Ibero-Romance derived creole languages, rather than focusing on abstract definitions that attempt to describe creole uni-

versals. Table 8.1 summarizes similarities and differences between the traditional Afro-Yungueño dialect and other relevant creole languages.

Under the criteria surveyed in the preceding paragraphs, Afro-Bolivian Spanish fits comfortably within the definitions of a creole language. The morphosyntactic reduction as compared to worldwide Spanish is characteristic of the second-language pidgin originally learned by speakers of African languages. One
cannot objectively rank the features found among creole languages in terms of
"creoleness". But, as Table 8.1 shows, at least impressionistically, Afro-
Yungueño Spanish is more creole-like than the Helvécia (Brazilian) Portuguese
dialect. At the same time, Afro-Yungueño Spanish seems less "deep" than the
creoles of Palenque (Colombia), São Tomé, or the heavily substratum-influenced
Chabacano varieties of Philippine Creole Spanish. On the creole "thermometer",
Afro-Yungueño Spanish probably falls just below Cape Verde *crioulo*. In comparative terms, Afro-Yungueño Spanish lies at about the same structural distance
from modern Spanish as Gullah does from English, or as Réunionais (Réunion
Island creole French) does from modern French. Once more, these comparative
data alone are insufficient to establish the typology of Afro-Yungueño as a creole; the comparisons are, however, highly suggestive.

The foregoing then raises the following question: is Afro-Yungueños Spanish
possibly an offspring of a pidgin once spoken by African-born slaves and their
immediate descendents? To answer this question, it is necessary to extrapolate
across a broad swath of colonial history for which few facts are known. On the
one hand, the traditional Afro-Bolivian dialect shows all the morphosyntactic
earmarks of second-language learners' strategies, and is consistent with virtually
all historical imitations and purported factual accounts of *bozal* Spanish. At the
same time, even the most traditional varieties contain more patrimonial Spanish
structures, particularly in terms of phrase- and sentence-level word order, than
might be expected if a rudimentary pidgin had become nativized into a creole
according to the prototypical scenario described above. Although much morphosyntactic approximation to modern Spanish has occurred since the post-1952
reforms,[3] there is no evidence to suggest that the "deepest" registers of the
dialect, still spoken today by some of the oldest Afro-Bolivians, were ever substantially more divergent from other varieties of Bolivian Spanish than they are
today. Put differently, the currently available evidence does not suggest that
Afro-Yungueño Spanish ever underwent decreolization.

---

[3] The Bolivian "revolution" of 1952 brought about sweeping reforms across the country,
and the Yungas were no exception. Two reforms were particularly important for Afro-Bolivians: the abolishment of the haciendas (which allowed Afro-Bolivians to become de facto
owners of small plots of land), and the establishment of schools in marginalized rural areas
such as the traditional Afro-Bolivian communities in the Yungas.

TABLE 8.1

Key structural features of Afro-Yungueño Spanish and selected creole languages

	Afro-Yungueño	Helvécia	Palenquero	Papiamentu	Chabacano	Gulf of Guinea	Cape Verde
null def. art.	yes	yes	yes	yes	no	yes	yes
invariant verb	yes	some	yes	yes	yes	yes	yes
TMA particles	maybe	no	yes	yes	yes	yes	yes
non-inverted questions	yes	yes	yes	yes	yes	yes	yes
pluralizing particle/3pl.	no	no	*ma*	3 pl. (*nan*)	*mga*	some 3 pl.	no
no gender concord in NPs	yes	some	yes	yes	yes	yes	yes
subject pronouns as object	no (except *yo* after prep.)	yes (except 1s.)	yes (except 1s.)	yes	no	some	no
'to have' as existential verb	some	yes	yes	yes	yes, in affirmative	yes	yes
negation	preposed (occasional double NEG with *nada*)	double NEG	postposed	preposed	preposed	double NEG/ postposed	preposed
NEG derived from *no/não*	yes	yes	yes	yes	*hendeq* and *no*	*na … f(a)*	yes
postposed NP as possessive	no	no	yes	no	no	yes	no
serial verbs	no	no	no	some	no	yes	few
predicate clefting	no	no	yes	yes	no	yes	no

I suggested in Chapter 1 that one reason for the preservation of the unique Afro-Bolivian Spanish dialect in the middle of a contemporary Spanish-speaking country well into the 21st century is found in the Afro- Yungas' earlier geolinguistic situation. That is, they were surrounded by essentially monolingual Aymara speakers, much as Sephardic Spanish survived for centuries surrounded by Greek, Turkish, Arabic, and several Baltic and Slavic languages. This leads me to assume that the contemporary Afro-Yungueño Spanish grammatical configurations are fundamentally the same as those that Afro-Bolivians introduced to their present homeland some 200 years ago. The absence of ready access to natively spoken varieties of Spanish for many generations allowed for fossilization of the language brought to the Yungas –a fossilization that under other circumstances would quickly have been superceded by a much closer approximation to monolingual Bolivian Spanish. Rather, much as occurred in Réunion French (Baker and Corne 1982), only partial restructuring of Spanish took place. The reasons are primarily demographic: in highland Bolivia (16th-18th centuries), just as in Réunion, the proportion of Africans to European settlers was relatively low, never approaching even half of the population. This situation would have stood in stark contrast to the demographic proportions found in plantation colonies such as Mauritius and Haiti, or in slave depot islands such as São Tomé and Curaçao. It was only the rapid displacement of Afro-Bolivians away from a primarily Spanish-speaking sociolinguistic environment that produced a contact vernacular that did not coalesce with regional Spanish until several centuries later. The presence of so much "standard" Spanish syntax in the traditional Afro-Yungueño dialect combined with severely reduced Spanish morphological paradigms suggests that even when access to Spanish speakers was increased, Afro-Bolivians in the Yungas did not relinquish much of their traditional dialect, whether as a deliberate act of cultural resistance or through a less clearly defined sense of membership in a speech community that coincided with black ethnicity (on this topic, see Schwegler and Morton 2003).

Ultimately, answers to the question of whether the contemporary Afro-Yungueño dialect results from the nativization of an earlier pidgin must rely on sociolinguistic history. In terms of the usual judicial criteria of means, motive, and opportunity, Afro-Bolivians learned a rudimentary Spanish pidgin during their first colonial experience, and they were subsequently encased in largely indigenous-speaking communities. Many generations later, they re-entered (though only partially so) the Spanish-speaking mainstream of Bolivia. The input to the aforementioned black box can only have been a learners' pidgin, characterized by minimal grammatical structures and similar to all beginners' Spanish pidgins worldwide. The output –the Afro-Yungueño dialect– has consolidated the grammatical reductions found in learners' pidgins in a fashion that is qualitatively and quantitatively different from any documented Aymara-Spanish inter-language. In the absence of any other viable scenario, Afro-Yungueño *Spanish must be viewed as the direct descendent of a colonial Afro-Hispanic pidgin.* One thing is for certain: Afro-Yungueño Spanish is the most radically restructured variety of Spanish spoken natively, not only in the contemporary Spanish-speaking world, but in all of the known history of the Spanish language.

8.4. Implicational relationships in Afro-Yungueño Spanish: possible decreolization

The traditional Afro-Yungueño dialect shows evidence of an early restructuring of Spanish in favor of simpler and morphologically less marked configurations. This proposal is strengthened by variational data from contemporary Afro-Bolivian speech. Although most speakers of traditional Afro-Yungueño Spanish are capable of switching with ease to close approximations of contemporary highland Bolivian Spanish, a noteworthy feature of the Afro-Yungueño speech community is the cline of morphosyntactic variation between the most restructured combinations and modern Spanish grammar. This is the signature behavior of decreolization, which takes place when a creole is in contact with its original lexifier language, typically in a sociolinguistically disadvantageous position, in which the creole language is stigmatized and deprived of official recognition.

Given the gradual displacement of the traditional Afro-Bolivian dialect by modern Bolivian Spanish over the past three generations, there is considerable morphosyntactic variation across recent generations. This variation is in turn correlated with exposure to modern Bolivian Spanish, in schools and in work environments. There are also regional isoglosses radiating outward from a geographic locus where the most traditional variety is spoken. This geographic locus is centered on the towns of Mururata and Chijchipa (Figure 8.1, p. 187).

The regional and generational variation is systematic enough so as to reveal unidirectional implicational relationships. Ranging from the most creole-like features to those that are very close to standard/regional Spanish, the Afro-Bolivian implicational scale operates as shown in Table 8.2 (p. 188).

8.5. Gender and number agreement in noun phrases: gradual decreolization?

In Afro-Yungueño Spanish (and judging by published examples, also in Helvécia and Angolan Portuguese), gender agreement is suspended more frequently than

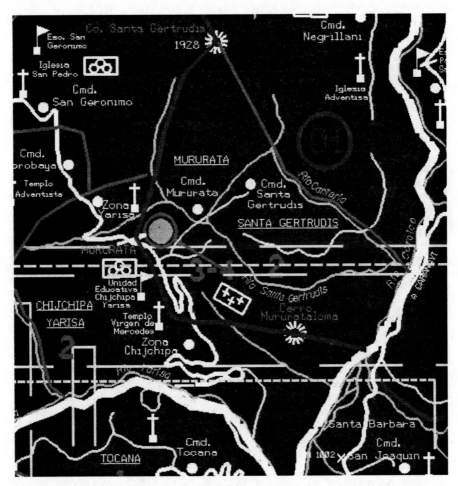

Figure 8.1[4]
Area of traditional Afro-Bolivian speech: Mururata, Chijchipa, Tocaña

number agreement, and in an implicational fashion. In other words, whereas an Afro-Bolivian speaker may produce combinations such as examples (4)-(6) where number (but not gender) is marked, there are no observed configurations such as *esa hierba* for plural *esas hierbas* 'those herbs'. Readers will note that

---

[4] The source is an electronic map prepared by the Instituto Nacional de Estadística for the 2001 census. I am grateful to the INE for providing me with the files for Nor Yungas and Sud Yungas, Departmento de La Paz.

TABLE 8.2
Implicational relationships in Afro-Yungueño speech

TRAIT	EXAMPLE	DEPTH OF FEATURE
NOUN PHRASE		
stripped plurals[5]	*unas muñeca*	↑
no gender concord in postverbal adjectives	*mujé alto*	
no gender concord in preverbal adjectives	*un mujé*	
invariant plurals	*lu patrón*	deepest
VERB PHRASE		
invariant 3 s. verb forms for 3 pl.	*eyu va trabajá*	↑
invariant 3 s. verb forms for 1 pl.	*nojotro va trabajá*	
invariant 3 s. verb forms for 1 s.	*yo va trabajá*	deepest

NOTE: Speakers who exhibit a given trait will also use all the traits found higher on the chart within the category of noun phrase or verb phrase, e.g., those who say *yo va trabajá* 'I am going to work' will also say *nojotro va trabajá* 'we are going to work', and those who say *lu mujé* 'the women' will also say *un mujé* 'a woman', and so forth.

The reverse implications do not hold: speakers who say *nojotro va trabajá* 'we are going to work' will not say *yo va trabajá* 'I am going to work', while those who say *mujé alto* 'tall woman' will not say *un mujé* 'a woman'.

in the examples that follow, only on the first element in the plural phrase carriers an overt plural marker (underlined). This is typical in traditional Afro-Yungueño speech.

(4)　*Esos hierba [esas hierbas]*　　'those herbs'
(5)　*Algunos enfermedá [algunas enfermedades]*　　'some illnesses'
(6)　*Luh persona mayó [las personas mayores]*　　'the adults'

---

[5] This means that a final plural /s/ is clearly discernible on the first element of the noun phrases (usually a determiner) and nowhere else.

From the perspective of restructuring, under imperfect language acquisition and subsequent convergence with modern Spanish, this suggests that number features are acquired before gender features, and that in the process of convergence (decreolization), number features will spread to extended projections such as pre- and post-nominal adjectives before gender features. This is not surprising in view of the fact that grammatical number marks a semantically prominent distinction (one versus many). In contrast, in Ibero-Romance, grammatical gender concordance is almost always semantically empty (hence "less prominent"). Even with semantically feminine nouns such as *mujer* 'woman', *yegua* 'mare', *gallina* 'hen', the feminine gender markers attached to determiners and adjectives in the noun phrase serve no semantic function. Experimental studies demonstrate that processing of grammatical gender in the absence of conceptual/biological information about the sex of the object is more costly; i.e., the processing of gender in *la casa* 'the house' requires more processing time than for *la mujer* 'the woman' (e.g., Vigliocco and Franck 1999).[6] The predominance of number over gender has been well documented cross-linguistically in first- and second-language acquisition as well as language impairment studies (e.g., De Vincenzi 1999; Di Domenico and De Vincenzi 1995; Eberhard 1997), and the decreolizing Afro-Bolivian data bear out this hierarchy. Moreover, there is much cross-linguistic experimental evidence that production of grammatical gender in bare nouns requires additional processing time (e.g., Cubelli et al. 2005 for Italian; also Schriefers and Jescheniak 1999). In other words, grammatical gender is selected by the speaker whether or not "needed" for the utterance about to be produced. This occurs independently of the phonological form of the word, i.e., whether or not one of the canonical *–o/–a* endings is present.[7] In addition "[...] to produce a given noun, the corresponding lexical-semantic and lexical-syntactic representations, specifying meaning and grammatical properties respectively, have to be selected before accessing its phonological form [...] the selection of semantic and grammatical features is conducted independently and [...] the selection of the lexical form of a given noun is achieved only when competition at both semantic and syntactic levels has been resolved" (Cubelli et al. 2005: 53). Cubelli et al. postulate that the semantic information is selected before the syntactic information. By extension, eliminating the grammatical gender category consequently eliminates the need

---

⁶ There are dissenting viewpoints, however. For example A. Domínguez et al. report experimental findings that suggest that in Spanish "gender information is accessed more straightforwardly than number in an inflected word" (1999: 495).

⁷ Cubelli et al. analyze this result as "reflecting a competitive lexical selection due to an abstract grammatical gender feature rather than to the morphological or phonological similarity of [the relevant nouns]" (2005: 52).

for gender selection, and produces a more efficient ("faster") processing strategy. De Vincenzi provides Italian experimental data that indicate that "number information is used in an earlier stage of antecedents identification (where syntactic information is used), while gender information is used at a later stage (where lexical and semantic information are used)" (1999: 551). She also suggests that while number heads an autonomous syntactic projection, gender never does so, not even in the case of variable gender. Finally, Caramazza et al. provide cross-linguistic information that production and processing of determiners is complicated by the necessity to retrieve gender and number information: "determiner selection in a given language occurs at the same point for *all* determiners, even though some of them could be selected earlier. In the case of Spanish, even though masculine determiners could be selected early, they are nevertheless selected at the same late point as feminine determiners" (2001: 223). Many of the L_2 Italian data on the acquisition of grammatical gender presented in Chini (1995) reinforce these observations. Afro-Yungueño Spanish reduces this complexity by effectively eliminating the gender and number marking on the determiners.

The processing of grammatical number, on the other hand, is not symmetric, in that there is experimental evidence suggesting that whereas plural is a semantically and syntactically marked category, words lacking a plural affix are not semantically singular but rather unmarked for number (cp. Berent et al. 2005). This hypothesis is supported by the Afro-Yungueño preference for invariant plurals of the sort *(luh) mujé [las mujeres]* 'the women', *luh varón [los varones]* 'the male children', which is common even in the most acrolectal forms of the dialect. Rather than representing a mismatch between semantic and syntactic features –a configuration that should augment rather than reduce production and processing difficulty– the bare plural is an unmarked form, whose plural reference can easily be extracted from the preceding plural determiner or from the surrounding discourse.

8.6. The Afro-Yungueño verb phrase: in the footsteps of decreolization

Together with the restructured noun phrase, the nature of the Afro-Yungueño verb phrase (VP) is the most significant departure from patrimonial Spanish patterns, and the strongest evidence for a *bozal* contact variety not derived from a simple imperfect acquisition of received Spanish. As shown in Chapter 4, in essence, the Afro-Yungueño VP shows some tense, mood, and aspect features (although the full range of Spanish "tenses" does not occur),[8] while there is no

---

[8] The Spanish verb system is traditionally described as tense-based, and terms like "present", "past", and "future" are used as descriptors. In reality, although tense is the dominant

agreement for person/number. No other variety of Spanish past or present departs from the full subject-verb agreement system inherited from Latin. Afro-Yungueño Spanish has more fully restructured the VP than, for instance, Helvécia Portuguese or vernacular Brazilian Portuguese, where some person and number agreement remains. In nearly all cases, the Afro-Yungueño verb lacking person and number agreement is derived from the Spanish 3rd person singular. The most "creole-like" combination in Helvécia Portuguese, the combination of first-person singular reference with third person-singular verb verbs (*eu trabalha* 'I work'), not found in even the most vernacular forms of other Brazilian dialects, only occurs at a 35% rate among speakers born before 1930, and virtually disappears among younger community members.[9] Comparative evidence from historical reproductions of *bozal* Spanish, and from contemporary second-language varieties of Spanish, as well as from the first stages of Spanish child language, confirm the unmarked status of the 3 s. verb form. This includes vestigial Spanish of such areas as the Philippines, Trinidad, the Isleños and Sabine River Spanish speakers of Louisiana, as well as transitional Spanish-English bilinguals throughout the United States (Lipski 1986d, 1990a, 1990b, 1993b, 1996b). The Spanish of Equatorial Guinea –the only officially Spanish-speaking nation in sub-Saharan Africa and where Spanish is a widely spoken second language– also exhibits frequent gravitation to the third-person singular as the default unmarked verb form, although Guineans seek to conjugate verbs correctly (Lipski 1985a). Early child language in both Spanish and Portuguese also favors the 3 s. as the unmarked form. For Portuguese, Simões (1976: 47) and Simões and Stoel-Gammon (1979) document such combinations as *eu gosta* 'I like', *eu viu* 'I saw'.[10]

In both Brazilian Portuguese and the Afro-Yungueño Spanish dialect, grammatically marked second person forms have disappeared: Brazilian Portuguese uses *você/vocês* for the familiar second-person, while traditional Afro-Yungueño Spanish uses only *oté/otene* for all second-person referents (see Chapter 3). Thus, from a morphological perspective, there are only two person markings: first person, and the remainder (including semantically second- and third-person referents). The preference for agreement in the first person singular as the first step in

---

trait, modal and aspectual distinctions are also signaled by certain paradigms (e.g., the subjunctive and conditional).

[9] Baxter (1997), Baxter and Lucchesi (1993), Baxter, Lucchesi and Guimarães (1997), Lucchesi (1998: 89), Mello et al. (1998). Naro (1998) has presented evidence of very occasional lapses of subject-verb agreement in contemporary and earlier European Portuguese, but these never involve the first person singular.

[10] Palenquero departs from this trend, in that many verbs are derived from the infinitive.

convergence with modern Spanish verb system is not surprising, given both the frequency of this combination and the uniquely personal nature of first-person reference. This is evidenced in Spanish and to a lesser extent in Portuguese by the number of verbs that have irregular forms only in the first-person singular (present indicative).[11]

In the third stage in the convergence of the Afro-Yungueño verb phrase with modern Spanish, subject-verb agreement occurs in all members of the paradigm except for the third-person plural: thus *eyu(s)come* 'they eat' lacks an agreement marker, while the corresponding 1st person singular and/or plural always carries one (cp. *yo como* 'I eat' and never **yo come* 'I eat'; *nojotro comemos* 'we eat' and never **nojotro come*).[12]

---

[11] Some Afro-Yungueño speakers effect most cases of subject-verb agreement when there is a single main verb, but suspend agreement on auxiliary verbs, particularly *ir* 'to go' in the periphrastic future combination *ir (a)* + INFINITIVE, and in *estar* + GERUND progressive combinations. This dichotomy is particularly frequent in Dorado Chico and surrounding communities. Examples of *va* + INFINITIVE include:

*¿de qué nojotro pobre **va** [vamos a] viví?*
'What are we poor folks going to live on?'

*lo que nojotro **ta** [estamos] hablando este rato*
'What we're talking about right now'

*qué día yo **va** í [voy a ir]*
'what day I'm going to go'

*eyo **va** [van a] leé, nojotro **va** [vamos a] leé*
'they are going to read, we are going to read'

Use of the 3rd person singular instead of the 1st person singular is also more common in the preterite than in the present tense. Baxter (1997), Baxter and Lucchesi (1993), Baxter et al. (1997) and Baxter in Mello et al. (1998: 126-127) document a similar tendency for the Brazilian Portuguese semicreole of Helvécia.

[12] There are additional configurations which, while not as consistently represented in the community as the examples displayed in the preceding sections, also demonstrate the gradual increase in morphological cohesion in the direction of full agreement systems. There are, for example, speakers who exhibit first person singular and plural subject-verb agreement in the present tense, but use invariant forms in the preterite and imperfect: *yo trabajo* 'I work' but *yo trabajó* 'I worked', etc. The privileged position of the present tense as regards full subject-verb agreement is also consistent with the prominence of the present tense as the most frequent in ordinary discourse, as well as the first tense to be mastered in both L1 and L2 acquisition. Baxter (1997: 281) also proposes the acquisitional order *person-number in present tense* > *person-number in preterite* for the Helvécia Portuguese dialect.

Comparative data from vernacular Brazilian Portuguese confirm that absence of subject-verb agreement in the first person singular is the most "creole-like" combination, found only in imitations of *bozal* or L2 Portuguese, and occasionally in Helvécia. *io sabi [eu sei]* 'I know', *io fas [eu faço]* 'I do'. This is the only known natively-spoken[13] Portuguese variety in which the 1st and 3rd person singular are homophonous, making this configuration the most "creole-like." Baxter (1997) observes that the first person singular is the earliest subject-verb agreement pattern to emerge during decreolization of the Helvécia dialect. Guy (2004: 132) notes that, in vernacular Brazilian Portuguese, subject-verb agreement rates in irregular verbs as well as verbs whose preterite forms are considerably different from the present forms (e.g., *fez–fizeram, falou–falaram, é–são*) are much higher than with regular verbs.[14] Guy speculates that this differential behavior is a leftover from a fully creolized language once spoken in Brazil, in which no subject-verb agreement existed:

> Subsequently, speakers who were in contact with standard Portuguese would have learned agreement in the way that is typical of second-language learners: acquire the most obvious features first. It would be highly salient to a standardizing learner that a plural verb form like *fizeram* occurs with a plural subject in place of singular *fez*, but rather obscure that *comem* is required instead of *come*.
>
> (Guy 2004: 132)

Guy's proposal is consistent with the notion that gradual decreolization is a function of parsing and processing strategies, as well as of greater exposure to the target language.

8.7. Further discussion: but is it really decreolization?

Some linguists have challenged the notion of a post-creole continuum as envisioned by De Camp (1971), Bickerton (1973, 1975), Rickford (1987), and others. Baker (1990, 1997) has countered that being in contact with the original lexifier language does not automatically trigger decreolization. Rather than

---

[13] In L2 vernacular Angolan Portuguese, the combination of 1ST SINGULAR SUBJECT + 3RD SINGULAR VERB is common (Lipski 1995c).

[14] In Spanish, there are no irregular finite verbs –in the preterite or other tenses– that drop the final syllable, as in Portuguese *fiz, fez*, etc. There are a few 2nd person singular imperative forms in which the final syllable of the finite form is missing: *haz* 'do' < *hacer, di* 'say' < *decir, pon* 'put' < *poner*, etc.

immediately seeking to learn "correct" versions of the superstrate language, emerging creole speakers seek to create a "medium for interethnic communication":

> [W]ith specific reference to slave plantation societies [...] slaves did not aspire to acquire the language of the plantation owner as such. Their aim was to communicate, particularly with their fellow workers. The most readily available lexical source for the MIC among a multilingual workforce was that of the language to which they were all exposed in the workplace, that of the plantation owner.
>
> (Baker 1997: 96)

Baker's conclusion is supported by historical records from several creole languages. These suggest that some sort of continuum between the basilectal creole language and the lexifier language may have existed from the outset, with no directional "decreolization" taking place subsequently.

At the same time, changes in attitudes towards traditional speech patterns, coupled with opportunities for acquiring a more "standard" version of the lexifier language in POST-slavery speech communities, can affect the resulting dialect. Afro-Bolivians in the Yungas were surrounded by monolingual Aymara speakers for at least two centuries; ambivalent attitudes (which, according to oral tradition, have existed for a long time) within each group limited linguistic contacts to a minimum, and in the absence of sustained contact with speakers of Spanish, the traditional Afro-Yungueño dialect survived as an enclave. Feelings of ethnic pride and a strong sense of identity as *negros* undoubtedly contributed to the retention of the traditional Afro-Bolivian dialect. At the same time, the conditions of virtual slavery that permeated the hacienda environment in the Yungas until the land reforms of 1952 would have undercut any incentives for Afro-Bolivians to "improve" their command of the landowners' language. After 1952 there finally arose educational opportunities, which engendered a sense of pride in literacy and in "being civilized" (the Afro-Bolivians' own term). This new sense of becoming integrated into modern Bolivian society made it more desirable for Afro-Yungueños to begin approximating national norms –linguistic and otherwise. Pride in having access to education competed with pride in an ethnically unique language; the former sentiment has ultimately prevailed, except for a scattering of tenaciously self-assertive speakers of the traditional dialect. Over the past three generations of Afro-Bolivians in the Yungas, one can observe a cline from essentially no morphological agreement among some of the oldest speakers to nearly full agreement among younger more educated speakers. This pattern is circumstantially consistent with decreolization and the formation of a post-creole continuum. Since information on Afro-Bolivians' attitudes towards their unique dialect during earlier generations is lacking, the equation cannot be completed. In the absence of data on earlier stages of the Afro-Yungueño dialect, and on the historical development of the Afro-Bolivian communities in the Yungas, any proposal regarding the historical trajectory of Afro-Yungueño Spanish will remain speculative.[15] Ultimately, the classification of Afro-Yungueño Spanish –as creole, semicreole, post-creole, or something else– is of less importance than the analysis of its structures, and its relationship to other Afro-Hispanic varieties, past and present.

8.8. The importance of Afro-Yungueño Spanish to Afro-Hispanic linguistics

The Afro-Yungueño Spanish dialect, now found only among what is apparently its last generation of fluent speakers, provides a critical link in the reconstruction of Afro-Hispanic language in colonial Spanish America. This may be the oldest surviving Afro-Hispanic language variety, going back at least to the 17th century if not earlier.[16] Do the Afro-Bolivian data represent the final stages in the decreolization of an earlier Palenquero-like Spanish creole? Or is Afro-Yungueño Spanish perhaps a remnant of a stable restructured (but not decreolized) variety of Spanish that co-existed with highland Bolivian Spanish since its inception? Chapter 3 (noun phrases), and Chapter 4 (verb phrase) provide hints that a full-fledged creole may once have existed in the speech areas that

---

[15] Although the aforementioned conditions provide a plausible scenario for the retention of the restructured dialect, in itself this does not necessarily imply that only the traditional variety existed until the 1950's. Even in very traditional communities such as Mururata, some of the oldest residents exhibit few of the traits of the traditional dialect; by their own accounts, these individuals acquired their idiolects well before the reforms of the mid 20th century. These same speakers assert that the speech of their parents and grandparents did not differ substantially from the patterns to be heard nowadays. These assertions remain to be verified, but it is evident that a simple model of decreolization is inadequate to account for the full range of variation in the Afro-Bolivian communities. Incidentally, this situation of multigenerational preservation of certain speech patterns mirror that of El Palenque de San Basilio, where the perhaps expected decreolization appears not to have occurred in the last 100 years or so (see Schwegler 2001).

[16] Palenquero appears to have its origins in a Portuguese-derived pidgin or creole (Schwegler 1996a), while Papiamentu has at least as much Portuguese content as Spanish, and may well derive from an originally Portuguese-based pidgin. The Afro-Yungueño dialect, on the other hand, shares almost none of the elements typically associated with Portuguese-derived pidgins and creoles, and which form the basis for monogenetic theories of Atlantic creoles (e.g., in Megenney 1984).

form the basis of this investigation. At the very least, the Afro-Yungueño dialect, both in terms of its external history and restructured "Spanish" grammar, qualifies as a *semicreole*, as defined by Holm: "when people with different first languages shift to a typologically distinct target language (itself an amalgam of dialects in contact, including fully restructured varieties) under social conditions that partially restrict their access to the target language as normally used among native speakers" (2000: 10).

Afro-Yungueño speech was always in contact with Spanish, but the contact was not intensive enough to prevent the partial restructuring of the originally L_2 Spanish spoken by *bozal* slaves. This partial restructuring is seen most clearly in the structure of the Afro-Yungueño noun phrase, and in verbal morphology. Afro-Yungueño Spanish is the only natively spoken variety of Spanish containing invariant verbs, stripped and invariant plurals, a restructured pronominal system, and lack of gender agreement in noun phrases. The Spanish article is also present in Afro-Yungueño speech, but often omitted in subject position when generic reference is intended. The presence of invariant plurals and the invariant plural article *lu/lo* are typical L_2 traits that fossilized in Afro-Yungueño speech, together with lack of consistent gender agreement. Innovative constructions such as possessives of the type *mi lu, su lu,* imperatives of the form *no qui* + INFINITIVE, the use of *nu hay* and *nu había* to express possession, and the placement of object clitics between auxiliary verbs and infinitives (*yo va ti disí* 'I'm going to tell you') suggest that more than fossilized learners' Spanish gave rise to Afro-Yungueño speech. The Afro-Yungueño verb system is a hybrid of canonical Spanish patterns and reduced L_2 paradigms. Spanish tense distinctions are normally maintained (although reduced to a subset of present and past indicative forms), while person and number morphology are reduced to the third person singular in most cases, this being the unmarked form in Spanish (cp. Bybee 1985: 50-51). The free alternation between progressive constructions with a fully realized gerund and eroded combinations that resemble the Spanish infinitive offers a model for how *ta* + INVARIANT VERB structures could arise in emergent Afro-Iberian creole languages.

In summary, the Afro-Yungueño dialect provides a miniature prototype of the sort of language that probably characterized most groups of African slaves in rural areas, from the beginning of the 16th century through the end of the 19th.[17]

---

[17] Naturally, the Aymara component of Afro-Bolivian Spanish is not typical of all Afro-Hispanic speech in Latin America, although Afro-Hispanic-indigenous hybrid combinations were probably more common than is suggested by available documentation (Lipski 2000b). Most of the characteristic Afro-Bolivian grammatical patterns are not attributable to contact with Aymara, so that Afro-Yungueño Spanish can reasonably be considered as a prototype for other Afro-Hispanic dialects.

The analysis of this dialect in the context of historical dialectology underscores the importance of studying other contemporary linguistic isolates, not just for their curiosity value but as microcosms that replicate more sweeping linguistic encounters, whose direct observation has been lost to time.

SAMPLE TRANSCRIPTIONS OF AFRO-BOLIVIAN SPANISH (YUNGAS)

Sample transcriptions

The following are sample transcriptions of Afro-Bolivian Spanish from the Yungas.[1] The transcriptions use Spanish orthography throughout, with characteristic phonetic traits of Afro-Yungueño Spanish indicated throughout the texts (e.g., loss of word-final /r/, aspiration and loss of word-final /s/, and realization of the palatal lateral /x/ as an approximant [φ]). Approximate English translations are given for each transcription.

Sample 1:
Mururata, male speaker in his early 50's

[1] *Yo subía pueh di abajo la escuela, cada mañana nojotro subía la escuela, pero lu malo, yo meaba peh la cama, yo meaba la cama;* [2] *yo subía un lau di pantalón, así pueh mojau; yo subía la escuela.* [3] *Y pa que gente no mi mira que yo, mi pantalón meau, yo lu puntiaba cun barro cun tierra ese lau pa qui disi p'aquí.* [4] *Disi yo cayó pa que no nota qui yo, mi pantalón ta mojau di meau; así pueh yo jondo, caracho.* [5] *Y diay mi mama mi mandaba por agua pueh la pozo.* [6] *Y diay yo peliaba cun mi lu hermano.* [7] *Yo lu quebraba, nojotro lu quebraba cántaro.* [8] *Mi mama cogía su palo nos hacía corré la*

[1] I came up from down [the hill] to school, every morning we came up to school, but the problem was that I wet the bed; [2] I would roll up one leg of my pants, it was all wet; I [then] came up to school. [3] And so that people wouldn't see that I had pissed in my pants I would spatter them with dirt right here on this side [of the leg], right here. [4] And I would say that I fell down so they couldn't see that my pants were soaked with piss; it was terrible. [5] And from then on my mother would send me for water from the well. [6] And from then on I would fight with my brothers. [7] We would break the water jugs. [8]

---

[1] As this book is going to press, Angola Maconde (2008) has just appeared, a history of the Dorado Chico community including transcribed oral narratives by many of the community's oldest residents. Some of the transcriptions are presented in the traditional Afro-Bolivian dialect of Dorado Chico.

chumi. **[9]** *Nojotro yegaba sin cántaro,*
sin agua. Así pueh nos pegaba. **[10]** *Ya*
nojotro yegaba, no cocinaba pueh. **[11]**
Nojotro tenía que í, sin comé eje día.
[12] *Nos bregaba. Nojotro peleaba sí.*
[13] *Eje cántaro cuando quebraba, nos*
sacaba la mano. Nos cortaba pueh
mano. **[14]** *Pa que no quebra mah disi,*
pa que no quebra más ...

    [15] *Yo fue más pobrecito pueh, yo*
no había mi tata, ca mi tata caminó
Caranaví cun otro mujé. **[16]** *Ya nojotro*
quedó pueh solo aqui, caray, ya cada
qui jue disjuili pueh yo nuhabía zapato
pueh pa vistí pueh, yo no había zapato
pa vistí. **[17]** *Lu qui tenía sus tata*
compró sus zapato; lus compraba
bandera, siempre había qui yevá
banderita la mano, ¿no ve? y yo
nuabía quen mi compra ni zapato ni
bandera caray, yo nuay zapato, ¿qué yo
hacía?
    [18] *Antes había sardina Lombarda*
¿no ve? ese yo lo tojeraba eje sardina
Lombarda, yo vistía en veh di zapato.
[19] *Mi pieh en eje tiempo fue chico no*
taba muy grandi. **[20]** *Yo vistía ese, lata*
di sardina en mi pie, uuh, contento,
zapato yo vio. Y luh demáh cun su lu
bandera pueh yo un había quien mi
compra bandera, empezaba yorá. **[21]**
Una lástima pueh yo crecía. **[22]** *Yo*
gritaba pueh ahora: "¿Quién pueh mi
compra bandera?" "¿Quién pueh mi
compra bandera?", yo decía. **[24]** *Yo nu*
había pueh yo nu había ni tata casi ni
mama, mi mama fue pobre nomás. **[24]**
Yo creció ya, este, yo creció pues, a la
bondá di Dios pueh; yo creció, pobrecito
pueh nojotro fue.

My mother would grab her stick and
chase us into the stand of trees. **[9]** We
would arrive without water jugs, without
water. As a result, she would beat us.
[10] When we arrived like that she
wouldn't cook. **[11]** We had to go
without food that day. **[12]** She scolded
us. We would fight. **[13]** When the
water jugs broke, she would take our
hand and cut it. **[14]** She said so
that we wouldn't break [the jugs] any
more.

    [15] I was very poor, I had no father
because my father ran off to Caranavi
with another woman. **[16]** We were left
alone, and every time there was a parade
I didn't have any shoes to wear, I didn't
have any shoes to wear.
[17] Those who had fathers would get
shoes, flags; they would buy [us] flags,
because we always had to wave a flag,
see? and I didn't have anyone to buy me
shoes or a flag, so what did I do?

    [18] Before there were Lombardi
sardines, see? and I would stomp those
sardine [cans] and I would wear them
instead of shoes. **[19]** My feet were
smaller then, and I was happy. **[20]** I
used to wear these, these sardine shoes,
uhh, happy [I was], I saw shoes [on my
feet]. And the rest had their flags, but I
didn't have anyone to buy me a flag, so I
would cry. **[21]** It was a shame how I
grew up. **[22]** I would yell: "Who will
buy me a flag?", "Who will buy me a
flag?" I would yell. **[23]** But I didn't
have a father and almost no mother, my
mother was very poor. **[24]** I grew up
through the grace of God; we were very
poor for sure.

Sample 2:
Mururata, female speaker in her late 40's

[1] *Yo acorda, siempre, un veh yo cun Juanita fue.* [2] *Nojotro no ha cuyuntao; pueh bien, juego nojotro tenía qui hacé cocé mote, ¿no ve?* [3] *No había jay recao, no había qui cocé mah eje mote, y tenía qui quedá un palo cuyuntao abajo.*

[4] *Y nojotro, ta pueh durmindo cuando mi mama subi cun su cincha nos pega.* [5] *Diji que poh nos ta pegando diji qui nojotro no cuyuntó juego; no había ni fósforo ni nada.* [6] *Nojotro Chijchipa, nojotro tenía que í cada sábado la rio buscá leña, pero cada sábado nojotro tenía qui í buscá leña, tuditu, ydiay.* [7] *Tudito tenía qui yevá coca, y mascá coca en eje playa di río andi, la río Yarisa, mascá coca bajá leña.* [8] *Y el cabo eh mal agüero, mal agüero es, no mascá coca la playa, noto [= nojotro] masacaba coca la playa, y así pueh genti muriu, así pueh genti muriu Chijchipa mal agüero eh.* [9] *Nojotro iba jarto – lu chica, lu mujé, nojotro iba por leña; luh hombre.* [10] *Pero tuitu yevaba coca, notro mascaba chiquitita jay notro fue, notro mascaba coca grave la río Yarisa, así como notro mascaba coca sí gente muriu, genti muriu, tudito dejó coca así.* [11] *Mal agüero també es, mal agüero es, nojotró dejó també, ya nojotro no mascó.* [12] *Así ya cada unu nojotro fue cambiando nustru vida, hemos ido cambiado, di mascá sí, pero ya no así. Mal agüero es, cosa di vicio parece que es mal agüero també.* [13] *Un viaje ya també, nojotro ya mi papa ya si fue pueh la comuna.* [14] *Ya mi mama muriu, nojotro ya ta*

[1] I remember one time, Juanita and I [were together]. [2] We hadn't saved the embers; alright, then, we had to prepare the fire to cook the *mote* [boiled corn mash], see? [3] There were no provisions, there was nothing to cook the *mote* with, we were supposed to leave a hot ember under [the stove].

[4] And we, we were asleep, when my mother came up with her belt and hit us. [5] She said she was hitting us because we hadn't saved the embers; there were neither matches nor anything else. [6] In Chijchipa we had to go to the river every Saturday for firewood, every Saturday we had to look for firewood, everybody. [7] Everybody had to take coca and chew coca there, there at the River Yarisa, chew coca and cut firewood. [8] But it's bad luck, bad luck, don't chew coca on the riverbank, we chewed coca on the riverbank, and people died like that, people died in Chijchipa, it's bad luck. [9] We all went – girls, [and] women; we went for firewood; the men [too]. [10] But everybody had coca, we chewed a little, we did, we chewed a lot of coca along the River Yarisa, just like we were chewing, people died, people died, everybody gave up coca. [11] It's bad luck too, it's bad luck, we gave it up too, we didn't chew any more. [12] So every one of us changed their life, we've changed, chew [a little], yes, but not like that, it's bad luck, it seems to be a kind of vice, bad luck too. [13] One time also, we, my father went to the community. [14] My mother died, we were sad. [15] Juanita came to school from the

pueh tristi. **[15]** *Juanita vini la escuela desdi la comuna, no conoce, desde la puente mah arriba, lejo jay fue.* **[16]** *... Sai salva Juanita, río taba yevando.* **[17]** *No qui mandá más a tu chiquita a escuela, río taba yevando, ta bien encontrá tu huahua.* **[18]** *Yo salvó disi ay Juanita disi no iba la escuela, mi hermana salio di escuela, pero mi hermana no sabe.*

community, don't you know, above the bridge, it was far away. **[16]** ... [I] went and saved Juanita, the river was carrying [her] off. **[17]** Don't send your kids to school any more, the river was carrying [her] off, it's good to find your child. **[18]** I saved [her], oh Juanita, [she] said [she] wasn't going to school, my sister left school, that's why my sister doesn't know [anything].

Sample 3:
Chijchipa, female speaker in her late 60's (J), with female speaker from Mururata, late 40's (A)

A: *Tudito nojotro va hablá; hermanita, ¿qué poh oté ta hacindo?*

We're all going to talk; what are you doing?

J: *Yo ta pueh trabajando lu chapiña, nomah, sentao, ayere yo fue ... a coreá.*

I'm chopping weeds, just sitting down, yesterday I went, to plant.

A: *¿Andi pueh oté corió?*

Where did you plant?

J: *A lo batio.*

In the low place.

A: *¿Oté ta coreá di agachao pueh?*

You are planting bent over, then?

J: *Agachao.*

Bent over.

A: *Ah, agachao; ¿y quién pueh ta ti ayudá?*

Ah, bent over, and who is helping you?

J: *Yo solo, yo solo fue; ninguno mi ayuda; ninguno mi ayuda, sí. ¿Quién va ayudá? Yo no mah fue. ¿Quién mi va ayudá?*

I alone, I went alone, nobody helps me, yes. Who is going to help? I went alone. Who is going to help me?

Sample 4:
Male speaker from Mururata, in his late 50's, describes the last black king, Rey Bonifacio Pinedo

[1] *Pa nojotro lu negro fue fiesta di Pascua.* [2] *Entonce, eyu pueh hacía fiesta y ese abuelo vistía disi, di rey.* [3] *Entonce di huahua chiquito, un huahua que tenía como cinco año, siete año ese huahua, tudito ese huahua iba delante.* [4] *Lu huahua iba agarrao así su capa, ¿no?* [5] *Así disi que era pueh, agarrao ese capa. Y ese abuelo iba disi regando plata, diez centavo; iba regalando pueh monedas iba regando; y lu huahua iba pueh recogé esus moneda, qui el rey regala, qui rey botaba.* [6] *Eso yo acuerda un poco, pero no tanto ...* [7] *Yu no acuerda, yu no acuerda eso; eso sí yo no acorda.* [8] *Si lo enterraba junto junto junto con el abuelo, o como sería pues, yo no acorda.* [9] *Yo fue huahua eje tiempo, chico yo jue.* [10] *Algo yo acorda, yo acorda cuando lo ehtaba yevando la pantión ...*

[1] For us black people, Easter was the feast day. [2] So then they celebrated and they say that old man [Bonifacio Pinedo, the last "king" of Mururata: JML] dressed up like a king. [3] Then a small child, a child who was five, [or] seven years old, all the children went in front. [4] The children would grab his cloak, right? [5] That's how they say it was, holding on to his cloak. And they say the old man would throw out coins, ten cents; he would throw these coins out; and the children would pick up those coins that the "king" was giving out, that the king was throwing. [6] I remember a little, but not much. [7] I don't remember at all, I don't remember that; that I really don't recall. [8] Whether they buried him along with his grandfather, I don't recall. [9] I was a child at that time, a child I was. [10] I remember something, I remember when they were taking him to the cemetery ...

Sample 5:
Female speaker from Santa Bárbara (now living in Coroico), in her early 70's

[1] *Ese tarde ya tiene qui yevá, tiene que yegá andi tata (d)i novia.* [2] *Ai ese duerme, siguiente día tiene qui cainá también.* [3] *Tiene qui bailá, cainá bailandu, tomandu; y tata tiene qui buscá este otro terno pa novia, otro ropa.* [4] *Había qui cambiá harto ese día.* [5] *Di eso de las cuatro las tres di la tardi ya, novia tenía que i a su casa.*

[1] That afternoon [the bridegroom] had to take, had to go to the home of the bride's father. [2] If he was sleeping, [then] the next day he had to rest as well. [3] He had to dance, rest dancing [and] drinking; and the bride's father had to find another jacket for the bride, other clothes. [4] They had to change clothes a lot that day. [5] Around three or four in the afternoon, the bride had to go to her house.

Sample 6:
Female speaker from Chijchipa (now living in Coroico), in her early 40's

[1] *Mi mama, cuando nojotro fue chiquitito, si ha casau con mi papá.* [2] *Y mi mama disi era chica catorce años mi papá disi qui tenía dieciseis año.* [3] *Disi qui mi mamá tenía huahuita, hartos hijitos.* [4] *A los treinta año mi mamá se ha muerto cun quince hijos ha dejadu.* [5] *Pero de los quince ha viviú tres; de los tres uno ha resultau larpa.* [6] *Después mi mamá disi como era chica no sabía y andaba preguntando tía mi huahua diji ta larpa. ¿Qué cosa será no?* [7] *Pero hay qui preguntá pues a loh qui sabe.* [8] *Nojotro lu genti antiguo, nojotro lu genti antiguo sabemo jay qué cosa es bueno.* [9] *Hay qui meté tijerita en la cintura cuando uno ehtá cun barriga.* [10] *Ahora si no sana, ... si no sana tu huahua hay qui í la cementerio recogé huesito.* [11] *Y esus huesito hay qui bañarlo envuelto en un trapo negro, hacelo tomá, con eso la huahua se sana.* [12] *Tampoco no es pa yevalo andi doctó, nada porque tampoco los doctó no sabe jay.*

[1] My mother, when we were small, married my father. [2] And they say my mother was a fourteen year old girl and they say my father was sixteen. [3] They say my mother had children, lots of children. [4] My mother died at age thirty leaving fifteen children. [5] But of the fifteen, [only] three lived. One of the three was premature and weak. [6] Then my mother said that since she was a girl, she didn't know [anything] and she went asking ma'am whether they say my child was a premature weakling. What could this be? [7] But you have to ask the people who know. [8] We old-timers, we old people know what is good. [9] You have to place scissors in your waist-band when you are pregnant. [10] Then if the child doesn't get well ... if your child doesn't get well, you have to go to the cemetery and collect little bones. [11] And you have to wash these bones wrapped up in a black cloth and have the child drink, with this the child will improve. [12] Nor should you take him to a doctor, the doctors don't know anything either.

Sample 7:
Male speaker from Chijchipa (now living in Coroico), in his late 70's

[1] *Yo quedó viudu.* [2] *Yo casi siete mes, siete año yo vivió con mi primer mujé.* [3] *Pero mi historia era lindo, fue pueh lindo mi historia.* [4] *A los seis mes ya yo casó cun otro mujé, ya yo casó cun otro mujé.* [5] *Pero después mi han criticau, disi viudu alegre. Disi eje mujé va murí disi este y el otro.* [6] *Di boca i genti no hay qui creyé.* [7] *Mira Juan, yo ta*

[1] I was widowed. [2] Almost seven months, seven years I lived with my first wife. [3] But my story was beautiful, story was beautiful. [4] Six months later, I married another woman, I married another woman. [5] But then I was criticized, [and] they called me the "merry widower." They said that woman is going to die, they said this and that.

treintaicinco año cun ese mujé, como no muriu. [8] *Gente antigo tenía mucho creencia, pero ese creencia no valía.*

[9] *Asuntu di bruju, había una señora, tenía un señora, un negra, compró pues su ropa di muerto.* [10] *Ante ropa di muerto era mortaja.* [11] *Compró su ropa di muerto.* [12] *Pa decí ele es achachila disi bruju bola disi porquí decimo, ponió su doh vela aquí.* [13] *Tiró pue la camino, en un lugar di río, lugar vacío que no había gente.* [14] *Cuando, un buen día d'eso, yo era chico:* [15] *Yo taba yendo cun mi awicho Grabiela, yindo di Santana yindo Mururata.* [16] *Haiga síu doce di la noche, en la mula loh doh montao, cuando nojotro yega di la río Yarisa ayá ariba.* [17] *Ta tirao pue así, blanco, tirao medio camino.* [18] *Mula paró y dos pie sopló no quería pasá.* [19] *Carajo no sé di cómo pueh.* [20] *Mi awicho Grabiela notó qui no jui alma, porque disi un poquito moviu.* [21] *Carajo mi awicho Grabiela la pegó un chicotazo a mula plano la pisó* [22]*¡Plan! awicho levantó, levantó pueh.* [23] *¡Disculpami! ¡no qui mi asentara cun mi awicho! Bajó, en la mula la muntú cun su palo.*

[6] You shouldn't believe what comes out of other people's mouth. [7] Look here, Juan, I was with that woman for thirty five years and she didn't die. [8] The old people had a lot of beliefs, but those beliefs were worthless.

[9] As regards witchcraft, there was a woman, there was a woman, a black woman, who had bought her burial clothes. [10] Before the burial clothing was a shroud. [11] She had bought her burial clothes. [12] They say she was a witch, an ancestral spirit, because we say, she lit her two candles. [13] She set out, a place along the river where there were no people. [14] One fine day, when I was a child [the following took place]: [15] I was going with my grandmother Gabriela, going from Santana to Mururata. [16] It must have been twelve midnight, the two of us riding a mule, when we got up to the Yarisa river. [17] She [the old lady] was there in the middle of the road, [all] pale. [18] The mule stopped, snorted, it didn't want to go on. [19] Damn, I don't know how. [20] My grandmother Gabriela saw that it wasn't a spirit because it moved a little. [21] Damn, my grandmother Gabriela whipped the mule, stomped him good. [22] Bam, the old lady got up. [23] Excuse me! Don't sit with my grandmother! [She] got down, [and] got her on the mule with her stick.

Sample 8:
Male speaker from Dorado Chico (now living in La Paz), in his mid 50's

[1] *Yo cuando era, cuando i síu chico, mi papá siempre mi daba jay tarea.* [2] *Yo tenía qui tené, yo tenía qui yená agua.* [3] *Esu era tudu lus tarde, tenia qui yená yo agua.* [4] *Y aparti di yená agua*

[1] When I was, when I was a child, my father always gave me chores. [2] I had to ..., I had to fill up [= fetch] water. [3] That was every afternoon, I had to fetch water. [4] And besides fetching water, we

teníamo dos tacho grandi. Cuando... pila no era jay cerca pila taba pueh lejo. [5] *Nos reuniamo nos juntamo luh chico porque nojotro nomá luh chico teníamo qui í a trayé agua.* [6] *A veces rompíamo pue esos tachu, y di aí a veces nuestru papá nos pegaba.* [7] *Nuestru mamá nos pegaba, saben jay que queré cortá mano cun cayana, cayana es ese tachu rompíu, con esu saben queré cortá mano cuando rompíamo tacho.* [8] *O sea hay qui í cun todo cuidado porque esus tachu era di barro, era di barro.* [9] *Ya no había jay esos baldi qui hay ahora di plástico.* [10] *Ay puru di barro era, oya di barro, tacho di barro, plato era di barro.* [11] *Cun esos cuchara di palo no era esuh cuchara di aluminio qui hay ahora era cuchara di palo.* [12] *Entonci pueh unu rompía oya o rompía esus tachu, papá te tira con la cuera.* [13] *Esus oya di barro, cada semana había qui subí.* [14] *Nojotro íbamo pa Arapata porque ahí venían luh viajero.* [15] *Esus papini charquini qui lu yaman ellus traían pues sus oya di, de aquí del altiplano.* [16] *Y esus viajero traían esus oya y había qui í a comprá.* [17] *A veces había, traían pueh unos chipa así, bien arreglau esos chipa, bien amarrao.* [18] *Y aí pue mi mamá mi papá mayormenti mi mamá iba comprá esus oya di barro.* [19] *Y esus oya di barro había qui pasa cun ..., había qui curá jay, había qui curá cun grasa calienti.* [20] *Había qui pasá por encima primero cun grasa caliente pa que no si rompa.* [21] *Graso di cerdo era pueh, grasa di cerdo, o mayormenti era grasa di vaca pero tenía qui sé grasa siempri.* [22] *O si no, tenía qui sé² grasa*

had two large jugs. [And this] when the water fountain was not close. [5] We children would get together [to go fetch water], because only we children had to go and bring water. [6] Sometimes we broke those jugs, and therefore our father sometimes beat us. [7] Our mother beat us, they would cut our hands with the pot shards, *cayana* is [from] that broken jug, with that they would cut our hands when we broke a jug. [8] So we had to be very careful, because those jugs were made of clay, they were of clay. [9] There weren't any of those plastic buckets like there are now. [10] Just clay, clay pots, clay jugs, clay plates. [11] With those wooden spoons, not aluminum spoons like there are now, wooden spoons. [12] So when one of us broke a pot or a jug father would hit us with his belt. [13] Those clay pots, every week we had to go. [14] We went to Arapata because the travelers came there. [5] Those *papini charquini* as they were called, they brought their pots from the Altiplano. [16] Those travelers brought their pots, and we had to buy [them]. [17] Sometimes they brought a net, those nets were really neat, really tied up. [18] And my father and my mother, mostly my mother bought those clay pots. [19] And those clay pots had to be rubbed with ..., they had to be cured, they had to be cured with hot grease. [20] First they had to be rubbed with hot grease so they wouldn't break. [21] Hog grease it was, hog grease or beef tallow, but it always had to be grease. [22] Or else, it always had to be grease, sometimes they even used chicken grease. [23] That chicken fat, we

---

² *tenía qui sé < tenía que ser.*

sempri, a veces hasta untu di gayina utilizaban. [23] Ese untu di gayina jay ese cebo. Había qui pasá alredidó tuditu oya pero calentando a la juego, ese untu, o ese cebo. [24] Entonce disi pueh qui era pa que oya no si rompa. [25] Entonces compraba oya; hacía eso di juntá cun ese grasa calentau. Y ya había pueh qui cociná; así oya aguantaba. [26] Sólo había qui tené cuidado la quiri pa qui no vaya cayí. [27] O cuando taba muy calienti pa bajá, había qui agarrá cun trapo sempre. [28] Porque si no se agarraba cun trapo caliente, ya pueh bien caliente, unu podía pueh rompé esu ya, vaciá tuditu ese comida qui taba cociná.

had to rub it all over the pot, but always [after first] heating it in the fire, that grease. [24] They said so the pot wouldn't break. [25] Then we bought the pots; and we rubbed them all over with hot grease, and then they were ready to be used for cooking; this way, the pots would last. [26] Only it was necessary to be careful with the cooking stand so they wouldn't fall over. [27] Or when they were too hot to take down, we always had to grab them with a rag. [28] Because if you didn't grab them with a rag –the really hot [pots], you could break them and spill all the food that was cooking.

BIBLIOGRAPHY

AILLÓN SORIA, Esther (2005): "La afro-andinización de los esclavos negros en las viñas de Cinti (Chuquisaca) siglos XVIII-XIX". *Raíces: revista boliviana de la fundación de afro descendientes* 2, 10-11.

ALARCÓN, Abel (³1997): "La cogida". In Soriano Badani, Armando (ed.): *Antología del cuento boliviano*. La Paz: Amigos del Libro, 24-28.

ALLEYNE, Mervyn (1980): *Comparative Afro-American*. Ann Arbor: Karoma.

ALTHOFF, Daniel (1994): "Afro-mestizo speech from Costa Chica, Guerrero: from Cuaji to Cuijla". *Language Problems and Language Planning* 18, 242-256.

AMARAL, Amadeu (1955): *O dialeto caipira*. São Paulo: Anhembi.

ANDRADE, G. de (1961): *Contos d'África, antologia de contos angolanos*. Sá da Bandeira: Publicaçoes Imbondeiro.

ANDREWS, George Reid (2004): *Afro-Latin America 1800-2000*. Oxford: Oxford University Press.

ANGOLA MACONDE, Juan (2000*)*: *Raíces de un pueblo: cultura afroboliviana*. La Paz: Producciones CIMA, Embajada de España, Cooperación.

— (2003): "Los Yungas: enclave africano". *Raíces: Revista boliviana de la fundación de afro descendientes* 1, 1, 3-9.

— (2006): "¿Dónde está mi pueblo?" *La Prensa* 6 de septiembre 2006, p. 12A. Available on line at: <www.laprensa.com.bo/20060906/opinion/opinion01.htm>.

— (2008): *Nuestra historia: comunidad Dorado Chico*. La Paz: Sindicato Agrario Dorado Chico/Traditions pour Demain.

— (MS): Unpublished manuscript. La Paz, Bolivia.

ANGOLA MACONDE, Juan & AGUILAR, Nelson (2005): "Diálogo con nuestros abuelos de Tocaña". *Raíces: revista boliviana de la fundación de afro descendientes* 2, 21-26.

ANON. (n.d.): "El afroboliviano". Available on line at: <www.afrosenandes.org/bolivia/afrobolivianos.html>.

ANON. (1647): "Sã aqui turo". University of Coimbra archives, manuscript #50, folios 18v-23v; recording on Roger Wagner Chorale, "Festival of early Latin American music" (Los Angeles: Eldorado, 1975), produced by the UCLA Latin American Center; also on the record "Native Angels" (San Antonio: Talking Taco Records, 1996).

ANON. (2002): "Afrobolivianos, 151 años libres, pero no iguales". *La Razón* (La Paz, Bolivia), November 26, 2002.

ANON. (2003): "Comunidad de afrobolivianos en Santa Cruz sueña con sede propia". Available on-line at: www.BoliviaHoy.com/modules/news/print.php?storyid=4402>.

ANON. (2004): "Una corriente de búsqueda mueve a los afrodescendientes". *La Razón* (La Paz, Bolivia), February 8, 2004. Availalbe at: <www.la-razon.com/Tendencias/Ferbrero/ten040208a.html>.

ARBELL, Mordechai (2002): *The Jewish Nation of the Caribbean. The Spanish-Portuguese Jewish Settlements in the Caribbean and the Guianas*. Jerusalem / New York: Gefen Publishing House.

ARELLANO, Ignacio & EICHMANN, Andrés (eds.) (2005): *Entremeses, loas y coloquios de Potosí (colección del convento de Santa Teresa)*. Madrid/Frankfurt: Iberoamericana/Vervuert.

AYALA LOAYZA, Juan Luis (1988): *Diccionario español-aymara, aymara-español*. Lima: J. Mejía Baca.

AZEVEDO, Milton (1984): "Loss of agreement in Caipira Portuguese". *Hispania* 67, 403-408.

BACARDÍ MOREAU, Emilio (1916-1917): *Doña Guiomar*. La Habana: Imp. El Siglo XX de A. Miranda.

BAKER, Philip (1990): "Off target?" *Journal of Pidgin and Creole Languages* 5, 107-119.

— (1997): "Directionality in pidginization and creolization". In Spears, Arthur & Winford, Donald (eds.): *The Structure and Status of Pidgins and Creoles*. Amsterdam: John Benjamins, 91-109.

BAKER, Philip & CORNE, Chris (1982): *Isle de France creole: affinities and origins*. Ann Arbor: Karoma.

BAL, Willy (1968): "O destino de palavras de origem portuguesa num dialecto quicongo". *Revista Portuguesa de Filologia* 15, 49-101.

— (1974): "Portuguese loan-words in Africa". *Aufsätze zur portugiesischen Kulturgeschichte* 13, 280-300.

BARANDA, Consolación (ed.) (1988): *Feliciano de Silva, Segunda Celestina*. Madrid: Cátedra.

BARRENA, Natalio (1957): *Gramática annobonesa*. Madrid: Instituto de Estudios Africanos.

BARRERA GUTIÉRREZ, Juan (1996): *Me avergüenzan tus polleras*. La Paz: Juventud.

— (2000a): *Rupertita la maestra mayor*. La Paz: Juventud.

— (2000b): *Cuidado con las gemelas*. La Paz: Juventud.

— (2001): *El matrimonio de la Rupertita*. La Paz: Juventud.

BAXTER, Alan (1992): "A contribuição das comunidades afrobrasileiras isoladas para o debate sobre a crioulização prévia: um exemplo do estado da Bahia". In d'Andrade, Ernesto & Kihm, Alain (eds.): *Actas do colóquio sobre crioulos de base lexical portuguesa*. Lisboa: Edições Colibrí, 7-36.

— (1997): "Creole-like features in the verb system of an Afro-Brazilian variety of Portuguese". In Spears & Winford (eds.) 1997: 265-288.

BAXTER, Alan & LUCCHESI, Dante (1993): "Procesos de descrioulização no sistema verbal de um dialeto rural brasileiro". *Papia* 2, 59-71.

BAXTER, Alan; LUCCHESI, Dante & GUIMARÃES, Maximiliano (1997): "Gender agreement as a "decreolizing" feature of an Afro-Brazilian dialect". *Journal of Pidgin and Creole Languages* 12, 1-57.

BECCO, Horacio Jorge (n. d.): *Negros y morenos en el cancionero rioplatense*. Buenos Aires: Sociedad Argentina de Americanistas.

BENÍTEZ DEL CRISTO, Ignacio (1930): "Los novios catedráticos". *Archivos del Folklore Cubano* 5, no. 2, 119-146.

BERENGUER Y SED, Antonio (1929): *Tradiciones villaclareñas,* vol. 1. La Habana: Imprenta y Papalería de Rambla, Bouza y Ca.

BERTONIO, Ludovico (1879): *Vocabulario de la lengua aymara.* Leipzig: B. G. Teubner [facsimile of original 1612 edition].

BIBANG OYEE, Julián-B. (2002): *El español guineano: interferencias, guineanismo.* Malabo: n.p.

BICKERTON, Derek (1973): "The nature of a creole continuum". *Language* 49, 640-669.

— (1975): *Dynamics of a Creole System.* Cambridge: Cambridge University Press.

— (1981): *Roots of Language.* Ann Arbor: Karoma.

BICKERTON, Derek & ESCALANTE, Aquiles (1970): "Palenquero: a Spanish-based creole of northern Colombia". *Lingua* 32, 254-267.

BINYÁN CARMONA, Narciso (1990): "¿Príncipes Kongos en Bolivia y Uruguay?" In Savoia, Rafael (ed.): *El negro en la historia: aportes para el conocimiento de las raíces en América Latina.* Quito: Centro Cultural Afro-Ecuatoriano, Departamento de Pastoral Afro-Ecuatoriano, 127-142.

BLYM, Hugo (1940): *Puna.* Santiago de Chile: Ercilla.

BONVINI, Emilio (2000): "La langue des «pretos velhos» (vieux noirs) au Brésil: un créole à base portugaise d'origine africaine ?" *Bulletin de la Société de Linguistique de Paris* 95, 1, 389-416.

BOTELHO GONSÁLVEZ, Raúl (1941): *Coca (motivos del Yunga paceño).* Santiago de Chile: Zig-Zag.

— (1945): *Altiplano: novela india.* Buenos Aires: Ayacucho.

— (1957): *Tierra chucara.* Santiago de Chile: Zig-Zag.

BOWSER, Frederick (1974): *The African Slave in colonial Peru 1524-1650.* Stanford: Stanford University Press.

BOYD-BOWMAN, Peter (1955): "Cómo obra la fonética infantil en la formación de los hipocorísticos". *Nueva Revista de Filología Hispánica* 9, 337-366.

BRIDIKHINA, Eugenia (1995): *La mujer negra en Bolivia.* La Paz: Ministerio de Desarrollo Humano.

BROCKINGTON, Lolita Gutiérrez (2006): *Blacks, Indians and Spaniards in the Eastern Andes: Reclaiming the Forgotten in Colonial Mizque, 1550-1782.* Lincoln: University of Nebraska Press.

BÜTTNER, Thomas; CONDORI CRUZ, Dionisio & LLANQUE, D. (1984): *Diccionario aymara-castellano = Arunakan liwru, aymara-kastillanu.* Lima/Puno: s.n.

BYBEE, Joan (1985): *Morphology: A Study of the Relation Between Meaning and Form.* Amsterdam: John Benjamins.

CAAMAÑO DE FERNÁNDEZ, Vicenta (1976): *La lengua campesina en la narrativa costumbrista dominicana.* Santo Domingo: Centurión.

CABRERA, Lydia (1971): *Ayapa: cuentos de jicotea.* Miami: Ediciones Universal.

— (1976): *Francisco y Francisca: chascarrillos de negros viejos.* Miami: C. R.

— (^{3}1983): *El monte.* Miami: C. R.

— (1989): *Los animales en el folklore y la magia de Cuba.* Miami: Ediciones Universal.

CABRERA PAZ, Manuel (1973): "Fragmento de poema". In Fernández de la Vega, Oscar & Pamies, Alberto (eds.): *Iniciación a la poesía afro-americana.* Miami: Ediciones Universal, 122-131.

212   John Lipski

CAICEDO, Miguel (1992): *El castellano en el Chocó (500 años)*. Medellín: Lealon.

CANFIELD, D. Lincoln (1981): *Spanish Pronunciation in the Americas*. Chicago: University of Chicago Press.

CANTO LARIOS, Gustavo del (2003): *Oro negro: una aproximación a la presencia de comunidades afrodescendientes en la ciudad de Arica y el Valle de Azapa*. Santiago: Semblanza.

CARAMAZZA, Alfonso; MIOZZO, Michele; COSTA, Albert; SCHILLER, Niels & ALARIO, F.-Xavier (2001): "A crosslinguistic study of determiner production". In Dupoux, Emmanuel (ed.): *Language, Brain, and Cognitive Development: Essays in Honor of Jacques Mehler*. Cambridge: MIT Press, 209-226.

CARDOSO, Boaventura (1977): *Dizanga dia muenhu*. São Paulo: Edições 70.

CARRASCO CANTOS, Pilar (1981): *Contribución al estudio del habla rural de Baeza (Jaén)*. Jaén: Instituto de Estudios Giennenses.

CARVAJAL CARVAJAL, Juan; HUANCA TÓRREZ, Vitaliano & VÁSQUEZ, Juana (1978): *Diccionario aymara-castellano*. La Paz: Instituto Nacional de Estudios Lingüísticos.

CARVALHO NETO, Paulo de (1965): *El negro uruguayo (hasta la abolición)*. Quito: Universitaria.

CASTELLANOS, Isabel (1990): "Grammatical structure, historical development, and religious usage of Afro-Cuban bozal speech". *Folklore Forum* 23, 1-2, 57-84.

CASTONGUAY, Luis (1987): *Vocabulario regional del oriente peruano*. Iquitos: Centro de Estudios Teológicos de la Amazonía.

CÉSAR, Amândio (1969a): *Contos portugueses do ultramar*, vol. 1. Porto: Portucalense.

— (1969b): *Contos portugueses do ultramar*, vol. 2. Porto: Portucalense.

CEASER, Mike (2000): "Son pocos, pero son. Afrobolivianos intentan mantener cultura y población frente a migración y matrimonios mixtos". *Noticias Aliadas.org*. December 4, 2000.

CENTRO PEDAGÓGICO Y CULTURAL SIMÓN I. PATIÑO (1998): *El tambor mayor: música y cantos de las comunidades negras de Bolivia*. La Paz: Fundación Simón I. Patiño.

CHINI, Marina (1995): *Genere grammaticale e acquisizione: aspetti della morfologia nominale in italiano L²*. Milano: Francoangeli.

CLARO, Samuel (1974): *Antología de la música colonial en América del Sur*. Santiago: Universidad de Chile.

COELHO, Adolfo (1967): "Os dialectos românicos ou neo-latinos na Africa, Asia e América". Published from 1880-1886 in the *Boletim da Sociedade de Geografia de Lisboa*. Reprinted in Morais-Barbosa, Jorge (ed.): *Estudos lingüísticos crioulos*. Lisboa: Academia Internacional da Cultura Portuguesa, 1-233.

COELLO VILA, Carlos (1996): "Bolivia". In Alvar, Manuel (ed.): *Manual de dialectología hispánica: el español de América*. Barcelona: Ariel, 169-183.

CÓRDOVA, Carlos Joaquín (1995): *El habla del Ecuador: diccionario de ecuatorianismos*, vol. 1. Cuenca: Universidad del Azuay.

CORTÉS, José Domingo (1875): *Bolivia: apuntes jeográficos, estadísticos, de costumbres descriptivos e históricos*. Paris: Librería Española de E. Denné Schmitz.

COSSÍO, José M. de (ed.) (1950): *Rodrigo de Reinosa*. Santander: Antología de Escritores y Artistas Montañeses XVI. Imp. y Enc. de la Librería Moderna.

COSTA ARDÚZ, Rolando (1997): *Monografía de la provincia Nor Yungas*. La Paz: Prefectura del Departamento de La Paz.

COTARI, Daniel; MEJÍA, Jaime & CARRASCO, Víctor (1978): *Diccionario aymara-castellano, castellano-aymara*. Cochabamba: Instituto de Idiomas, Padres de Maryknoll.

COUTO, Hildo Honório do (1998): "Falar capelinhense: um dialeto conservador do interior de Minas Gerais". In Grosse & Zimmermann (eds.) 1998: 371-391.

CRESPO, Alberto (1977): *Esclavos negros en Bolivia*. La Paz: Academia Nacional de Ciencias de Bolivia.

CRETO GANGÁ [Bartolomé José CRESPO Y BORBÓN] (1975): "Un ajiaco o la boda de Pancha Jutía y Canuto Raspadura". In Leal, Rine (ed.): *Teatro bufo siglo XIX, antología*, vol. 1. La Habana: Arte y Literatura, 47-93.

CRUZ, Mary (1974): *Creto Gangá*. La Habana: Instituto Cubano del Libro 'Contemporáneos.'

CRUZ, Sor Juana Inés de la (1952): *Obras completas de Sor Juana Inés de la Cruz*. Vol. 2: *Villancicos y letras sacras*. México, D.F.: Fondo de Cultura Económica.

CUBA, María del Carmen (1996): *El castellano hablado en Chincha*. Lima: Universidad Nacional Mayor de San Marcos, Escuela de Posgrado.

CUBELLI, Roberto; LOTTO, Lorella; PAOLIERI, Daniela; GIRELLI, Massimo & JOB, Remo (2005): "Grammatical gender is selected in bare noun production: evidence from the picture-word interference paradigm". *Journal of Memory and Language* 53, 42-59.

CUCHE, Denys (1981): *Perou nègre*. Paris: L'Harmattan.

DE CAMP, David (1971): "Towards a generative analysis of a post-creole continuum". In Hymes, Dell (ed.): *Pidginization and Creolization of Languages*. Cambridge: Cambridge University Press, 349-370.

DEGRAFF, Michel (2005): "Linguists' most dangerous myth: the fallacy of Creolist Exceptionalism". *Language in Society* 34, 533-591.

DE LA ROSA SÁNCHEZ, Manuel Antonio (1988): "El juego de los tambores congos (tradición oral afromestiza de Panamá)". In Quartucci, Guillermo (ed.): *Segundo Congreso Nacional Asociación Latinoamericana de Estudios Afroasiáticos, Universidad Veracruzana, Jalapa, Veracruz, 3 al 5 de julio de 1985*. México, D.F.: El Colegio de México, 153-177.

DE VINCENZI, Marica (1999): "Differences between the morphology of gender and number: evidence from establishing coreferences". *Journal of Psycholinguistic Research* 28, 537-553.

DEZA GALINDO, Juan Francisco (1989): *Nuevo diccionario aymara-castellano/castellano-aymara*. Lima: Consejo Nacional de Ciencias y Tecnología CONCYTEC.

DI DOMENICO, Elisa & DE VICENZI, Marica (1995): "Gender and number in the retrieval of pronoun antecedents: differences in use and representation." In Nash, L.; Tsoules, F. & Zribi-Herts, A. (eds.): *Actes du deuxième colloque "Langues et grammaire"*, Paris 8 juin 1995, 95-109.

DÍAZ, Jesús (1966): *Los años duros*. La Habana: Casa de la Américas.

DÍAZ VILLAMIL, Antonio (1946): *La niña de sus ojos*. La Paz: Juventud.

— (³1986): *La Rosita*. La Paz: Popular.

— (³1987): *Plebe*. La Paz: Popular.

214 John Lipski

DOMÍNGUEZ, Alberto; CUETOS, Fernando & SEGUI, Juan (1999): "The processing of grammatical gender and number in Spanish". *Journal of Psycholinguistic Research* 28, 485-498.

DOMÍNGUEZ, Luis Arturo (1989): *Vivencia de un rito loango en el Tambú*. Caracas: Talleres de Hijos de Ramiro Paz.

DOMÍNGUEZ CONDEZO, Víctor (1990): *Problemas de interferencia quechua-español*. Huanuco: Facultad de Educación, UNHV.

DROLET, Patricia (1980a): *The Congo ritual of northeastern Panama: an Afro-American expressive structure of cultural adaptation*. Ph. D. dissertation, University of Illinois.

— (1980b): *El ritual congo del noroeste de Panamá: una estructura afro-americana expresiva de adaptación cultural*. Panamá: Instituto Nacional de Cultura.

EBBING, Juan Enrique (1965): *Gramática y diccionario aimara*. La Paz: Don Bosco.

EBERHARD, Kathleen M. (1997): "The marked effect of number in subject-verb agreement". *Journal of Memory and Language* 36, 147-164.

ELTIS, David; BEHRENDT, Stephen; RICHARDSON, David & KLEIN, Herbert (eds.) (1999): *The Trans-Atlantic Slave Trade: A Database on CD-ROM*. Cambridge: Cambridge University Press.

ERICKSON, Curtis (1986): "La "f" y la "j" en el español del oriente peruano". In Moreno de Alba, José (ed.): *Actas del II Congreso Internacional sobre el Español de América*. México, D.F.: Universidad Nacional Autónoma de México, 301-306.

ESCALANTE, Aquiles (1954): "Notas sobre El Palenque de San Basilio, una comunidad negra en Colombia". *Divulgaciones Etnológicas* (Barranquilla) 3, 207-359.

ESCOBAR, Alberto (1978): *Variaciones sociolingüísticas del castellano en el Perú*. Lima: Instituto de Estudios Peruanos.

ESTRADA Y ZENEA, Ildefonso (1980): *El quitrín*. La Habana: Letras Cubanas.

FEIJÓO, Samuel (ed.) (1979): *Cuentos cubanos de humor*. La Habana: Letras Cubanas.

— (ed.) (1980): *Cuarteta y décima*. La Habana: Letras Cubanas.

FERRAZ, Luis Ivens (1979): *The creole of São Tomé*. Johannesburg: Witwatersrand University Press.

— (1984): "The substrate of Annobonese". *African Studies* 43, 119-136.

FERREIRA, Carlota da Silveira (1985): "Remanescentes de um falar crioulo brasileiro". *Revista Lusitana* (nova série), Lisboa, 5, 21-34

FLÓREZ, Luis (1950): "El habla del Chocó". *Thesaurus* 6, 110-116.

— (1951): *La pronunciación del español en Bogotá*. Bogotá: Instituto Caro y Cuervo.

FORTÚN DE PONCE, Julia Elena (1957): *La navidad en Bolivia*. La Paz: Ministerio de Educación.

FRANCESCHI, Víctor (1956): *Carbones*. Panama: Departamento de Bellas Artes y Publicaciones del Ministerio de Educación.

FRIEDEMANN, Nina S. de & PATIÑO ROSSELLI, Carlos (1983): *Lengua y sociedad en el Palenque de San Basilio*. Bogotá: Instituto Caro y Cuervo.

FUENTES GUERRA, Jesús & SCHWEGLER, Armin (2005): *Lengua y ritos del Palo Monte Mayombe: dioses cubanos y sus fuentes africanas*. Madrid/Frankfurt: Iberoamericana/Vervuert.

GARCÍA, Juan (1982): *La poesía negrista en el Ecuador*. Esmeraldas: Banco Central del Ecuador.

GARRISON, Rob (1999): "Bolivia". In Appiah, Kwame Anthony and Gates, Henry Louis, Jr. (eds.): *Africana: the encyclopedia of the African and African American experience*. New York: Basic-Civitas Books, 280-284.

GELABERT, Francisco de Paula (1875): *Cuadros de costumbres cubanas*. La Habana: Imprenta de la Botica de Santo Domingo.

GOBIERNO MUNICIPAL DE LA PAZ (1993): *El negro no es un color, es una saya*. La Paz: Gobierno Municipal de La Paz.

GÓMEZ BACARREZA, Donato (1999): *Diccionario básico del idioma aymara*. La Paz: Instituto de Estudios Bolivianos.

GÓNDOLA SOLÍS, Nolis Boris (^{2}2005): *El revellín de los bumbales*. Colón: Biblioteca Siglo XXI, Imprenta Colón. (1st ed. n. d., n. p.)

GREEN, Katherine (1997): *Non-standard Dominican Spanish: evidence of partial restructuring*. Ph. D. dissertation, City University of New York.

— (1999): "The creole pronoun *i* in non-standard Dominican Spanish". In Zimmermann, Klaus (ed.): *Lenguas criollas de base lexical española y portuguesa*. Madrid/Frankfurt: Iberoamericana/Vervuert, 373-387.

— (2001): "The past tense marker *a*: Palenquero in San Cristóbal (Dominican Republic)". In Moñino, Yves & Schwegler, Armin (eds.): *Palenque, Cartagena y Afro-Caribe: historia y lengua*. Tübingen: Niemeyer, 137-148.

GROSSE, Sybille and ZIMMERMANN, Klaus (eds.) (1988): *«Substandard» e mudança no português do Brasil*. Frankfurt: TFM.

GUEVARA, Darío (1968): *Lenguaje vernáculo de la poesía popular ecuatoriana*. Quito: Universitaria.

GUIRAO, Ramón (1938): *Órbita de la poesía afrocubana 1928-1937*. La Habana: Ucar García.

GÜNTHER, Wilfried (1973): *Das portugiesische Kreolisch der Jlha do Príncipe*. Marburg an der Lahn: Selbstverlag.

GUY, Gregory (1981): "Parallel variability in American dialects of Spanish and Portuguese". In Sankoff, David & Cedergren, Henrietta (eds.): *Variation Omnibus (NWAVE 8)*. Edmonton / Carbondale: Linguistic Research, 85-96.

— (2004): "Muitas línguas: the linguistic impact of Africans in colonial Brazil". In Curto, José C. & Lovejoy, Paul E. (eds.): *Enslaving Connections: Changing Cultures of Africa and Brazil during the Era of Slavery*. Amherst, NY: Humanity Books, 125-137.

HALL, Robert (1966): *Pidgin and Creole Languages*. Ithaca: Cornell University Press.

HARTH-TERRÉ, Emilio (1971): *Presencia del negro en el virreinato del Perú*. Lima: Universitaria.

— (1973): *Negros e indios: un estamento social ignorado del Perú colonial*. Lima: Juan Mejía Baca.

HATHERLY, Ana (1990): *Poemas em língua de preto dos séculos XVII e XVIII*. Lisboa: Quimera.

HENRÍQUEZ UREÑA, Max (1966): *Panorama histórico de la literatura dominicana*. Santo Domingo: Librería Dominicana.

HERRERA, Mariano (1964): *Después de la zeta*. La Habana: Ediciones R.

HOCHBERG, Judith (1986): "Functional compensation for /s/ deletion in Puerto Rican Spanish". *Language* 62, 609-621.

HOLM, John (1987): "Creole influence on popular Brazilian Portuguese". In Gilbert, Glenn (ed.): *Pidgin and Creole Languages: Essays in Memory of John E. Reinecke*. Honolulu: University of Hawaii Press, 406-429.

— (1988): *Pidgins and Creoles*. Vol. 1: *Theory and Structure*. Cambridge: Cambridge University Press.

— (2000): *An Introduction to Pidgins and Creoles*. Cambridge: Cambridge University Press.

— (2004): *Languages in Contact: The Partial Restructuring of Vernaculars*. Cambridge: Cambridge University Press.

HUALDE, José Ignacio & Schwegler, Armin (2008): "Intonation in Palenquero". *Journal of Pidgin and Creole Languages* 23, 1-31.

HUDSON, Rex & HANRATTY, Dennis ([3]1991): *Bolivia: A Country study*. Washington: Library of Congress, Federal Division.

IZNAGA, Alcides (1970): *Las cercas caminaban*. La Habana: Unión de Escritores y Artistas de Cuba.

JARAMILLO DE LUBENSKY, María (1992): *Diccionario de ecuatorianismos en la literatura*. Quito: Casa de la Cultura Ecuatoriana.

JEROSLOW, Elizabeth (1974): *Rural Cearense Portuguese: A study of one variety of non-standard Brazilian speech*. Ph. D. dissertation, Cornell University.

JIMÉNEZ PASTRANA, Juan (1983): *Los chinos en la historia de Cuba: 1847-1930*. La Habana: Editorial de Ciencias Sociales.

JOLY, Luz Graciela (1981): *The Ritual Play of the Congos of North-central Panama: Its Sociolinguistic Implications*. Austin, Texas: Southwest Educational Development Laboratory, Sociolinguistic Working Papers, no. 85.

— (1984): "Implicaciones sociolingüísticas del juego de Congos en la Costa Abajo de Panamá". *Revista Lotería* 338-339, 22-55.

JONES, Adam (1995): "Female slave-owners on the Gold Coast: just a matter of money". In Palmié, Stephan (ed.): *Slave Cultures and the Cultures of Slavery*. Knoxville: University of Tennessee Press, 100-112.

KOOPMAN, Hilda & LEFEBVRE, Claire (1981): "Haitian creole *pu*". In Muysken, Pieter (ed.): *Generative Studies in Creole Languages*. Dordrecht: Foris, 201-223.

LAIME AJACOPA, Teófilo (2005): *Castellano andino de los bilingües: un lenguaje desde la pragmática y la semántica*. La Paz: Imprenta Offset Visión.

LAPRADE, Richard (1976): *Some salient dialectal features of La Paz Spanish*. M. A. thesis, University of Florida.

— (1981): "Some cases of Aymara influence on La Paz Spanish". In Hardman, M. J. (ed.): *The Aymara Language in its Social and Cultural Context*. Gainesville: University Presses of Florida, 207-227.

LARIBE, Lucette (1968): *Nombre de Dios et les "regnes de Congos"*. Panama: Alliance Française Panamá.

— (1969): *Les "regnes de Congos" de Nombre de Dios*. Panama: Alliance Française Panamá.

LAUREL, Tomás Ávila (2000): *Áwala cu sangui*. Malabo: Ediciones Pángola.

LAYME PAIRUMANI, Félix (³2004): *Diccionario bilingüe: aymara castellano, castellano aymara*. La Paz: Consejo Educativo Aymara.

LAYME PAIRUMANI, Félix; LAYME AJACOPA, Teófilo; APAZA MAMANI, Damián & LÓPEZ APAZA, Primitiva (1992): *Diccionario castellano-aimara*. La Paz: Presencia.

LEITE DE VASCONCELLOS, José (1901) : *Esquisse d'une dialectologie portugaise*. Paris: Aillaud & Co.

LEMA G., Ana María (2005): "Los esclavos en los Yungas a fines del siglo XVIII hasta 1830". *Raíces: revista boliviana de la fundación de afro descendientes* 2, 8-9.

LÉONS, Madeline Barbara (1998): "Stratification and pluralism in the Bolivian Yungas". In Whitten, Norman E., Jr. and Torres, Arlene (eds.): *Blackness in Latin America and the Caribbean: social dynamics and cultural transformations, volume 1, Central America and Northern and Western South America*. Bloomington and Indianapolis: Indiana University Press, 335-356.

LEONS, William (1984a): "The politics of revolution: continuities and discontinuities in a Bolivian community". In *Anthropological Investigations in Bolivia*. Greeley, CO: University of Northern Colorado, Museum of Anthropology, Miscellaneous series No. 58, 1-12.

— (1984b): "Pluralism and mobility in a Bolivian community". *Anthropological Investigations in Bolivia*. Greeley, CO: University of Northern Colorado, Museum of Anthropology, Miscellaneous series No. 58, 13-27.

— (1984c): "Some notes on the demographic history of the Negro in the Bolivian Yungas". *Anthropological Investigations in Bolivia*. Greeley, CO: University of Northern Colorado, Museum of Anthropology, Miscellaneous series No. 58, 28-36.

LEYTON, Presbítero Raúl (1967): "Alko Rancho". In *Cuentistas bolivianos* 1965. Oruro: Universidad Técnica de Oruro, 73-97.

LIPSKI, John (1983): "La norma culta y la norma radiofónica: /s/ y /n/ en español". *Language Problems and Language Planning* 7, 239-262.

— (1984): "On the weakening of /s/ in Latin American Spanish". *Zeitschrift für Dialektologie und Linguistik* 51, 31-43.

— (1985a): *The Spanish of Equatorial Guinea*. Tübingen: Max Niemeyer.

— (1985b): "Black Spanish: the last frontier of Afro America". *Crítica* 2, 1, 53-75.

— (1986a): "Golden Age 'black Spanish': existence and coexistence". *Afro-Hispanic Review* 5, 1-2, 7-12.

— (1986b): "On the weakening of /s/ in *bozal* Spanish". *Neophilologus* 70, 208-216.

— (1986c): "Modern African Spanish phonetics: common features and historical antecedents". *General Linguistics* 26, 182-195.

— (1986d): "Creole Spanish and vestigial Spanish: evolutionary parallels". *Linguistics* 23, 963-984.

— (1986e): "Lingüística afroecuatoriana: el Valle del Chota". *Anuario de Lingüística Hispánica* 2, 153-176.

— (1986f): "Convergence and divergence in *bozal* Spanish". *Journal of Pidgin and Creole Languages* 1, 171 203.

— (1986g): "Sobre la construcción *ta* + INFINITIVO en el español 'bozal.'" *Lingüística Española Actual* 8, 73-92.

— (1986h): "The *negros congos* of Panama: Afro-Hispanic creole language and culture". *Journal of Black Studies* 16, 409-428.

— (1986i): "El lenguaje de los *negros congos* de Panamá". *Lexis* 10, 53-76.

— (1987a): "The Chota Valley: Afro-Hispanic language in highland Ecuador". *Latin American Research Review* 22, 155-170.

— (1987b): "The construction *ta* + INFINITIVE in Caribbean *bozal* Spanish". *Romance Philology* 40, 431-450.

— (1988): "On the reduction of /s/ in 'black' Spanish". In Staczek, John (ed.): *On Spanish, Portuguese, and Catalan Linguistics*. Washington: Georgetown University Press.

— (1989a): *The speech of THE NEGROS CONGOS of Panama*. Amsterdam: John Benjamins.

— (1989b): "/s/-voicing in Ecuadoran Spanish". *Lingua* 79, 49-71.

— (1990a): "Trinidad Spanish: implications for Afro-Hispanic language". *Nieuwe West-Indische Gids* 62, 7-26.

— (1990b): *The Language of the ISLEÑOS: Vestigial Spanish in Louisiana*. Baton Rouge: Louisiana State University Press.

— (1990c): "Aspects of Ecuadorian vowel reduction". *Hispanic Linguistics* 4, 1-19.

— (1991): "Origen y evolución de la partícula *ta* en los criollos afrohispánicos". *Papia* 1, 2, 16-41.

— (1992a): "Origin and development of *ta* in Afro-Hispanic creoles". In Byrne, Francis & Holm, John (eds.): *Atlantic Meets Pacific: A Global View of Pidginization and Creolization*. Amsterdam: John Benjamins, 217-231.

— (1992b): "Sobre el español *bozal* del Siglo de Oro: existencia y coexistencia". *Scripta philologica in honorem Juan M. Lope Blanch*, vol. 1. México, D.F.: Universidad Nacional Autónoma de México, 383-396.

— (1992c): "Spontaneous nasalization in Afro-Hispanic language". *Journal of Pidgin and Creole Languages* 7, 261-305.

— (1993a): *On the Non-creole Basis for Afro-Caribbean Spanish*. Research Paper No. 24, Latin American Institute, University of New Mexico.

— (1993b): "Creoloid phenomena in the Spanish of transitional bilinguals". In Roca, Ana & Lipski, John (eds.): *Spanish in the United States: Linguistic Contact and Diversity*. Berlin: Mouton de Gruyter, 155-182.

— (1994): "El español afroperuano: eslabón entre Africa y América". *Anuario de Lingüística Hispánica* 10, 179-216

— (1995a): "Literary 'Africanized' Spanish as a research tool: dating consonant reduction". *Romance Philology* 49, 130-167.

— (1995b): "[round] and [labial] in Spanish and the 'free-form' syllable". *Linguistics* 33, 283-304.

— (1995c): "Portuguese language in Angola: luso-creoles' missing link?" Presented at the annual meeting of the American Association of Teachers of Spanish and Portuguese (AATSP), San Diego, California, August 1995. Available on line at: <http://www.personal.psu.edu/jml34/papers.htm>.

— (1995d): "Spanish hypocoristics: towards a unified prosodic analysis". *Hispanic Linguistics* 6/7, 387-434.

— (1996a): "Contactos de criollos en el Caribe hispánico: contribuciones al español *bozal*". *América Negra* 11, 31-60.

— (1996b): "Los dialectos vestigiales del español en los Estados Unidos: estado de la cuestión". *Signo y Seña* 6, 459-489.

— (1997): "El lenguaje de los *negros congos* de Panamá y el *lumbalú* palenquero: función sociolingüística de criptolectos afrohispánicos". *América Negra* 14, 147-165.

— (1998a): "Latin American Spanish: creolization and the African connection". *PALARA* (Publications of The Afro-Latin American Research Association) 2, 54-78.

— (1998b): "El español *bozal*". In Perl, Matthias & Schwegler, Armin (eds.): *América negra: panorámica actual de los estudios lingüísticos sobre variedades criollas y afrohispanas*. Madrid/Frankfurt: Iberoamericana/Vervuert, 293-327.

— (1998c): "El español de los braceros chinos y la problemática del lenguaje *bozal*". *Montalbán* 31, 101-139.

— (1999a): "Creole-to-creole contacts in the Spanish Caribbean: the genesis of Afro Hispanic language". *Publications of the Afro-Latin American Research Association (PALARA)* 3, 5-46.

— (1999b): "Chinese-Cuban pidgin Spanish: implications for the Afro-creole debate". In Rickford, John & Romain, Suzanne (eds.): *Creole Genesis, Attitudes and Discourse*. Amsterdam: John Benjamins, 215-233.

— (1999c): "Evolución de los verbos copulativos en el español *bozal*". In Zimmermann, Klaus (ed.): *Lenguas criollas de base lexical española y portuguesa*. Madrid/Frankfurt: Iberoamericana/Vervuert, 145-176.

— (1999d): "Sobre la valoración popular y la investigación empírica del 'español negro' caribeño". In Perl, Matthias & Pörtl, Klaus (eds.): *Identidad cultural y lingüística en Colombia, Venezuela y en el Caribe hispánico*. Tübingen: Max Niemeyer, 271-295.

— (2000a): "Strategies of double negation in Spanish and Portuguese". Presented at Spanish Linguistics Symposium, Indiana University-Bloomington, November, 2000. Available on line at: <www.personal.psu.edu/jml34/papers.htm>.

— (2000b): "Afro-Asian and Afro-indigenous linguistic contacts in Spanish America". Presented at the Annual Meeting, Afro-Latin American Research Association (ALARA), Port-au-Prince, Haiti, August, 2000. Available on line at: <www.personal.psu.edu/jml34/papers.htm>.

— (2001): "Panorama del lenguaje afrorrioplatense: vías de evolución fonética". *Anuario de Lingüística Hispánica* 14, 281-315

— (2002a): "Contacto de criollos y la génesis del español (afro)caribeño". In Díaz, Norma; Ludwig, Ralph & Pfänder, Stefan (eds.): *La Romania americana: procesos lingüísticos en situaciones de contacto*. Madrid/Frankfurt: Iberoamericana/Vervuert, 53-95.

— (2002b): "Epenthesis vs. elision in Afro-Iberian language: a constraint-based approach to creole phonology". In Satterfield, Teresa; Tortora, Christina & Cresti, Diana (eds.): *Current Issues in Romance Languages*. Amsterdam: John Benjamins, 173-188.

— (2002c): "Génesis y evolución de la cópula en los criollos afro-ibéricos". In Moñino, Yves & Schwegler, Armin (eds.): *Palenque, Cartagena y Afro-Caribe: historia y lengua*. Tübingen: Niemeyer, 65-101.

— (2002d): "'Partial' Spanish: strategies of pidginization and simplification (from Lingua Franca to 'Gringo Lingo')". In Wiltshire, Caroline & Camps, Joaquim (eds.): *Romance Phonology and Variation*. Amsterdam: John Benjamins, 117-143.

— (2004): "Nuevas perspectivas sobre el español afrodominicano". In Valdés Bernal, Sergio (ed.): *Pensamiento lingüístico sobre el Caribe insular hispánica*. Santo Domingo: Academia de Ciencias de la República Dominicana, 505-552.

— (2005): *A History of Afro-Hispanic Language: Five Centuries and Five Continents.* Cambridge: Cambridge University Press.

— (2007): "Castile and the hydra: the diversification of Spanish in Latin America". Presented at the conference Iberian Imperialism and Language Evolution in Latin America, University of Chicago, April 13, 2007. Available on line at: <www.personal.psu. edu/jml34/papers.htm>.

— (Forthcoming): "El lenguaje afromexicano en el contexto de la lingüística afrohispánica". *PALARA (Publications of the Afro-Latin American Research Association).*

LIPSKI, John & SANTORO, Salvatore (2007): "Zamgoangueño creole Spanish". In Holm, John & Patrick, Peter (eds.): *Comparative Creole Syntax: Parallel Outlines of 18 Creole Grammars.* London: Battlebridge Publications, 373-398.

LLANOS MOSCOCO, Ramiro & SORUCO ARROYO, Carlos (2004): *Reconocimiento étnico y jurídico de la comunidad afrodescendiente.* La Paz: Comunidad de Derechos Humanos, Capítulo Boliviano de Derechos Hmanos Democracia y Desarrollo.

LÓPEZ, José Florencio [Jacan] (1879): *Nadie sabe para quién trabaja.* Matanzas: Imprenta El Ferro-Carril.

LORENZINO, Gerardo (1998): *The Angola Creole Portuguese of São Tomé: Its Grammar and Sociolinguistic History.* Munich: Lincom Europa.

LUCCA, Manuel de (1983): *Diccionario aymara-castellano, castellano-aymara.* La Paz: Comisión de Alfabetización y Literatura en Aymara.

LUCCHESI, Dante (1998): "A constitução histórica do português brasileiro como um processo bipolarizador: tendências atuais de mudança nas normas culta e popular". In Grosse & Zimmermann (eds.) 1998: 73-99.

LUCERO MAMANI, Virginia (2003): *Uso de las concordancias nominales del castellano en las expresiones de estudiantes bilingües de lingüística.* Tesis de grado, Universidad Mayor de San Andrés (La Paz).

MACHADO, Juan Pedro (2000): *The Afro-Paraguayan Community of Cambacuá.* London: Minority Rights Group and Mundo Afro.

MACHADO FILHO, Aires da Mata (1964): *O negro e o garimpo em Minas Gerais.* Rio de Janeiro: Editôra Civilização Brasileira.

MALDONADO CHALÁ, Olga Lidia (2006): *Vocablos que hacen particular el habla de los afro choteños y que aún se encuentran presentes en las personas mayores.* Tesis de Diploma Superior en Estudios de la Cultura, Mención Diáspora Andina, Universidad Andina Simón Bolívar, Sede Ecuador.

MANSOUR, Mónica (1973): *La poesía negrista.* México, D.F.: ERA.

MARTINS, Manuel de Morais (1958a): "Contribução para o estudo da influência do português na língua quicongo". *Garcia de Orta* 6, 33-51.

— (1958b): *Contacto de culturas no Congo português.* Lisboa: Junta de Investigações de Ultramar.

MAURER, Philippe (1988): *Les modifications temporelles et modales du verbe dans le papiamento de Curaçao.* Hamburg: Helmut Buske.

— (1995): *L'angolar: un créole afro-portugais parlé à São Tomé*. Hamburg: Helmut Buske.

MEDINA, Jorge (2004): "La situación de la comunidad afro en Bolivia". In *Los afroandinos de los siglos XVI al XX*. San Borja, Peru: UNESCO, 120-127.

MEGENNEY, William (1984): "Traces of Portuguese in three Caribbean creoles: evidence in support of the monogenetic theory". *Hispanic Linguistics* 1, 177-189.

— (1986): *El palenquero: un lenguaje post-criollo colombiano*. Bogotá: Instituto Caro y Cuervo.

— (1989): "An etiology of /-s/ deletion in the Hispanic Caribbean: internal process or substratum influence?" In *Estudios sobre el español de América y lingüística afroamericana*. Bogotá: Instituto Caro y Cuervo, 200-327.

— (1990): *África en Santo Domingo: la herencia lingüística*. Santo Domingo: Museo del Hombre Dominicano.

— (1993): "Helvecian Portuguese: vernacular dialect or creole?" In Milleret, Margo & Eakin, Marshall (eds.): *Homenagem a Alexandrino Severino: Essays on the Portuguese Speaking World*. Austin: Host Publications, 114-131.

— (1994): "Creoloid Portuguese: the search for Brazilian Palenqueros". *Diaspora* 3, 3, 1-36.

MELLADO Y MONTAÑA, Manuel (1975): "La casa de Taita Andrés, semi-parodia de la casa de Campo. Juguete cómico del género bufo en un acto". In Leal, Rine (ed.): *Teatro bufo siglo XIX*, vol. 1. La Habana: Arte y Literatura, 263-303.

MELLO, Heliana. R. de; BAXTER, Alan, HOLM, John & MEGENNEY, William (1998): "O português vernacular do Brasil". In Perl, Mattias & Schwegler, Armin (eds.): *América negra: panorámica actual de los estudios lingüísticos sobre variedades criollas y afrohispanas*. Madrid/Frankfurt: Iberoamericana/Vervuert, 71-137. [pp. 97-134, Baxter's Morfossintaxe.]

MENDES, Orlando (1981): *Portagem*. Maputo: Edições 70.

MENDONÇA, Renato (1935): *A influência africana no português do Brasil*. São Paulo: Companhia Editora Nacional.

MENDOZA, Aída (1976): *Sistema fonológico del castellano y variantes regionales*. Lima: Inide.

— (1978): "Variantes fonéticas regionales". In *Lingüística y educación: Actas del IV Congreso Internacional de la ALFAL*. Lima: ALFAL/Universidad Nacional Mayor de San Marcos, 445-456.

MENDOZA, José (1991): *El castellano hablado en La Paz: sintaxis divergente*. La Paz: Universidad Mayor de San Andrés.

MENDOZA LÓPEZ, Max (1970): "La Lisa ttaku". *Cuentos bolivianos: IV Concurso Nacional de Cuento 1968*, Oruro: Universitaria, Universidad Técnica de Oruro, 59-76.

MENESES, Raúl (1945): *En Bolivia está Yungas*. Chulumani: Imprenta Económica.

— (1948a): "Provincia Nor Yungas". In *La Paz en su IV Centenario 1548-1948*, vol. 1. Buenos Aires: Imprenta López, 159-183.

— (1948b): "Provincia Sud Yungas". In *La Paz en su IV Centenario 1548-1948*, vol. 1. Buenos Aires: Imprenta López, 185-217.

MILLONES SANTAGADEA, Luis (1973): *Minorías étnicas en el Perú*. Lima: Pontificia Universidad Católica del Perú.

MINORITY RIGHTS GROUP (ed.) (1995): *No Longer Invisible: Afro-Latin Americans Today*. London: Minority Rights Publications.

MIRANDA S., Pedro (1970): *Diccionario breve castellano – aymara y aymara – castellano*. La Paz: El Siglo.

MONTAÑO ARAGÓN, Mario (1992): "La familia negra en Bolivia". In *Guía etnográfica lingüística de Bolivia (tribus del altiplano y valles)*, primera parte, vol. 3. La Paz: Don Bosco, 211-285.

MONTES GIRALDO, José Joaquín (1962): "Sobre el habla de San Basilio de Palenque (Bolívar, Colombia)". *Thesaurus* 17, 446-450.

— (1974): "El habla del Chocó: notas breves". *Thesaurus* 29, 409-428.

MOODIE, Sylvia (MS): "Basilectal survivals in post creole Caribbean Spanish". Unpublished manuscript, University of the West Indies, St. Augustine, Trinidad.

MORÚA DELGADO, Martín (1975): *La familia Unzúazu*. La Habana: Arte y Literatura.

MOSONYI, Esteban Emilio; HERNÁNDEZ, María & ALVARADO, Elizabeth (1983): "Informe preliminar sobre la especificidad antropolingüística del "luango" de Barlovento". In *Actas del III Encuentro de Lingüistas*. Caracas: Instituto Pedagógico de Caracas, Departmento de Castellano, Literatura y Latín, Departamento de Idiomas Modernas, 159-167.

MOYA, Ruth (1981): *El quichua en el español de Quito*. Otavalo: Instituto Otavaleño de Antropología.

MOYA CORRAL, Juan Antonio (1979): *La pronunciación del español en Jaén*. Granada: Universidad de Granada.

MUFWENE, Salikoko (1997): "Jargons, pidgins, creoles, and koines: what are they?". In Spears & Winford (eds.) 1997: 35-70.

MÜHLHÄUSLER, Peter (1997): *Pidgin and Creole Linguistics*. London: University of Westminster Press.

NARO, Anthony (1978): "A study on the origins of pidginization". *Language* 45, 314-347.

— (1998): "O uso da concordância verbal no português *substandard* do Brasil: atualidade e origens". In Grosse & Zimmermann (eds.) 1998: 139-151.

NEWMAN, Roger (1966): *Land reform in Bolivia's Yungas*. M. A. thesis, Columbia University.

OCHOA, Gabriel (ed.) (1914): *Obras dramáticas del siglo XVI*. Madrid: n. p.

ORTIZ LÓPEZ, Luis (1998): *Huellas etno-sociolingüísticas bozales y afrocubanas*. Madrid/Frankfurt: Iberoamericana/Vervuert.

OTHEGUY, Ricardo & ZENTELLA, Ana Celia (2007): "Apuntes preliminarios sobre nivelación y contacto en el uso pronominal del español en Nueva York". In Potowski, Kim & Cameron, Richard (eds.): *Spanish in Contact: Educational, Linguistic, and Social Perspectives*. Amsterdam: John Benjamins, 273-293.

PADILLA OSINAGA, Paz ([3]1997): "Tiodor". In Soriano Badani, Armando (ed.): *Antología del cuento boliviano*. La Paz: Amigos del Libro, 317-321.

PAREDES, Manuel Rigoberto (1971): *Vocabulario de la lengua aymara*. La Paz: Ediciones Isla.

PAREDES-CANDIA, Antonio (1967): *Diccionario del folklore boliviano*. Sucre: Universidad Mayor de San Francisco Xavier de Chuquisaca. 2 vols.

— (1987): *Tradiciones de Bolivia*. La Paz: Popular.

— (⁴1988a): *Cuentos populares bolivianos (de la tradición oral)*. La Paz: Popular.

— (²1988b): *Zambo Salvito*. La Paz: Popular.

PENNY, Ralph (1991): *A History of the Spanish Language*. Cambridge: Cambridge University Press.

PEÑAHERRERA DE COSTALES, Piedad & COSTALES SAMANIEGO, Alfredo (1959): *Coangue o historia cultural y social de los negros del Chota y Salinas*. Quito: Llacta.

PEREDA VALDÉS, Ildefonso (1965): *El negro en el Uruguay: pasado y presente*. Montevideo: Revista del Instituto Histórico y Geográfico del Uruguay, no. 25.

PERL, Matthias (1989): "Algunos resultados de la comparación de fenómenos morfosintácticos del "habla bozal," de la "linguagem dos musseques, " del "palenquero, " y de lenguas criollas de base portuguesa". In *Estudios sobre español de América y lingüística afroamericana*. Bogotá: Instituto Caro y Cuervo, 368-380.

PIKE, Ruth (1967): "Sevillian society in the sixteenth century: slaves and freedmen". *Hispanic American Historical Review* 47, 344-359.

PIZARROSO CUENCA, Arturo (1977): *La cultura negra en Bolivia*. La Paz: Ediciones Isla.

PLAZA MARTÍNEZ, Pedro & CARVAJAL CARVAJAL, Juan (1985): *Etnias y lenguas de Bolivia*. La Paz: Instituto Boliviano de Cultura.

PORTUGAL ORTIZ, Max (1977): *La esclavitud negra en las épocas colonial y nacional de Bolivia*. La Paz: Instituto Boliviano de Cultura.

POWE, Edward (1998): *The Black and Indigenous Lore of Bolivia, Peru & Ecuador*. Madison, WI: Armchair Travelers.

PRESTOL CASTILLO, Freddy (1986): *Pablo Mamá*. Santo Domingo: Taller.

QUEVEDO, Francisco de (1988): *Obras completas*, vol. 1. Prosa. Madrid: Aguilar.

QUILIS, Antonio (2001): "Notas gramaticales sobre la lengua española de Bolivia". *Lexis* 25, nos. 1-2, 201-221.

QUILIS, Antonio & CASADO-FRESNILLO, Celia (1995): *La lengua española en Guinea Ecuatorial*. Madrid: Universidad Nacional de Educación a Distancia.

RAIMUNDO, Jacques (1933): *O elemento afro-negro na língua portuguesa*. Rio de Janeiro: Renascença Editôra.

RAMOS, Arthur (1935): *O folk-lore negro do Brasil*. Rio de Janeiro: Civilização Brasileira.

REY GUTIÉRREZ, Mónica. (1998): *La saya como medio de comunicación y expresión cultural en la comunidad afroboliviana*. Tesis de licenciatura, Facultad de Ciencias Sociales, Carrera de Comunicación Social, Universidad Mayor de San Andrés, La Paz.

RIBAS, Oscar (²1969): *Uanga feitiço*. Luanda: Tip. Angolana.

RICKFORD, John (1987): *Dimensions of a Creole Continuum*. Stanford: Stanford University Press.

ROCHA, Jofre (1977): *Estórias do musseque*. São Paulo: Edições 70.

RODRIGUES, Ana Natal (1974): *O dialeto caipira na regiao de Piracicaba*. São Paulo: Atica.

ROMAINE, Suzanne (1988): *Pidgin and Creole Languges*. London and New York: Longman.

ROSS, Elena (1958): *Diccionario castellayo-aymara-castellano*. La Paz: Misión Cristiana Pro-Alfabetización, Christian Literacy Mission.

ROSSBACH DE OLMOS, Lioba (2007): "Expresiones controvertidas: Afrobolivianos y su cultura entre presentaciones y representaciones". *Indiana* 24, 173-190.

ROUT, Leslie (1976): *The African Experience in Spanish America, 1502 to the Present Day*. Cambridge: Cambridge University Press.

RUIZ GARCÍA, Armanda (1957): *Más allá de la nada*. Santa Clara: Offset Cancio.

RUIZ GARCÍA, Marta (2000): *El español popular del Chocó: evidencia de una reestructuración parcial*. Ph. D. dissertation, University of New Mexico.

SALMÓN, Raúl (1969): *Teatro boliviano*. La Paz: Los Amigos del Libro.

— (^{3}1988): *Joven, rica y plebeya*. La Paz: Juventud.

— (1989): *Escuela de pillos*. La Paz: Juventud.

— (^{6}1998): *Miss Ch'ijini*. La Paz: Juventud.

— (^{8}1999a): *Plato paceño*. La Paz: Juventud.

— (1999b): *La birlocha de la esquina*. La Paz: Juventud.

SALVADOR PLANS, Antonio (1981): "¿Tres pueblos de habla extremeña en Andalucía? Estudio lingüístico". *Anuario de Estudios Filológicos* 4, 221-231.

SANABRIA FERNÁNDEZ, Hernando (1988): *El habla popular de Santa Cruz*. La Paz: Juventud.

SÁNCHEZ, Walter (1998): "Los sonidos del tambor mayor: presencia, imágenes acústicas y representaciones de los negros en Bolivia". In booklet accompanying the CD *El tambor mayor* (Centro Pedagógico y Cultural Simón I Patiño 1998), 7-124.

SÁNCHEZ MALDONADO, Benjamín (1961): "Los hijos de Thalía o bufos de fin del siglo". In *Teatro bufo, siete obras*, vol. 1 (no editor listed). Santa Clara: Universidad Central de las Villas, 217-255.

SANTA CRUZ, María de (1908): *Historias campesinas*. La Habana: Imprenta y Librería de M. Ricoy.

SARRÓ LÓPEZ, Pilar (1988): "Notas sobre la morfosintaxis del habla de las negras de Lope de Rueda". In Ariza, M.; Salvador, A. & Viudas, A. (eds.): *Actas del I Congreso Internacional de Historia de la Lengua Española*, vol. 1. Madrid: Arco, 601-610.

SCHRIEFERS, Herbert & JESCHENIAK, Jörg (1999): "Representation and processing of grammatical gender in language production: a review". *Journal of Psycholinguistic Research* 28, 575-600.

SCHUCHARDT, Hugo (1888): "Beiträge zur Kenntnis des kreolischen Romanisch. Vol. 1: Allgemeineres über das Negerportugiesische". *Zeitschrift für romanische Philologie* 12, 242-254.

SCHWEGLER, Armin (1991a): "El español del Chocó". *América Negra* 2, 85-119.

— (1991b): "Predicate negation in contemporary Brazilian Portuguese – A linguistic change in progress". *Orbis* 34, 187-214.

— (1994): "Black Spanish of highland Ecuador: new data and fuel for controversy about the origin(s) of Caribbean Spanish". Presented at the XXIV Linguistic Symposium on Romance Languages, University of California Los Angeles and University of Southern California, March 1994.

—(1996a): *"Chi ma nkongo": lengua y rito ancestrales en El Palenque de San Basilio (Colombia)*. Madrid/Frankfurt: Iberoamericana/Vervuert. 2 vols.

— (1996b): "La doble negación dominicana y la génesis del español caribeño". *Hispanic Linguistics* 8, 247-315.

— (1999): "Monogenesis revisited: the Spanish perspective". In Rickford, John & Romaine, Suzanne (eds.): *Creole Genesis, Attitudes and Discourse*. Amsterdam: John Benjamins, 235-262.

— (2001): "The myth of decreolization: The anomalous case of Palenquero". *Degrees of restructuring in creole languages*, ed. Ingrid Neumann-Holzschuh & Edgar Schneider. Amsterdam: John Benjamins. 409-436.

— (2002): "On the (African) origins of Palenquero subject pronouns". *Diachronica* 19, 273-332.

— (2006): "Habla bozal: Captivating new evidence from a contemporary source (Afro-Cuban "Palo Monte")". In Fuller, Janet & Thornburg, Linda (eds.): *Studies in Contact Linguistics: Essays in Honor of Glenn G. Gilbert*. New York: Peter Lang, 71-101.

— (2007): "A fresh consensus in the making: Plural *MA* and bare nouns in Palenquero". In Mihatsch, Wiltrud & Sokol, Monika (eds.): *Language contact and language change in the Caribbean and beyond – Lenguas en contacto y cambio lingüístico en el Caribe y más allá*. Frankfurt: Peter Lang, 59-75.

SCHWEGLER, Armin & MORTON, Thomas (2003): "Vernacular Spanish in a microcosm: *Kateyano* in El Palenque de San Basilio (Colombia)". *Revista Internacional de Lingüística Iberoamericana* 1, 97-159.

SEVCIK, Amy (1999): *Farsa de Lucrecia – Tragedia de la castidad, de Juan Pastor, mitad del siglo XVI*. Available at: <http://parnaseo.uv.es/Lemir/Textos/Lucrecia/Lucrecia.html>.

SIMÕES, Maria Cecília Perroni (1976): "Descrição do sistema verbal de uma criança brasileira com dois anos". In *I Encontro Nacional de Lingüística, conferéncias*. Rio de Janeiro: Pontifícia Universidade Católica de Rio de Janeiro, Departamento de Letras, 45-55.

SIMÕES, Maria Cecília Perroni & STOEL-GAMMON, Carol (1979): "The acquisition of inflections in Portuguese: a study of the development of person markers on verbs". *Journal of Child Language* 6, 53-67.

SMITH, Ronald (1975): *The society of los Congos of Panama*. Ph. D. dissertation, Indiana University.

SOJO, Juan Pablo (1986): *Estudios del folklore venezolano*. Los Teques: Biblioteca de Autores y Temas Mirandinos, Instituto Autónomo Biblioteca Nacional y de Servicios de Biblioteca.

SOLER PUIG, José (1975): *Bertillón 166*. La Habana: Editorial de Arte y Literatura.

SOROMENHO, Castro (^{2}1979): *A chaga*. Lisboa: Livraria Sá da Costa Editora.

SPEARS, Arthur & WINFORD, Donald (eds.) (1997): *The Structure and Status of Pidgins and Creoles*. Amsterdam: John Benjamins.

SPEDDING, Alison (1995): "Bolivia". In Minority Rights Group (ed.) 1995: 319-344.

STRATFORD, Billie Dale (1989): *Structure and use of Altiplano Spanish*. Ph. D. dissertation, University of Florida.

— (1991): "Tense in Altiplano Spanish". In Klee, Carol & Ramos-García, Luis (eds.): *Sociolinguistics of the Spanish-speaking World*. Tempe: Bilingual Review Press, 163-181.

SUÁREZ Y ROMERO, Anselmo (^{2}1947): *Francisco*. La Habana: Ministerio de Educación.

TARIFA ASCARRUNZ, Erasmo (1990): *Diccionario aymara castellano*. La Paz: Instituto Internacional de Integración Convenio Andrés Bello.

TEJEIRA JAÉN, Bertilda (1974): "Los congos de Chepo". *Patrimonio Histórico* 1, no. 3, 129-148.

TEJERIZO ROBLES, Germán (1989): *Villancicos barrocos en la Capilla Real de Granada (500 letrillas cantadas la noche de Navidad 1673 a 1830)*. Vol 1. Sevilla: Junta de Andalucía, Consejería de Cultura.

TEMPLEMAN, Robert (1994): "Afro-Bolivians". In Wilbert, Johannes (ed.): *Encyclopedia of world cultures, vol. 7: South America*. Boston: G. K. Hall and New York: Macmillan, 7-10.

— (1998): "We are the people of the *Yungas*, we are the *saya* race". In Whitten, Norman E., Jr. and Torres, Arlene (eds.): *Blackness in Latin Amereica and the Caribbean: social dynamics and cultural transformations, volume 1, Central America and Northern and Western South America*. Bloomington and Indianapolis: Indiana University Press, 426-444.

TINHORÃO, José Ramos (1988): *Os negros em Portugal*. Lisboa: Caminho.

TOMPKINS, William (1981): *The musical traditions of the blacks of coastal Peru*. Ph. D. dissertation, University of California, Los Angeles.

TOSCANO MATEUS, Humberto (1953): *El español del Ecuador*. Madrid: Consejo Superior de Investigación Científica.

XITU, Uanhenga [Agostinho MENDES DE CARVALHO] (1977): *Mestre Tamoda e outros contos*. São Paulo, Edições 70.

— (1979): *Maka na sanzala (mafuta)*. São Paulo: Edições 70.

VAN DEN BERG, Hans (1985): *Diccionario religioso aymara*. Iquitos: Centro de Estudios Teológicos de la Amazonía (CETA) and Puno: Instituto de Estudios Aymaras (IDEA).

VEGA CARPIO, Lope de (1893): *Obras de Lope de Vega*. Madrid: Real Academia Española.

VICENTE, Gil (1912): *Obras de Gil Vicente*. Coimbra: França Amado.

VIEIRA, José Luandino (1974): *Velhas estórias*. Lisboa: Plátano Editora.

— (1980): *A vida verdadeira de Domingos Xavier*. São Paulo: Editora Atica.

— (1982): *Luuanda*. São Paulo: Editora Atica.

— ([5]1985): *Vidas novas*. Luanda: União dos Escritores Angolanos.

VIGLIOCCO, Gabriella & FRANCK, Julie (1999): "When sex and syntax go hand in hand: gender agreement in language production". *Journal of Memory and Language* 40, 455-478.

VILLA, Ignacio (1938a): "Drumi, Mobila". In Guirao (ed.) 1938: 183-186.

— (1938b): "Calota ta morí". In Guirao (ed.) 1938: 183-186.

VILLAVERDE, Cirilo (1979): *Cecilia Valdés*. Critical edition by Raimundo Lazo. México, D.F.: Porrúa.

— (1981): *Excursión a Vuelta Abajo*. La Habana: Letras Cubanas.

WILDER CERVANTES B., Jorge (2001): *La saguchera de la esquina*. La Paz: Juventud.

YAPITA, Juan de Dios ([2]1979): *Vocabulario castellano inglés aymara*. Oruro: Indicep.

ZELINSKY, Wilbur (1949): "The historical geography of the Negro population of Latin America". *Journal of Negro History* 34, 2, 153-221.

ZELL, Rosa Hilda (1953): "La sombra del caudillo". In Bueno, Salvador (ed.): *Antología del cuento en Cuba (1902-1952)*. La Habana: Dirección de Cultura del Ministerio de Educación, Ediciones del Cincuentenario, 293-295.

ZIEGLER, Douglas-Val (1976): *A preliminary study of Afro-Cuban creole*. M. A. thesis, University of Rochester.